Civilization & Science
in Conflict or Collaboration?

*The Ciba Foundation for the promotion of international cooperation in
medical and chemical research is a scientific and educational charity established by
CIBA Limited – now CIBA-GEIGY Limited – of Basle. The Foundation operates
independently in London under English trust law.*

*Ciba Foundation Symposia are published in collaboration with
Associated Scientific Publishers (Elsevier Scientific Publishing, Excerpta Medica,
North-Holland Publishing Company) in Amsterdam.*

Associated Scientific Publishers, P.O. Box 3489, Amsterdam

Civilization &
Science
in Conflict or Collaboration?

A Ciba Foundation Symposium

1972

Elsevier · Excerpta Medica · North-Holland
Associated Scientific Publishers · Amsterdam · London · New York

ISBN Excerpta Medica 90 219 4001 9
ISBN American Elsevier 0-444-10351-1

Library of Congress Catalog Card Number 77-188826

Published in 1972 by Associated Scientific Publishers, P.O. Box 3489, Amsterdam, and 52 Vanderbilt Avenue, New York, N. Y. 10017.
Suggested series entry for library catalogues: Ciba Foundation Symposia.

Printed in the Netherlands by Mouton & Co., The Hague

Contents

Contributors

Symposium on Civilization and Science: in Conflict or Collaboration?
held at the Ciba Foundation, London, 28th-30th June 1971

Chairman: H. BLOCH Vice-President, Swiss National Science Foundation;
 Director, Friedrich Miescher-Institut, Basle

SIR ERIC ASHBY Master of Clare College, Cambridge; Chancellor, Queen's
 University of Belfast; Chairman of the Royal Commission on
 Environmental Pollution

H. BONDI Chief Scientific Adviser, Ministry of Defence, London; formerly
 Director-General, European Space Research Organization

F. BOURLIÈRE Professor of Medical Biology, Faculty of Medicine,
 University of Paris; Chairman, ICSU International Biological
 Programme

J. F. BROCK Honorary Professor of History and Philosophy of Medicine
 (formerly Professor of Medicine), University of Cape Town

SIR ALAN BULLOCK Vice-Chancellor, and Master of St Catherine's College,
 Oxford University

C. FREEMAN Director, Science Policy Research Unit, and Reginald M.
 Phillips Professor in Science Policy, University of Sussex

JUNE GOODFIELD-TOULMIN Professor of Philosophy and Human Medicine,
 Michigan State University

H. G. JOHNSON Professor of Economics, University of Chicago and
 London School of Economics

F. A. LONG Henry R. Luce Professor of Science and Society, and Director,
 Program on Science, Technology and Society, Cornell University,
 Ithaca, N.Y.

GAUTAM MATHUR Professor and Head of the Department of Economics,
 and former Dean, Faculty of Social Sciences, Osmania University,
 Hyderabad, India

LADY MEDAWAR Executive Chairman, Margaret Pyke Centre, and
    former Chairman, Family Planning Association, London
SIR PETER MEDAWAR Former Director, National Institute for Medical
    Research, now at MRC Clinical Research Centre, Northwick Park,
    London; Nobel Laureate 1960
G. PELLETIER Federal Secretary of State, Canada
G. W. RATHENAU Director, Philips Research Laboratories, Eindhoven
    and Professor, University of Amsterdam
M. ROCHE President, Consejo Nacional de Investigaciones Científicas
    y Tecnólógicas, Caracas, Venezuela
E. SHILS Professor of Sociology and Social Thought, University of Chicago,
    and Visiting Professor of Social Anthropology, University College
    London; founder and editor of *Minerva*
H. THIEMANN Director-General, Battelle Research Centre, Geneva
M. TODA Professor of Psychology, Faculty of Letters,
    Hokkaido University, Japan
LORD TODD Master of Christ's College, and former Professor of Organic
    Chemistry, Cambridge University; Chancellor, University of Strathclyde,
    Glasgow; Nobel Laureate 1957
S. E. TOULMIN Professor of Philosophy, Michigan State University, and
    Visiting Professor, Science Policy Research Unit, University of Sussex
A. M. WEINBERG Director, Oak Ridge National Laboratory, Tennessee
SIR JOHN WOLFENDEN Director, The British Museum, London; former
    Vice-Chancellor, Reading University

Editors: G. E. W. WOLSTENHOLME and MAEVE O'CONNOR

The problem defined

HUBERT BLOCH

The establishment of research priorities, the evaluation of scientific projects, science policy in the context of various social and political systems, and policies affecting research institutions were among the important issues raised and exhaustively reviewed at the Ciba Foundation symposium on *Decision Making in National Science Policy* held in 1967.[2] Today, not only are these issues still with us but newer and more disturbing problems are giving the decision makers for science policy, and the rest of us, more to review exhaustively than any experts can manage.

In most countries, science budgets have not received the expected increases but have even been reduced, rendering the competition for funds fiercer and the need for guidelines for intelligent policy decisions more acute. Also, a world-wide anti-science movement has since emerged, which contrasts our technological world with all its shortcomings and imminent dangers with a romanticized view of the past seen as a bucolic golden age ruined by the advance of science.

The question of the worthwhileness of scientific activities was almost taboo when it was mentioned at that meeting in 1967.[9] But now powerful voices from scientific as well as non-scientific quarters are saying that scientists should become more socially responsible, that science should be tolerated and supported only as long as its results are socially relevant, and that science must be constitutionalized and controlled if it is not to destroy our civilization.[3, 5, 7] It is said that the scientist's lack of values has left him helpless to prevent science from being used for exploitation and destruction.[1] And in the minds of many, science, all the way from nuclear physics and engineering to biology and medicine, has become a most dangerous evil.

This is the framework for the present symposium, and clearly we must address ourselves to the more elusive questions before we can continue the discussion on decision-making. What is the impact of science on the quality of life, on our work and leisure, on our environment, on human values—in short, on civilization? How does scientific progress influence civilization and how do the two interact to determine each other's course? To what extent is science involved in, or even responsible for, present world crises? Where does the scientist's responsibility for the consequences of his efforts begin and end? To whom is he responsible? How free is he, or should he be, in choosing his subjects and carrying out his work? And who should tell him what he can and what he cannot do?

Surely the new antagonistic forces alone, and all the turmoil they produce, are sufficient reason to hold this symposium and ask such questions. And indeed meetings of a similar character are now continually being arranged by many types of concerned groups. It is irrelevant whether the recent Pugwash Conference at Frascati on *Social Aspects of Technological Change* was one where scientists could relieve their remorse—like the Victorian businessman's attendance at church on Sunday, in Dr Shils' words[8]—or whether the Weizmann Institute's symposium on *The Impact of Science on Society*, which is taking place in Brussels at the same time as we are meeting here in London, was similarly motivated. It is a fact that in the world today such topics appear to be uppermost in the minds of scientists as well as non-scientists, and they will be pursued until some answers are found.

What, then, are the actual problems with which the scientific community must concern itself? Many of us are confronted with them in our everyday lives:

As university teachers we are faced with student militancy and forced to justify an activity that for centuries was unchallenged and came to be regarded as one of the most highly respected and most securely protected ways of life.

As science administrators and members of research councils we are confronted with the impossible task of wisely allocating funds that are in too short supply to satisfy all legitimate needs.

As scientists in industry we are accused of wilfully contributing for the sake of profit to the destruction of our environment and the exhaustion of the world's natural resources.

As scientists in government we are accused of lending our professional competence to helping to achieve military goals aimed directly at destroying whole populations.

As doctors we are accused of abusing our skills by not penetrating to the real causes of our patients' illnesses, but merely treating them for their symptoms in order to return them as soon as possible to a disease-producing society.

As biologists we are accused of plotting to use our recently acquired fundamental knowledge for the perversion of the human race by biomedical and genetic engineering.

These are some expressions of the antagonistic forces with which the scientific community is faced. We may find that some accusations have a base in reality and some have not. We may find answers to some and none to others. But where can we begin our search?

We could start by asking, what are the yardsticks by which the value of scientific projects is measured? Quality is probably the first, and everyone agrees that only good scientists and scientifically sound projects ought to be supported. But our agreement probably ends there. By what criteria are we to distinguish between good projects belonging to different disciplines? Clearly, the inherent quality of research project A is an insufficient criterion to rank it before or after an equally good project B, if A, for example, belongs to astronomy and B to enzymology. Ways must be found to compare the value of research of the A type and research of the B type. But immediately we come upon other questions. The value for what and for whom? For the promotion of knowledge? For the advancement of science? For the good of a particular university? For the power of a nation? For the health of mankind? For our happiness and well-being? And to whom should it be left to answer these questions? To the scientific community? To governments? To supra-national bodies?

These are not new questions. They are indeed difficult. They reflect an ill-defined but strongly felt *malaise* about the role of science in society and about the scientist's responsibility for the technological application of the results of his work. It behoves us to recognize this *malaise*. Its aetiology is clear: it lies in the contribution of science to the deterioration of our world— or rather in the uncontrolled application of scientific technology that leads to the now well-known problems of environmental pollution, the use of science for war and destruction, and the social implications of the by-products and side-effects of medical progress—and in the fact that science and technology have failed in many people's view to make our lives happier and more meaningful.

But while the diagnosis of the *malaise* and its aetiology are clear, its therapy is much less obvious. I have thought about three areas in which the scientific community could rally its own resources and begin to work on some therapeutic measures. They are the elaboration of a practical system to evaluate scientific projects, the creation of mechanisms permitting the relative significance of scientific results to be assessed and the construction of safeguards against the growing dangers of specialization.

Evaluation of scientific projects

Wherever science is supposed to serve specific interests, such as industrial or military goals, bodies and procedures exist to evaluate progress and review the significance of research at regular intervals. Such bodies and procedures are, however, almost non-existent for so-called basic research projects. Here every scientist individually tries to sell his projects as best as he can to the granting agency to which he applies. True, the quality of his project is reviewed, but its significance is usually much less considered. I am often surprised at the discrepancy between the short time spent on reflecting on the significance of a planned piece of research and the length of time that is afterwards required to execute the work. A serious attempt ought to be made to rank all publicly supported research projects in order of importance according to criteria such as their originality, their contribution to knowledge, their social significance, their applicability in agriculture or in medicine, their potential industrial value and their practical effects, good or bad, on the so-called quality of life. Where such value scales exist on national levels, they are subject to frequent reclassification according to political and emotional pressures. Here an international, less variable and less vulnerable scale of values might be formulated and defended by appropriate multidisciplinary groups, perhaps under the sponsorship of UNESCO. In spite of working on a world-wide scale, such bodies could still adjust their priority listings to regional needs.

Relative significance of scientific results

A continuing ranking of the relative significance of scientific results appears necessary because individual scientists are rarely able to judge the consequences of their work beyond the narrow limits of their fields.[11] However, an elite of the international scientific community could be charged to carry out a continuing interdisciplinary evaluation of the practical implications of all scientific progress. Conclusions could be published regularly, so that government agencies and the public would be informed of the possible consequences of the work they sponsor and be guided in making decisions.

Such regular evaluation would be merely informative but the considered judgement of independent groups of experts might carry enough weight to make scientists themselves, as well as their sponsors, conscious of the long-range implications of research. Here I should like to emphasize that although the evaluation of the consequences and social effects of science is a task for scientists, including social scientists, the implementation of their findings is a political act and calls for decisions by the representatives of the public—government executives, city mayors, politicians. Implementation requires in addition the willingness of the citizenry to foot the bill for decisions that place a greater financial burden on individuals and on their community. In the end it is always the citizen who pays the bill, be it as taxpayer or as consumer.

Safeguards against specialization

It is obvious that, like most other occupations, science is becoming increasingly specialized and fragmented. Scientists, just like assembly-line or office workers in large organizations, are physically and emotionally separated from the end-product of their work. To many of them its usefulness remains unclear. This is particularly true for scientists in government and industry. They may lack the pertinent information and the necessary understanding and, what is worse, they are not even clearly aware of these shortcomings and therefore make no attempt to remedy them. I submit that it is the task of the universities not to foster specialization but to resist it, to train their science students in such a way as to prevent them from becoming assembly-line workers. Every single teaching subject can be put into its broader context, even at the expense of specialization. This would have the added beneficial effect that the professors would be forced to think about and answer questions relating to the wider significance of their own endeavours.

One might object that these three suggestions, if implemented, would lead to censorship and *dirigisme* and that they could curtail the freedom of science and hamper its progress. I do not think such a fear is justified, because already under our present system no scientist, unless he finances his research from his own independent means, is entirely free to do what he wants. The implementation of these suggestions would, however, give the scientist a greater awareness of the social and cultural significance of his work.

Although scientific research is wasteful by nature and research projects—in contrast to development projects—cannot be accurately planned and justified in detail, scientists cannot escape the responsibility of justifying their social role. Scientists have taken their own infallibility and the paramount importance of their work for granted for too long, and much wasteful nonsense has been produced in the name of science.[6] Every scientist who uses public funds for his research should be prepared to defend his expenditure, not only within the scientific context but also in terms of the contribution he hopes to make to the social well-being of his country and the world. This should not be interpreted as a call for applied as opposed to pure science. It is a claim, however, that scientists should be requested to defend their work on social grounds, just as they are traditionally used to doing on scientific grounds, as long as they are using public funds.

Many of us are engaged in the battle of defending science, perhaps to keep it on its traditional lofty pedestal and save it from the bloodier battles below. We are defending science essentially by extolling its past achievements and by telling people that thanks to science 'they never had it so good'.[4, 10] But in defending science should we not use a different approach, not starting from the axiomatic position that science *must* remain as it is, must continue to be supported, must concern itself with the same areas as hitherto, must give the scientists complete freedom to do what they want, or that we must *a priori* agree that *all* scientific subjects and disciplines are equally worthy of support? Perhaps after discussing the subject we may conclude that there are other and better ways of defending science than those we have used so far, and that perhaps even the curtailment of funds and the questioning of the wisdom of some of the past performances of science may not be as bad as they seem.

Finally, a short word on 'secrecy and science', because this has some bearing on the contribution of science to civilization. In essence and in the long run, secrecy and science are mutually exclusive, because non-secrecy is one of the essential and vital characteristics of science. However, a certain degree of short-term secrecy is common to all scientists. Most of them keep their results to themselves until these can be published or patented. Also, in the present social and political context, some secrecy will always overshadow certain projects belonging to either military or industrial and even academic research. Curiously enough, this is as true in the socialist as in the capitalist world, or perhaps it applies even more in the former. This state of affairs will not change as long as scientists are willing or can be compelled to undertake classified work, or as long as the prevailing system of academic prizes, recognition and promotion rewards those who are first to come forward with scientific results. It is therefore entirely up to the scientific community itself whether secrecy in scientific matters is tolerated and accepted—the scientists themselves are the only ones who could, if they wished, force their establishments to change.

Because of the various points just mentioned, science policy-making will be under scrutiny for some time to come. The main goal, as I see it, of any science policy should be to reintegrate science into our civilization, to place it exactly where it belongs in the scale of human values—not too low and not too high, to construct solid safeguards that should prevent science from destroying the very society which supports it and to instil in the scientists a refreshing and much-needed measure of humility.

Bibliography

1. BLACKBURN, T. R. (1971) Sensuous-intellectual complementarity in science. *Science, 172*, 1003–1007.
2. DE REUCK, A., GOLDSMITH, M., and KNIGHT, J., (ed.) (1968) In *Ciba Foundation and Science of Science Foundation Symposium on Decision Making in National Science Policy.* London: Churchill.
3. DUBOS, R. (1970) *Reason Awake–Science for Man.* New York: Columbia University Press.
4. HANDLER, P. (1970) Science's continuing role. *Bio-Science, 20*, 1101–1106.
5. MUMFORD, L. (1970) *The Myth of the Machine: The Pentagon of Power.* New York: Harcourt Brace Jovanovitch.
6. NIEBURG, H. L. (1966) *In the Name of Science.* Chicago: Quadrangle Books.
7. ROSZAK, T. (1969) *The Making of a Counter Culture.* Garden City, N.Y.: Doubleday.
8. SHILS, E. (1971) Of pride and men of little faith. *Minerva, 9*, 1–6.
9. WEINBERG, A. M. (1968) The philosophy and practice of national science policy. In *Ciba Foundation and Science of Science Foundation Symposium on Decision Making in National Science Policy*, pp. 26–43. Ed. A. de Reuck, M. Goldsmith and J. Knight. London: Churchill.
10. WEINBERG, A. M. (1970) In defense of science. *Science, 167*, 141–145.
11. ZUCKERMAN, S. (1970) *Beyond the Ivory Tower.* London: Weidenfeld and Nicolson.

Some reflections on science and civilization

P. B. AND J. S. MEDAWAR

At present we are going through a bad period in the relations between science and civilized society. People generally have become increasingly aware and resentful of the havoc that may be wrought by a technology that develops without social censorship. Worse still, a new mood of despondency and help-lessness has descended upon us, for the equal of which we should have to go back to the early days of the 17th century.[5]

It has come to be felt that there is some *essential* malefaction about the progress of science and technology: that they lurch forward like some great Behemoth trampling down in its pathway almost everything that makes for civilized life. We have been given the privilege of thinking aloud on this subject and told that some measure of overlap between what we say and what others may say later is not necessarily undesirable. Our plan is to discuss some of the psychological elements that enter into the present tendency to repudiate science and all its works, and then discuss the shape of possible solutions to these embarrassments.

Relations between science and society in the 17th century

If we say that the relations between science and society are now going through a bad period, we are under an obligation to say when we think the relationship was a cordial one. The first period in which it was so was in the 1620s when Francis Bacon most winningly and indeed irresistibly talked people into believing that science was something that would work for 'the merit and emolument of man'. The second, surely, was during the 19th century—the epoch of the great civil engineers when it was taken altogether for granted that science was the principal agency of progress and that science and civilization stood shoulder to shoulder. But even then there were rancorous voices. Magee[3] has wittily reminded us that the proposal in 1848 to lay London's first main sewer was vehemently opposed by much established opinion, notably by *The Times* which appeared to feel that to die in one's own way without civic interference was one of the elementary liberties of mankind: 'We prefer to take our chance with cholera and the rest than to be bullied into health. England wants to be clean but not to be cleaned by Chadwick'. (We can take it that the Prince Consort, who died of typhoid in 1861, did not share this bizarre preference.)

Let us now consider some of the psychological elements that enter into the present anti-scientific mood—we say 'psychological' to distinguish them from the sense of resentment people justifiably feel about the ecological depredations of modern technology. The first we shall call 'Mumfordry', by which we mean nothing more serious than a certain propensity to think the worst about science and technology.

In an article published in 1966 Lewis Mumford[6] quoted a lengthy passage from Edward McCurdy's translation of Leonardo's notebooks (London 1908, p. 266), a passage which describes the fearful and irresistible rampaging of a black-faced monster with swollen and bloodshot eyes and ghastly features— a monster from which the populace defended themselves in vain:

'Oh, wretched folk for you there avail not the impregnable fortresses nor the lofty walls of your cities nor the being together in great numbers nor your houses or palaces! There remained not any place unless it were the tiny holes and subterranean caverns where after the manner of crabs and crickets and creatures like these you might find safety and a means of escape. Oh, how many wretched mothers and fathers were deprived of their children, how many unhappy women were deprived of their companions! In truth . . . I do not believe that ever since the world was created has there been witnessed such lamentation and wailing of people accompanied by so great terror. In truth the human species is in such a plight that has need to envy every other race of creatures.

' I know not what to do or say for everywhere I seem to find myself swimming with bent head within the mighty throat and remaining indistinguishable in death buried within the huge belly'.

Lewis Mumford surmises that this nightmare represents the 'reverse side of Leonardo's hopeful anticipations of the future'. It is Leonardo's premonition of the despoliation that the advances of modern science and technology may wreak upon the earth and its inhabitants. But 'there is no way of proving this', Mumford concedes, and we therefore diffidently submit an alternative interpretation: that in this passage Leonardo is describing the devastation consequent upon the spread of a bubonic plague of Levantine or, perhaps, Libyan origin. For justice's sake it must be added that the advances of science and technology have virtually eliminated bubonic plague from the western world.

The kind of attitude which Mumford's interpretation of this passage from Leonardo illustrates can only be sustained if we systematically neglect the benefactions of science—for example, being alive and well instead of ill or dead—and pay attention only to the miscarriages of technology. Advances in medicine and the possibilities of human happiness created by the relief of suffering are a great embarrassment to those determined to think nothing but evil of science and technology. Their only recourse is to point to the population problem as the direct consequence of medicine and medical technology and to say or imply that modern drugs cause as many ailments as they cure. In spite of these dissonant voices, most people believe as we do that medical science has a moral credit balance.

Science and the mastery of nature

A second element in the revulsion of many thoughtful people from science —and a factor which has had a thoroughly mischievous effect for reasons we shall try to explain—is the ideology of the mastery or domination of Nature. 'Bacon's fundamental maxim' said an 18th century philosopher 'is that knowledge is power: every accession man gains to his knowledge is an accession to his power; and extends the limits of his empire over the world which he inhabits'. There are passages in Bacon which fully bear out this judgement. However, in the context of Bacon's own thought the ideology of mastery and domination is not particularly offensive because it is bound up with his own special concept of experimentation as an alternative to the passive contemplation of the information that nature spontaneously proffers us. The idea of mastery makes a brief appearance in the writing of Marx[4] and of Freud.[1] The 'conquest of infectious disease' is fair enough, because bacteria are indeed inimical to us. On the other hand the 'conquest of space' rings quite false. The main objection to the ideology of mastery and warfare is that it dulls the sensibilities and seems to condone or in some perverse way even to justify the worst excesses of environmental despoliation. One hopes that these unpleasant figures of speech have not taken so deep a hold that they cannot be uprooted from popular writing and popular thought. It is *understanding,* not mastery, that should be the declared ambition of scientific research.

Does science pay?

Another factor which makes for uneasy relations between technology and civilized life is the tendency, especially prevalent in England, to make economic return or cost-effectiveness the ultimate measure of the worthwhileness of any enterprise. (The password into this area of thought is 'does it pay?') A purely economic system of mensuration is not conducive to the welfare of the environment. The purification and the safe disposal of toxic effluents are costly obligations and the cost-effectiveness of many manufacturing procedures is greatly improved when these obligations are disregarded or circumvented.

Is society sick?

Some thinkers of the 20th century have professed to discern a serious social ailment in modern civilized society. Both Keynes and Freud have had civilization on the couch. J. M. Keynes[2] diagnosed 'a nervous breakdown' and Freud [1] 'a neurosis'. Keynes believed of mankind that we had been 'expressly evolved by Nature with all our impulses and deepest instincts' for the purpose of solving the economic problem, the problem of keeping our heads above water in a hostile and competitive world. The economic problem was approaching solution, so Keynes goes on to say, 'I think with dread of the readjustment of the habits and instincts of the ordinary man bred into him for countless generations that he may be asked to discard within a few decades. . . . Must we not expect a general nervous breakdown?' Keynes likens the plight of civilized society to that of a suburban housewife who has been relieved of economic and of some domestic cares by a prosperous husband and for whom the enjoyment of a nervous ailment is now the only remaining métier.

Keynes's argument is a relic—the last, one hopes—of social Darwinism and Freud's is based on a misunderstanding, forgivable because at that time widely prevalent, of the true scope and significance of Haeckel's recapitulation theory. Both arguments are unconvincing. The idea that civilized society can suffer from an ailment is a figure of speech which can easily lead us astray. It is fair enough to speak of society suffering from a 'disorder' because orderliness is one of the defining characteristic of a civilized society but we shall depress ourselves unduly if we see ourselves as sitting anxiously by civilization's bedside. It really makes no more sense to speak of civilization suffering a nervous breakdown than to speak of it having a headache or a bad back. The disorders of society are peculiar to and distinctive of society, e.g. an unfavourable trade balance, unemployment or over-population. They are particular disorders, moreover, for which we should seek particular remedies. The misuse of the organismic conception of society must bear some part of the blame for the current feeling of helplessness and despondency about how matters can be remedied.

Utopia and Arcadia

Let us now consider the shape of possible solutions of our present dilemma, which is that we have become increasingly dependent on science and increasingly resentful of the fact that we are so. In the early 17th century, when people in England got fed up with the state of the nation and the quality of life they could and did emigrate to America, but no one today would have recourse to such a solution because America is in a worse plight than we are in most matters to do with the bad relations between science and civilized life.

From the 16th century onwards, however, imaginative writers and philosophers have entertained purely notional solutions of the dilemma. These notional solutions or daydreams of a better world are roughly speaking of two kinds: Utopian and Arcadian.

The old Utopias—Utopia itself, the new Atlantis, Christianopolis and the City of the Sun—were ectopic civilizations discovered by chance in far-off seas. In Utopia man has become the landlord of the domain in which he was formerly a mere tenant. He arranges matters in such a way that people live in amity and under the protection of justice and enjoy all the benefactions that an enlightened technology can bestow upon them—though a technology still so rudimentary that it could not have the grievous side-effects we now deplore. It is worth remembering that the old Utopias did not repudiate science and technology but on the contrary put them to work for the common good. In Utopia it is assumed that men improve themselves by their own exertions and that the qualities of character and mind that make for civilized living will eventually become second nature.

Scientists are Utopian by temperament. If asked why they do what they are doing one suspects most of them would answer that they hoped their work would one day make the world a better place to live in. And that is the essence of Utopianism. A civilized world is not 'given', but something men can make for themselves—an audacious and irreverent idea in its time.

Arcadian thought is closely bound up with the legend of a Golden Age in which human beings lived in a state of natural happiness and innocence, tranquillity and peace—a state from which they have since undergone a grievous decline. In Arcadia human beings retreat into a tranquil pastoral world where peace of mind is not threatened, intellectual aspiration is not called for and virtue it not at risk. But an Arcadian society is anarchic (a fatal objection). Everything that is implied by authority is replaced by everything that is implied by fraternity. Arcadia is a world without ambition and without accomplishment. Anarchy is perhaps the sociological equivalent of solipsism. Just as it is normally regarded as fatal to the pretensions of any theory of knowledge to show that it leads to solipsism, so, it seems, is it fatal to the pretensions of any social system to show that it leads to or implies a state of anarchy.

Practical remedies

Let us therefore turn away from notional solutions to practicalities. If we can agree that civilized society is not the victim of any one ailment, we shall not look for any one remedy. It is not one thing that is wrong with modern society but a multitude of particular things and for these we must find a multitude of particular remedies. Pollution, for example, is always pollution of something by something at some particular time and place. Each individual contribution to pollution must be sought out and remedied. If a town is intoxicating itself with smoke then smokeless fuel must be introduced borough by borough until the nuisance has abated.

Sweden has set a notable example of 'piecemeal social engineering' in its conservation programme for Lake Vättern, which was being slowly polluted out of existence and rendered progressively more unfit to supply water to the municipalities round its shore or to sustain a char fishing industry. The major sources of pollution were identified as sewage from holiday camps and lakeshore holiday homes, fermentation liquids from silos and effluents from the regional paper and pulp industry. At considerable expense each source of contamination was studied and as far as possible remedied.

It is a heartening story because it shows how evils of technological origin can be mitigated by technological means. This applies even to the greatest evil of all, the overpopulation problem. We believe that one day a medically inoffensive means will be found of preventing conception and that in spite of administrative difficulties and doctrinal barriers it will come into general use. Nevertheless, we fully concur with Professor Paul Ehrlich's judgement that our entire economic system, based as it is upon overproduction, over-consumption and waste is unsound and must eventually be supplanted by something more like a spaceship economy distinguished by frugality, recycling and above all forethought.

The future

We conclude with a statement of belief which, like all such statements, is essentially a fragment of autobiography.

We believe that technological remedies can be found for evils of technological origin and are prepared to marvel at people who think otherwise. One had hoped that a journey to the far side of the moon had convinced everyone that any accomplishment which is not at odds with the laws of physics is within human capability. (It was some such thought I (P.B.M.) had in mind when I chose a Baconian motto for my Presidential Address to the British Association[5] in 1969: 'On "The Effecting of All Things Possible"'.) As to the anti-scientific mood, we can only hope that it will disappear along with the grounds that justify it, unless indeed its causes lie deeper and are less easily eradicable than we have supposed them to be. But of course nothing will happen unless there is widespread public determination that technology must remain subject to rules of social morality and be kept under constant surveillance so that its miscarriages can be prevented or cured. There is already evidence that this new mood of determination is growing. Last year was European Conservation Year. In England a Ministry for the Environment is a promising beginning; the United States has recently held a nationwide Earth Day and the World Health Organization is convening a conference in Stockholm in 1972 on the general theme of man and his environment.

We have said nothing about incentives. There is a widespread feeling that just as politicians and schoolteachers of the wrong kind have found it fairly easy to inculcate ideas of nationalism and patriotism in the narrow sense into schoolchildren, so they might now make amends by inculcating the same sentiments about the earth as a whole. What should the new *ism* be called—terrestrialism? (but that is too much of a mouthful)—and in what terms should children henceforward be encouraged to declare their allegiance to the world they are to live in?

Discussion

Toulmin: Most of the evils at which Sir Peter's Arcadians gripe are the result not of science but of 19th-century industrialization, combined with overpopulation; and 19th-century technology, represented by William Blake's 'dark satanic mills', was the product of mature capitalism rather than of science. The more genuinely 'science-based' technological innovations are, the less—I suspect—they tend to pollute. Most of the ghastliness of pollution has happened where technology has gone ahead without the safeguards that proper scientific thought could give. Science can and should be used to provide proper control; so what we need is more science rather than less. The view of science as a source of evil is a historically unfounded one that we should all fight against.

Weinberg: We as scientists are accused of being irresponsible by the counter-culture, whose recipe for solving the problem is to go back to Arcadia. But it is not the social responsibility of scientists which is faulty; as Dr Toulmin says, it is our technology that is faulted, is tainted. Our task is to remove the taints of this faulted technology.

Freeman: We should beware of ridiculing the 'Arcadian' view as fuddy-duddy and reactionary. Some of the unpleasant things we see today, while not directly the result of 'science', would not be there but for scientific knowledge. It is certainly naive to see science as an evil come into the world, but although the anti-personnel mine, for example, is an invention which is not based on new science, other modern weapons would not have been possible without the development of new scientific knowledge, and we cannot dismiss this. Our political systems have not kept up with the speed of scientific and technical change. We have to learn to use science as a means of improving and conserving the quality of life. This will mean new political institutions for assessing and licensing new science and technology. Uncontrolled *laissez-innover* is no more acceptable than uncontrolled *laissez-faire*.

Medawar: I didn't want to imply that the Arcadian view was fuddy-duddy and ineffectual. It derives from a very long-established and respected humanistic and literary tradition, and its greatest literary exponent was of course J.-J. Rousseau. But it is simply not *technologically* feasible to put the clock back since the whole pattern and tempo of life adjusts itself to the prevailing technology. For example it is not realistic to shun travelling by air; the present tempo of life obliges us to use aeroplanes and society will not work if we pretend that its technological apparatus doesn't exist.

Weinberg: The real question is whether a stable society is any longer possible in the face of the extreme compression of events and awareness of them produced by our highly developed technologies of communication. The tragic killing of students at Kent State University in May 1970 occurred in the afternoon and by 7 p.m. every household in the United States was seeing it on television. Even thirty years ago there would have been more attenuation than this between an event, the public reactions to it, and its social consequences.

Professor Bloch rightly argued that the world does not owe science (or scientists) a living, and that science must justify its continuing public support. How should allocations be made to science, and priorities set within science? Science does *not* operate as a market economy; hence allocations, and the discussions and criteria leading to them, cannot be made by any remote body making decisions on high. This simply would not work. The essence of the problem of priorities is to raise the intellectual level of the political process by which allocations are actually made. One of the important criteria for deciding which scientific projects should be pursued is what I call their connectedness: the science that matters, that is important, is the science that makes a difference to the larger community of *science* outside the field under scrutiny.

Bloch: But when the fall-out to the scientific community is long delayed, people will start questioning the usefulness of that project.

Weinberg: Certainly. Einstein, and Planck's quantum theory, are examples of this from the past. But Einstein was cheap science; space research is not.

Bloch: Nor is biology now.

Brock: If a young student of science were here he would be asking what the social relevance of a scientific project is, but I don't think this is what you mean by 'connectedness' in evaluating the worth of a particular scientific study?

Weinberg: No. I mean that one must evaluate one part of science by its relevance to the rest of science.

Long: I would like to broaden Dr Weinberg's notions of instability to include the seriousness of the increased rate of social change which technology has brought to the world. I am also uneasy about one of the challenges that Professor Bloch listed (p. 2). He sees assessment of the impacts of science and technology as a task for scientists but I think it may rather be a task for a much broader political grouping. Scientists can properly ask for a role, but it should not be so broad as to include prime responsibility for making technological assessments.

Bloch: I do not know whether I can fully agree. I feel that scientists should not merely ask for a role in assessing the impacts of science and technology on society. They should be forced to share the responsibility in this assessment. On the other hand, science and technology cannot alone be blamed for the present disruption of our societal structure. The decay of forces such as religion which for centuries gave society its stability is only indirectly due to technological progress. But since science is of such paramount importance in our present-day social and economic structure and since scientists are by their very command of modern technology called upon to be among the leaders of society, the scientists have in my opinion no choice but to accept the challenge and to play a leading role.

Roche: I come from an underdeveloped country, Venezuela, and we are shocked by the reaction against science. But we note that this reaction is restricted to a small corner of the world (the United States, and Europe, seen as a small peninsula of Asia!) and that, in fact, 90 per cent of the world's people still passionately desire science and a share in it as a source of human happiness; we even wish for pollution, as a sure sign of prosperity!

Science is ambivalent in its outcome and it is difficult to know what will result eventually from basic research. To control it is tantamount to castrating it. Let us limit ourselves to redirecting the application of science and leave basic science alone.

June Goodfield-Toulmin: You have rightly reminded us that current anti-scientific views are restricted to a very small part of the world. Perhaps this reaction is an inevitable one when science, which was expected to solve all problems, not only appears to have failed but even to have made more. Yet while science was riding what I call the 'post-sputnik' bandwagon, we were never pulled back from our dreams of a collective Utopia. We never heard much from the scientists themselves about either the complexity of our problems or the limits to the contributions science could make towards solving them.

Wolfenden: Professor Bloch distinguished carefully between science and scientists, on the one hand, and technology and technologists on the other; but the distinction seems to be becoming blurred in subsequent statements. As an Arcadian, a humanist, I want to ask naively whether or not we are maintaining a difference between science and technology.

Weinberg: This comes back to the distinction between the Baconian and Newtonian views of science. The Baconian view is that science aims to make two blades of grass grow where one grew before (this is how Dean Swift put it). The Newtonian view is that we do science for the glory of the intellect, of the intellectual construct. With respect to the support of science, society takes the Baconian view, that science is done in order to 'master' nature.

Derek Price has argued[5] that the connections between science and technology are very frail and that they only occur because both subjects meander and so they accidentally intertwine. I disagree: we scientists cannot buy out so cheaply! The connections between modern technology and science are integral connections. To the general public, technology and science are as one. Because technology has had many deleterious side-effects, the public has cast blame on the scientist as well as the technologist. We may not enjoy being in that cauldron, but we are in it!

Bloch: I am glad to hear you say that. Lord Todd might add the further distinction between technologists and technicians; maybe the latter are the scapegoats we are searching for!

Rathenau: We hear a great deal about the bad results of science in the past, which led to the development of technology and to the ever-increasing population which now constitutes a major problem, but what do we see for the future? Is stability possible in the future *without* science? Surely the answer is that it is not. Dr Jay Forrester at the Massachusetts Institute of Technology has been calculating by a computer model the dynamics of the world to come, including many feedback loops and non-linear relationships which govern social processes.[1, 2] His model predicts catastrophe if measures are not taken carefully. Unless such models are acted upon *now* by populations and politicians, it is difficult to see how catastrophe can be avoided.

Medawar: Professor Bloch said that science is becoming more specialized and more fragmented. This is not true of biology, the branch of science I know best. Biology is now more integrated, more close-knit and more of a whole than it has ever been.

Weinberg: Science has become more integrated, but at a higher level of abstraction. In the process, we lose detail that at one time gave much charm to science. There is a beautiful discussion of integration of science in *The Art of the Soluble*.[3]

Medawar: One of my purposes in that book was to deplore class distinction between pure and applied science—the latter with its connotation of overalls and oily rags and the unspiritual things that engineers are thought to do. I would emphasize what Dr Rathenau said: we are in a mess, and only technology can get us out of it.

Thiemann: The problem of increasing interdependence in the world has already been raised. Dr Forrester's model [1, 2] to which Dr Rathenau referred considers just this fact. Two forces, both increasing exponentially—population and capital—have essentially been considered. Forrester says there are three things which could limit the exponential growth: the natural resources, the availability of arable land, and pollution. World population was low when man was still a hunter but when he began to cultivate the land it increased considerably.

In modern times, science and technology have allowed further increases in population and there is today no precise information about the biological limit to total population. We do not yet understand the new stabilizing factors and this is why dynamic world models are being used to try to understand such factors.

Dr Roche referred to the attitudes to science in the underdeveloped countries. Only a quarter of the world's population consumes 85 per cent of the world's resources. Limited natural resources mean that the underdeveloped part of the world does not at present achieve the same high standard of living as the developed world. The question humanity may face is whether to go on at a high population level, say 20 000 million people with a fairly low standard of living, or whether to try to keep the population down to, say, 5000 to 6000 million with a relatively high standard of living. What will the new regulating forces be? It is a tremendous new challenge for the scientist and the technologist to find solutions to this problem. However, the time lag between recognition of a problem and implementation of practical solutions is nearly a whole generation. Therefore action should be taken now.

Mathur: Perhaps we have been a bit hard on Mumford. He was not originally anti-science. In fact in *Technics and Civilization*,[4] published in 1934, he divided technical progress into three phases. The period of preparation or Eotechnic Phase apart, the drawbacks of technological expansion may be witnessed in the second or Paleo-Economic Phase. But as regards the third phase, the Neotechnic Phase, Mumford was full of adulation. He likened looking at a modern laboratory or an automated chemicals factory to the aesthetic experience of being in a temple. We have no quarrel with Mumford on the point about the undesirable effects of ill-planned use of technology, coupled with the baser elements of the profit motive. But the original Mumford formulation was not hostile to the modern aspects of scientific progress, which he had accepted as part of civilization.

Bibliography

1. FREUD, S. (1965) *Civilization and its Discontents*, ed. J. Strachey. London: Hogarth Press and Institute of Psychoanalysis.
2. KEYNES, J. M. (1930) Economic possibilities for our grandchildren. *The Nation and Athenaeum*, October 18, 96–97.
3. MAGEE, B. (1965) *Towards Two Thousand*. London: MacDonald.
4. McLELLAN, C. (1970) Marx and the missing link. *Encounter*, November [and his forthcoming edition of Marx's *Grundrisse*].

5. MEDAWAR, P. B. (1969/70) On 'The effecting of all things possible'. *The Advancement of Science, 26*, No. 127, 1–9.
6. MUMFORD, L. (1966) *New York Review of Books*, 29th December.

Discussion

1. FORRESTER, J. (1971) Counterintuitive behavior of social systems. *Technology Review, 73*, No. 3, 52–68.
2. FORRESTER, J. (1971) *World Dynamics*. Cambridge, Mass.: Wright-Allen Press.
3. MEDAWAR, P. (1969) *The Art of the Soluble*. London: Methuen.
4. MUMFORD, L. (1934) *Technics and Civilization*. New York: Harcourt Brace.
5. PRICE, D. J. DE SOLLA (1965) Is technology historically independent of science? A study in statistical historiography. *Technology and Culture, 6*, 553–568 (winter).

The historical background
to the anti-science movement

STEPHEN TOULMIN

To those of us who grew up, as I did myself, within the sub-culture of science, and who have learned to love and value the intellectual enterprise of science as we conceive it, the anti-scientific rhetoric of the contemporary counter-culture comes at first as a puzzle or as an irritation, rather than as a genuine challenge. In our own minds we are entirely clear that the activity of scientific research, and the knowledge at which it aims, are good in themselves; and we find it hard to summon up the patience required to justify this obvious proposition in public yet again—especially to people whose motives, honesty and powers of self-criticism we are at least half tempted to doubt. On the contrary: these suspicions seem to justify us, instead, in shutting our eyes to the whole phenomenon. Perhaps it is one more superficial and transitory feature of the late 20th century scene: along with drugs, long hair and ungrateful students.

If we do take this easy way out, however, we are liable to overlook some important and urgent questions; and history will not deal kindly with us. For in one respect, at least, Anti-Science is indeed like long hair and drugs. It may or may not be superficial, but at any rate it is not transitory. (When did you last look at a picture of Thomas Henry Huxley, or read de Quincey's *Confessions of an Opium-Eater*?) Rather, all three are things that come and go—recurrent if not permanent features of human experience, which are normally there below the surface, and have occasionally blown up to serious proportions. And I do not think we shall understand the anti-science movement properly unless we look at it in its longer-term historical context: unless we are prepared, first to recognize it as the contemporary expression of deeper-seated and longer-standing attitudes and interests, and then to ask ourselves whether some of those attitudes and interests are not, after all, as legitimate and respectable as our own.

Looking back at the whole history of public attitudes to science, in fact, I have sometimes wondered whether they were not a generational or secular phenomenon, as predictable as the tides. Throughout the last half-millennium, at least, anti-scientific attitudes seem to have peaked at intervals of 130 years or so, if not every 65 or 30–35 years. (In this as in so many other ways, for instance, life in the 1960s was a kind of replay of life in the 1830s . . .) So it is worth trying to see whether we can learn anything about our own situation today, by considering it alongside earlier similar situations. Today's LSD and cannabis are the counterparts of de Quincey's opium, and of the laudanum that would have raised no eyebrows even in Mrs Gaskell's Cranford; so can we not see today's anti-science, similarly, as a recurrent expression of the same preoccupations that underlay the hostility of Goethe, Schiller and William Blake to the Newtonian science of their time? Or the scorn of Jonathan Swift for the activities of the early Royal Society? Or the insistence of Michel de Montaigne that intellectual life should be focused on matters of humane concern, rather than on hubristic attempts to theorize about aspects of nature quite foreign to human needs?

Asking these questions compels us to admit, at any rate, that we are here dealing with something more than a flash-in-the-pan. And, if we can once bring ourselves to take the present-day reaction against science a little more seriously, this may help us, in turn, to recognize the genuine conflicts of interests which power the continuing pendulum-swing of general public sympathies and attitudes first towards, then away from, that science about whose virtues we ourselves may have no doubts.

Actually, there are certain common topics to be found in both the literature of the counter-culture today and its forerunners in earlier periods; and I shall begin by saying something about these parallels. In some other respects (I shall concede later) our own period is also unique—what historical period isn't? Still, we should try to understand the particular grounds of complaint levelled against science today, not as something entirely unique and unparalleled, but rather as a reformulation, within the special context of the present time, of certain older and more general lines of criticism. Let me begin, too, by stating these heads of complaint in their own terms—taking them just as they come, without trimming off the rhetorical excrescences or sugar-coating them. Of course, they all involve exaggerations of one kind or another; but we can go on later and sort out the grain of truth in each complaint from the intolerable deal of chaff surrounding it. If we take this course, I believe, we shall end by recognizing that—after all—there is more to the complaints than we were at first inclined to admit: that, in certain respects, we had this present anti-scientific reaction coming to us.

At least five themes recur again and again, at every stage in the anti-science debate. First, one can pick up the theme of *Humanism*. This can be traced back eventually as far as Socrates. Socrates dissociated himself from the scientific interests of the pre-Socratics (and, by implication, from those of his own pupil, Plato) by emphasizing the primacy of humane issues, in language very much like that of Montaigne in the 16th century A.D. Both Socrates and Montaigne were inclined to scepticism about the possibility of genuine scientific knowledge: even if there *were* any fundamental laws or principles to nature, they claimed, man probably had no hope of discovering them. But this epistemological position was, at least in part, an excuse for their own entirely worthy preoccupations with questions about society, ethics and human relationships. Montaigne particularly was speaking for a much larger group as well as for himself. The 16th-century humanists in general were neutral, when not actually hostile, to science. In this, they were quite unlike their scientifically minded successors of the 17th century. If anything, they would have felt much more sympathy for Swift's brutal caricature of the Royal Society men, in his *Voyage to Laputa*, with its attacks on the obscene and humanly irrelevant subjects chosen for research by the Robert Boyles and other scientific *virtuosi* of the 1660s and after.

The scientific ideas of the classical Greeks had been kept more or less alive throughout the Middle Ages, but the humanists were busy rediscovering the poets, the tragedians, the essayists and historians of antiquity: and the effect of this rediscovery did much more for the European sensibility than a Harvey or a Galileo could do. (It is in the 16th century, in fact, that one should probably look for the historical roots of that cleavage between the sciences and the humanities about which there has been so much discussion in the years since 1945.) The humanists tended—like the romantics of the early 19th century—to go on and pillory the scientists for being indifferent, and even callous, about humane issues, with the same kind of passion as any of today's anti-scientists denouncing nerve-gas research or the alliance between official science and the military-industrial complex. But a side-effect of these exaggerated attacks, at every stage, has been to stir the public consciences of the scientists themselves: there was, for instance, a curious and little-studied movement among mid-19th-century German scientists, led by Rudolph Virchow, to democratize and humanize science, which seems to have been a direct response to the complaints of the romantics about science during the 1830s and 1840s.

Then there is the recurring theme of *Individualism*. Again and again, literature and the fine arts have been presented by anti-scientists as superior to science, just because they give scope to the individual personality of the writer or artist; whereas scientific research is (by their account) an essentially conformist, collectivist mode of activity, in which the character and personal preoccupations of the individual scientist are suppressed in favour of communally imposed questions, procedures and orthodoxies. So in science (the argument runs) we are continually elevating the mean opinion of the professional group over the ideas of the individual, from whom alone any real originality or vision can be hoped. (This is a theme that unites Blake, Kierkegaard and Heidegger with many of our contemporaries: I have come across it, in odd forms, even among some younger research scientists today.)

Closely connected with this is a third theme: that of *Imagination*. Science is allegedly at fault because it limits itself to stereotyped and mechanical modes of argument, and so deprives itself of the creative powers that belong properly only to imaginative thought or fantasy. This theme you will recognize as common form among all the romantics of the early 19th century. Blake is again the most striking example, but Goethe and Schiller say the same; and so, too, do many of their present-day successors. In its extreme form, this argument has even turned into an attack on reason or rationality itself. Here—I have to admit—some of my colleagues in philosophy of science are partly to blame. By making exaggerated claims about the scope of formal logic in science, they have given the anti-science people a pretext for dismissing all scientific thought as drily and uncreatively 'logical'; and this has been made an excuse, in turn, for talking as though only 'irrationality' could be either artistically or intellectually creative.

A fourth, related theme—characteristic of Goethe, in particular, but familiar in many others—is that of *Quality versus Quantity*. The scientist is said to concern himself only with what is common to many different individual things, with general properties, and—for preference—with quantifiable or statistical magnitudes. This leads him to be indifferent to the qualitative features in which every individual differs from his fellows. Goethe, of course, believed that science—if properly conducted—could be redeemed from this charge. It was 'Newtonian' science that was specifically guilty of ignoring the individual, of subordinating qualitative differences to quantitative uniformities, of killing the animal whose life it pretended to explain, of breaking up into a spectrum (and so destroying) the whiteness of light, which needed rather to be studied in its primal integrity, and so on . . . Instead, the scientist should cultivate more of the clinical, personal, humane insight into his objects of study that a good doctor brings to his individual patients; and so transform himself (one might say) into an artist of the intellect—developing a feeling for the personality and uniqueness of each colour, leaf, human being, or meteorological event, without which he could not seriously claim to 'understand' it. The established Newtonian way only encouraged a callous concern with multiplicity, averages, collectives; and, in so doing, reinforced the tendency of the Newtonians towards an inhumane indifference.

Along with this complaint goes the other traditional Romantic attack, on the *Abstract* character of scientific ideas and inquiries. Scientists are not prepared to take the actual course of events, or the problems that arise within it, as they find it. They begin by imposing certain arbitrary theoretical demands and standards on the variety of nature, and they are then prepared to pay serious attention only to those aspects of nature which they choose to accept as 'significant' by those standards. A true humanism, by contrast, will be prepared to accept each new concrete situation in all its complexity and variety, as it arises, and deal with it accordingly. It will approach the task of building a dam, governing a village or treating an invalid, not with the abstract and self-limited attitudes of a scientist engaged in research into the strength of materials, the nature of social cohesion or the pathology of diabetes, but rather with an open-minded sensitivity to any and all aspects of the region, community or individual whose welfare is directly at risk.

Clearly, these five grounds of attack dovetail and reinforce one another. The humanist's preoccupation with concrete and specific problems of welfare and personal relations feeds his distrust of that abstract, statistical and generalizing approach which is crucial to theoretical progress in science; and the same hostility to 'cold-blooded rationality' plays into the hands of the romantic, with his emphasis on the creative imagination of the individual and his distrust of the logical and the methodical aspects of science. Together all five have played a powerful part in the whole syndrome of anti-science as it has recurred down the centuries; and with up-to-date variations they still play a part today. Science—or Technology, to give Beelzebub another of his names—is depicted as an abstract, logical, mechanical, cold-blooded, generalizing activity, given over to collectivist policies and practices devised solely for their technical efficiency and without regard for their effect on all the heterogeneous flesh-and-blood individuals at the receiving end. For lack of personal insight, emotional imagination or a feeling for the specific impact of his activities on real individuals, the scientist goes his indifferent way, regarding his fellow-men simply as so much extra subject-matter for social and technological experimentation.

All of this is, no doubt, very unjust and exaggerated. Of course, we may reply, the scientist's approach to his problems—the manner in which he selects topics for research, the terms in which he poses his questions and the rest—must, in the nature of the case, be guided by the objective demands of the theoretical situation in his field of inquiry. He cannot afford to be distracted from problems of crucial significance for the progress of his scientific field, however abstract and 'humanly irrelevant' they may appear, by the fact that other more practical issues may appeal more directly to his warm heart. (Indeed, it will be no sort of human kindness for him to let himself be distracted in this way, since the only long-run hope of dealing effectively with the humanly relevant issues is to tackle the theoretically crucial ones first.) So it just doesn't follow from the scientist's abstract approach that he himself is necessarily anti-humane. On the contrary, he may perfectly well be attacking the intellectually urgent problems in—say—physiology out of a higher and more realistic sense of compassion for the suffering men who can be successfully helped only *after* we have a better theoretical understanding.

Similarly, the fact that the professional activities demanded of a scientist, in the pursuit of his particular natural science, are single-valued and single-minded—even, as John Ziman likes to put it, 'monastic'—does not mean that in the rest of his life a scientist is obliged to suppress his personality or live anything less than a rich individual life. How else could a J. B. S. Haldane or a Frederick Lindemann get so far in science? Nor, for that matter, does a scientist's professional need to be 'numerate', and to concern himself with quantitative measures and general correlations, mean that he is necessarily—or can even afford to be—indifferent and insensitive to the details of individual cases. Absolute honesty about the facts of some individual case may, in fact, be the very thing which shows up a new problem or anomaly. In each case, accordingly, the points at which the romantic anti-scientist takes issue with science refer at first to some quite genuine aspect of science: but, in each case, he at once lapses into a misrepresentation of this point for the sake of rhetorical effect.

We *may* reply in this way, I say. But can we really, in all candour and sincerity, give this reply and leave matters at that? Maybe the romantic too often lets himself be tempted into reckless exaggeration. Maybe all that he criticizes in science 'ain't *necessarily* so'. But can we really cross our hearts and swear that it isn't *in fact* so? Just because all these defects that the romantic sees in science do have a grain of truth behind them—just because science is, in the nature of the case, abstract, quantitative and the rest—is there not a genuine risk that scientists may tend, more often then they should, to behave in fact in the ways the anti-scientist alleges that they necessarily behave? For example, remember that terrible remark of Oppenheimer's, about scientists being ready to attack any problem that is 'technically sweet' . . . . Of course, he should never have said it (I mean, of course it was a mistake for him to *admit* it); but isn't that just the kind of handle the anti-scientist is entitled to take hold of, in order to justify his claim that science is cold-blooded, and doesn't care about humane consequences? And let us be honest about the attitude the profession *in fact* adopts towards its mavericks: the Lindemanns, the Haldanes, the Bernals. Certainly, as an apprentice-scientist in a government research establishment during the Second World War, I was left in no doubt of what to think about Lord Cherwell for having let himself be drawn into playing the politician as well as the scientist. And can we really swear that the respectable majority of the profession hasn't let a collective suspicion of eccentricity and individuality colour its views about J. D. Bernal and J. B. S. Haldane too? No doubt, a scientist isn't *necessarily* penalized for being a complex, versatile, eccentric individual with lots of extra-scientific interests. But it certainly doesn't help him a bit.

The question we must, at this point, try to face squarely is: 'Why did the makers of the counter-culture *automatically* regard science as being on the side of the enemy?' Men like Ted Roszak are certainly too intelligent, knowledgeable and critical to fall for the rhetoric of their own wilder propagandists. So why didn't they see and acknowledge that the ideals of science are really on the side of imagination, humanity and individual integrity, just as much as those of literature and the fine arts? If we put the question in this way, then there is only one candid answer. Over the last thirty or forty years, the profession of science has lost its public reputation for living up to the proper ideals of its own occupation. I emphasize: this is not a remark about individual scientists, but one about the 'image' which the profession has, somehow or other, managed to get itself. Notice: it is not the ideals of science that the advocates of the counter-culture are angry about—how could they be? Nor is it individual scientists—they would be only too happy to recruit as many scientists as possible under a new, Virchow-like flag. It is the scientific profession they are attacking: and attacking as guilty of a renewed *trahison des clercs*—that is, for having delivered over to the temporal powers an enterprise which should be guided rather by perennial values. And it is only if we are ready to admit this sad fact that we can understand (I believe) the full virulence of the contemporary reaction against science.

What is new about the present situation, then, is not the standing risks to which scientists are—and always have been—exposed as a result of the

monasticism of their work. Rather, it is the fact that science has at last
achieved a position in which it is a significant political factor in its own right.
And the sharper edge which the anti-science movement has developed in the
last few years reflects (in my view) the particular manner in which the
scientific profession itself has, on the whole, responded to this new position of
political influence. As to the quality of this response, I suggest that you read
Vannevar Bush's recent memoirs, *Pieces of the Action*.[2] Let me say: I always
was, and in some ways still am, a great admirer of Vannevar Bush's work, but
it was a great shock to read his own recollections of that work. For they reveal
quite devastatingly the uncriticized presuppositions of the Scientific Establishment. Not the shadow of a doubt seems to cross his mind, either, whether
science is entitled to special public support on a scale that the fine arts and
other such activities are not; or, that the inner self-selected caucus of the
National Academy of Sciences, of which he was a member, was entitled to
co-opt other individuals of its kind to give unaccountable behind-the-scenes
advice to Government; or that, in technical matters of science and technology—however vast their potential effects on everyone else's lives—such
behind-the-scenes influence can be properly exercised without any kind of
democratic control. The low point for me is a passage in which Bush[1] justifies
the decision to drop the atomic bomb:

'By that time I knew that civilization faced an utterly new era, and I felt
that it might as well face it squarely .... If for no other reason I would
justify the use of the bomb at Hiroshima and Nagasaki because it was the
only way in which the dilemma could be presented with adequate impact on
World Consciousness'.

This is an argument which I sincerely hope that God Himself would not
have the gall to use. (Or, to pass from the grave to the light-hearted, let me just
recall that splendid remark of a prominent member of Congress reported by
Jerome Wiesner—that the unique thing about the scientific pork-barrel was
that the pigs themselves were running it.)

Still, one doesn't need to go to the Presidential level in order to see what
the counter-culture people are getting at. Something of the same political
transformation has gone much deeper. One only has to read the average
research-grant application of the 1960s in order to see the point. For, as so
many of my scientific colleagues candidly admit, it has been very important
throughout these last ten or fifteen years for scientists to know just what kind
of implied promises to hold out in their applications to each of the granting
agencies—whether keeping up with the Russians, or helping to cure fatal
diseases, or (nowadays) solving the problems of the 'urban environment'—
even when they also knew, perfectly well, that these implied promises were

empty. Consciousness of one's own pure motives has been held to excuse any such minor dishonesty.

If I cite American examples, this is—as always—simply because the acuteness of the problems affecting the scientific profession, and also the degree of awareness of them, have been greater there than elsewhere. There was even a stage around 1965-66, before the Vietnam business soured the attitudes of public-minded scientists from George Kistiakowsky down, when the problem of creating some better institutional control over the funding and application of science and technology was beginning to be tackled seriously. Scientists in general in the United States finally began to recognize that it was just not good enough to operate the public policy of science entirely *sub rosa,* through the back door of the Executive Mansion; and Kistiakowsky's Committee on Science and Public Policy was beginning to develop effective links with Congress which might have introduced some first element of democratic control into the situation.

Now, however, things seem to have moved far beyond the point they were at, even in the mid-1960s. I believe one can fairly regard the main thrust of the counter-culture attack on science and technology as one more aspect of the same general uprising of the people at the receiving end of political and economic change as that which Ralph Nader has come to speak for in the consumer movement. For in their own way—surely—the leaders of the scientific profession have operated, in their political role, as 'irresponsibly' as the board of General Motors in its economic and managerial roles. I am using the word 'irresponsibly' here in its primary, straightforward sense: that is, they have not been *answerable* in any way to the people whose lives have been affected by their political actions. The shortcomings in the present situation thus spring from political—not technical—defects in the institutions of policy-making, not from any lack of satisfactory criteria of choice.

In this situation, one can understand the temptation to which Jacob Bronowski yielded in 1970, when he publicly called for science to cut its links with government.[1] But that seems to me only an inadequate, partial and unrealistic response to the problems we now face. The British Society for Social Responsibility in Science, which Bronowski was addressing, can hardly be content simply to wash its hands of the only effective machinery for social and political action. More important: I think we should be taking up seriously again the debate that was broken off around 1967, about the ways in which the giving of scientific and technological advice to policy-makers can be set within some new institutional framework, which will allow a better measure of criticism and control on behalf of the people who will have to live with the consequence of that advice. The problem of 'humanizing' science is not that ot giving science itself new and more humane ideals. Nor is it the problem of making individual scientists more humane. It is that of creating a framework of institutions for policy-making within which the *human interests* of the non-scientific majority can be properly defended, wherever the effects of scientific and technological advice will bear upon their personal lives and happiness.

One last word: there may well be a case for disestablishing science at the same time. By this I mean: there may well be a case for arguing that such bodies as the National Academy of Science cannot perform, at one and the same time, the two separate functions of representing the interests of the scientific profession *to* government, and also of giving *sub rosa* advice as and when required *by* government. And there may well be a case, also, for trying to work our way back to a situation in which the financial support of pure science is once again put on the same basis as that of art or literature or education. But that is another story. . . . In the meantime, it can do us no harm to remind ourselves that the next major advances in scientific thought may well be going to come, not from any generously-funded 'research project', but—as they have so often done before—from the late 20th-century counterpart of a country house in Kent, or the Swiss Patent Office, or a monastery in Bohemia.

Bibliography

1. BRONOWSKI, J. (1971) The disestablishment of science. In *The Social Impact of Modern Biology*, pp. 233–243. Ed. W. Fuller. London: Routledge & Kegan Paul.
2. BUSH, V. (1970) *Pieces of the Action*. New York: Morrow.

See pp. 49-59 for further discussion of points raised in this paper.

Anti-science: observations on the recent 'crisis' of science

EDWARD SHILS

The 'crisis'

It appears that, precipitously from its high estate and great glory, science has come into a crisis. This is said by scientists of eminence and not just by excitable publicistic hangers-on of the 'science industry'. When the term 'crisis' is used it is usually meant that what is in 'crisis' is in danger; by danger is meant that its continued existence is less probable, that it is falling into a state of disorder, that its future existence will be constricted, that it will not be able to perform its tasks as effectively as it had hitherto. In the case of an intellectual activity, a crisis can be purely intellectual. Science would be in an intellectual crisis if it were shown that it had been proceeding erroneously, that its discoveries had been shown to be illusions, that it had exhausted its problems and, finding nothing more worthwhile to work on, had descended to trivialities of no intellectual consequence, or finally that it could make no progress in the solution of the scientific problems which it undertook to study.

Science could also be in a crisis if interest in it declined to the point where minds of superior capacity no longer wished to engage in its cultivation. It would be in a crisis if the institutions in which it was performed became incapable of fostering its pursuit. If the institutions of science were so organized that important problems of science could not be studied effectively as a result of the way in which the power to make decisions was organized, or as a result of the practices of recruitment, recognition, promotion, and allocation of resources, or as a result of the unmanageability of the literature of science or its excessively professional specialization, then, despite the availability of numerous important problems intellectually susceptible to fruitful investigation, science would be in a serious crisis.

Science could also be in a crisis as a result of a markedly diminishing appreciation of its value—intellectual and practical—among the laity on whom it depends for manpower, financial support, and respect. The crisis of science in these last few years appears in some measure to be of this latter sort. This does not mean that the crisis of science could not be severe. The future of science could be greatly imperilled if young persons of talent did not show themselves willing to undergo the discipline required in becoming well qualified to carry on the work of science. The future of science could be endangered by a great shrinkage in the funds available for research and training. The future of science could be endangered if political and public opinion turned against it—denying its value, either as truth or as a source of valuable technology or because it was thought to have pernicious moral and social consequences. If there were a powerful critical revulsion from science on the part of its lay patrons, both immediate and indirect, and its potential recruits, this could do much harm to science. Such a revulsion would indeed be severe enough to be called a crisis.

Finally, if practising scientists themselves, not just those individuals who might become scientists in the future but those already working in science, lost their belief in the worthwhileness of scientific work, then science would be in a bad way. If a significantly large number of well-established scientists were to decide that it is intellectually or morally wrong to conduct scientific investigation along traditional lines, or that because of pernicious consequences which flow from it into other spheres of life they should give up science, and if they were to make their reasons known, they might endanger science by demoralizing some of its less well-established practitioners, by discouraging young persons from entering it and by dissuading its patrons and appreciators from supporting it.

The crisis in context

The recent alarm among scientists and the friends of science about the crisis of science must be viewed in a wider context.

Many scientists and many politicians and publicists have lived in the twenty-five or more years since the end of the Second World War in a situation in which science seemed to have been elevated to the centre and foundation of our existence. Not only had it replaced theology as the 'queen of the sciences'—this had happened a long time before—but it had been made into the arbiter of the destiny of man. Science was elevated into the source of industrial development. Attention was focused on those industries called science-based industries; then the entire society was alleged to be on the verge of becoming science-based. Practically every human activity was regarded as sooner or later coming under the guidance—not just the scrutiny but the guidance—of scientific knowledge.

Infectious diseases were considered to have been overcome; degenerative diseases were being struggled against with reasonable prospects of success. Agricultural productivity was the beneficiary of scientific research. Military security was made to appear to be dependent on scientific research. One need not go on to enumerate the technological and intellectual triumphs of scientific research. All this redounded to the prosperity and prestige of science and scientists. Scientists became the heroes of the age. The press and television devoted much space and time to honouring them and to describing in popular form their achievements. Governments showed themselves to be unprecedentedly generous to them. Resources for research were placed at their disposal with unprecedented lavishness. Even very poor countries like India strained themselves to provide ample facilities for research. In the rich countries, almost anything a qualified scientist wished to do would be paid for—if not he could go to the United States where he could get what was lacking at home.

Scientists lived in a state of euphoria. Yet at the same time, outside the scientific community uneasiness began to be felt, though not the same kind of uneasiness as had been experienced by educated non-scientists in the 19th century when science began its institutionally organized forward march. In the 19th and early 20th centuries, as more and more of human life came under the glass of scientific understanding, various defences had been put up to delimit the dominion of scientific *understanding*.* But the expanding dominion of science in the 19th and early 20th centuries had been mainly a cognitive expansion. It had scarcely involved *control* of the foundations of man's existence. The expansion of the dominion of science in the Second World War went further. It brought with it our expectation that the future would be not just the epoch of the universal sway of scientific *knowledge*. Science in the new epoch would become increasingly the source of practical decisions and the basis of power. The future of our societies would be under the rule of science and that meant the rule of scientists. The 'post-industrial society' would not only be brought about by the progress of scientific knowledge

---

* The German distinction between *Geistes-* and *Naturwissenschaften* had been one such defence. It is not one which has had many devotees recently. The theological defence resting on the distinction of the proper spheres of reason and science on the one hand, and of revelations and faith on the other, has had even fewer.

derived from organized research; it would also be governed on the basis of scientific knowledge. 'Needs' would be satisfied by what science disclosed would most adequately satisfy them. The 'real needs' would even be discovered by scientific research.

The tellers of Gothic tales—not just the writers of what is acknowledged to be (science) fiction but publicists of science and enthusiastic scientists— filled in some of the details of the scientific post-industrial society with accounts of bio-engineering, genetic engineering and self-sustaining, self-directing computers free of human controllers. It should be said again that many, perhaps most, scientists have not held this view. But something like this has been asserted by the heralds of science, by 'science writers' and by enthusiasts among scientists. Most of us have frequently heard some of our colleagues say things like this and even when those speaking on behalf of this 'promise' of science were not scientists, the credit or discredit for the aspiration went to science.

No very great power of logical reasoning and imagination would have been required to put all these bits of loose talk together to create the phantasm of a body of scientists with nearly limitless powers but without clearly visible moral restraints and willing and nearly ready to put the human race under their control. In the background of these developments and claims lay slumbering the atomic bomb. Most sensitive and informed persons know nowadays that the hair on which their life hangs has grown especially thin since 1945. It is true that nuclear weapons have not been used in war since August of that year and although in the two long and difficult wars which the United States has fought in Asia since then, nuclear weapons have not been used, the terror of nuclear weapons exists among us and the prominence of great scientists in their creation is not lost, even if not often articulated.

What has been articulated, alongside of and often in the same minds as great awe and admiration, is a repugnance towards scientists for having, in collaboration with businessmen and the military, polluted the atmosphere and the waters, eroded and scarred the earth's surface, damaged its plant and insect life. Some deep-lying fantasy of a 'natural nature', harmonious and perfectly equilibrated, doing no damage to any species until man intervened, has been evoked and perturbed.

Some politicians, especially those annoyed with the military and its industrial suppliers, have, as part of their campaign against their adversaries, taken out some of their vexation on scientists who have worked under military auspices—although certainly not always on problems of military technology. It must be remembered that intellectuals in most countries have had very troubled relations with politicians and that in the United States these relationships were more strained than in most other countries until the rise of the new liberalism of Woodrow Wilson. Since then they have had marked ups and downs. The kind of sentiment which came to the surface during the ascendancy of the first Senator McCarthy is the product of an old tradition; it is always ready to re-emerge. The rise of scientists to a position of centrality stirred these latent sentiments.

The strain of resentment against the scientists which came to the visible surface in the last few years has drawn reinforcements from academic and other critics of the 'flying professors'. The 'flying professors' have been to a large extent scientists serving on advisory boards and panels. The resentment against them in the academic world came largely from the humanities departments, members of which believed that they were being slighted by the reigning powers of the national government, despite the equal beauty of their eyes. They felt that there was an overtone derogatory to their own status in the preferment accorded the scientists, the preferment consisting of the grant of large sums for research, appointments to advisory posts, the opportunity to associate with the powerful. It became widely believed that university teachers in the sciences did not attend to their teaching responsibilities because they were so engrossed in their research and in their consultations with governments.* Commentators on the higher educational system of the United States often referred to this dereliction from duty.

Thus the prototypical science professor at the major university in the United States came to be impugned. He was charged with being concerned only with his own research, his own university department, his own generation of scientists, his own protégés, etc. The 'scientific community' came to be seen as the 'scientific establishment' looking exclusively after its own interests. Even a noted sociologist chimed in with the 'Matthew effect' which declared that those scientists already at the top of their respective disciplines gain more prominence, more credit for achievement, more honours, better appointments, etc., while the others, presumably with equal natural endowment, suffer further the slings of outrageous fortune. This was not merely the fantasy of a sociologist. A similar attitude began to be more emphatically expressed within the scientific community itself. Members of and spokesmen for universities which were far down on the list of eminence of achievement

---

* I find it amusing to notice that among the main seedbeds of complaints against teachers for having failed to live up to their obligations as teachers and to teach 'relevant' stuff are English and sociology departments. The former had no 'flying professors', the latter very few. Yet the scientific departments of the universities have not been much troubled by the demands of students for more attention, better teaching and more 'relevant' courses of study!

began to complain that under the existing system of the award of grants, the 'elite universities' got the lion's share. They implied that this share was not merited but came their way because of their prestige and because the panels of advisers who reviewed applications had been elected from those 'elite universities'—again, mainly on account of their prestige.

Naturally congressmen, concerned for the welfare and gratitude of their constituencies, echoed and intensified these complaints. The rupture of the unity of the scientific community—previously unbroken except for the widespread revulsion against Dr Edward Teller—was aggravated by the war in Vietnam and by the student disorders.

This brief and rough sketch of the state of opinion which confronts science today must be appreciated in all its paradoxicality. Ten years ago, scientists were glorified but their glory was not without qualifications. These qualifications have become more pronounced in the past few years. These qualifications are the platform of anti-science. Do they mean that science is in a crisis?

How serious is the crisis?

I do not think that science is in a serious crisis. It is true that the criteria are ambiguous and the evidence vague and fragmentary. Nonetheless it does not seem to me that science is in grave danger. Intellectually, it seems to be in a condition of great fertility. It is also very well financed despite the howls of calamity which I hear. Its *primary* institutional structure seems, on the evidence of its accomplishment, to be sound. (This does not mean that the primary institutional structure, that is laboratories, training arrangements and communications, are perfect!) Although science seems to be in good condition intellectually, there is much criticism both from the outside and from within the ranks of scientists, including some of those at the very highest ranks. Science, scientists and the institutional setting of science are being criticized, more voluminously and more harshly than they have been for a very long time. The criticism of science is certainly not new; hostility towards scientists is not new; lack of interest in science is not new. But there has been a change of mood in the last half-dozen years which is markedly different from the attitude which has prevailed in most countries for at least the past three decades.

Some of the criticisms which have been directed against science and scientists in this most recent period are no more than the reiteration of criticisms which have been directed against science for at least a century and a half. I refer here particularly to the criticism of science for disregarding wholeness, for practising objectivity or detachment and dispassionateness, for denying and suppressing individuality, and so on. Not all of the criticisms are reiterations. Some are fairly new and are responses to the new situation of science since its great expansion in the past three decades.

What is striking about these newer critiques is that they leave the intellectual side of science relatively untouched. The validity of the findings of science is left pretty well unquestioned; the reliability of the methods of science has been immune from doubt. It is not alleged that science has reached a dead-end and that it is incapable of going on to make further important discoveries. In general the purely intellectual reputation of science has never been better and its intellectual prospects seem to be regarded as no less favourable than they have ever been.

In the 19th century, when science was criticized, its truths were denied—because it impugned or denied the geological, palaeontological, biological and historical beliefs which formed major parts of the Christian intellectual tradition. On the surface, and perhaps more deeply, science is no longer an object of hostility on the grounds that it destroys non-scientific beliefs. Nor is the procedure of science criticized for entering into spheres of existence where it is claimed to be unqualified to enter. The human mind, human behaviour, social organization—spheres which it was once thought science was not qualified to enter or where if it did enter it was claimed that it would do harm—are also now thought to be proper objects of scientific analysis. The challenging but feeble social and behavioural sciences are now thought likely to benefit by the extension of scientific modes of analyses beyond their traditional subject matters.

The crisis, such as it is, is a crisis in the external institutional relations of science. It is a crisis in the external technological, economic and political relations of science—not in its external intellectual relations. It is also a crisis of the wider institutional setting of science, that is, of the institutional arrangements which mediate between scientific work and the society external to it.

The economic crisis of science

The external relations of science which have been criticized in the recent wave of anti-science are economic, technological, political and organizational. These are all linked with each other in various ways by the critics whose criticism helps to constitute the 'crisis' of science in the minds of those who deplore the crisis and wish that it did not exist. I shall deal with the economic crisis of science first because it is probably the simplest and most straightforward. It is also more independent of the technological, political and organizational phenomena with which the anti-science movement is concerned.

It is said by scientists and by the publicists who observe and write about science that science has come into a crisis because it is not receiving the amount of financial support which scientists think it ought to have. The support has either ceased to grow at the same rate as over the preceding quarter of a century (i.e. after the Second World War when it grew manyfold), or it has ceased to grow at all and has even decreased by a very small fraction. There is no doubt that this has caused considerable consternation among scientists in the United States and the United Kingdom. All around one hears statements like: 'This is a fatal blow to X' (i.e. the particular branch of science cultivated by the speaker), or 'The United States will lose its world leadership in Z' (again, the particular field of the speaker).

The restriction of funds is variously interpreted as a result of the effective competition of other fields of governmental expenditure, or as a failure on the part of government to understand how important the research field in question is. More generally many scientists seem to believe that the restrictions are evidence that science has fallen from the favour which it had until very recently enjoyed. Indeed the restriction in funds is made into the symbol of the generalized anti-science attitude which is manifested over a far wider front of the external relation of science than that of 'mere' finance.

The technological relations of science

The technological relations of science had been until recently a major source of the pride of scientists—or at least, so they said. They have surely provided one of the major motives of the financial support of science. The integration of the results of research into the technology of economic growth, material well-being and military action has been put forward by scientists to justify their claims for financial and moral support. The friends of science outside the scientific community have nearly always cited this technological relevance as the justification for the support of research; so did scientists. Regardless of their privately held beliefs, scientists seldom referred to the intrinsic value of man's knowledge of the universe. They had become very used to thinking of science in utilitarian terms, whether as a result of deep conviction or of the rhetoric of application for financial support. There were very few scientists who did not regard, either in their innermost conviction or in their claims for support, the utilitarian-technological justification for scientific research as the right one.

There was a happy coincidence of interests. Industrialists, military men, politicians, publicists and other leaders of public opinion and those sections of the citizenry interested enough to have an opinion all wanted the technological—industrial, military, medical, etc.—benefits of research. The scientists were pleased to conduct the research, as long as they were free to work on what they wished to work on and were amply supported. Basic research which had no immediately intended or tangible technological benefits enjoyed the status of the ultimate source of the practical benefit and it therefore also came in for ample support.

For a long time this relationship was unquestioned. Even that small, courageous and public-spirited group of American scientists who had first opposed the use of nuclear weapons against the Japanese and then contended for international control and a related domestic control of the uses of atomic energy raised no questions about this relationship. The Pugwash movement raised no questions about the relationship either.

There had been some discussion about the moral obligations of scientists to concern themselves with the consequences or the applications of their scientific discoveries but this discussion seldom, as far as I can recall, raised questions about the relationship between scientists and their governmental and private patrons. Then things began to change. The growing concern about pollution of air and water by radioactivity and industrial waste-substances mounted into *crescendo*. The use of insecticides in agriculture, and of defoliants and napalm in Vietnam, raised the question much more acutely and urgently. Research on substances for purposes of chemical and biological warfare came under passionate attack. Whereas at the beginning criticism had been directed towards the 'users' of the products derived from scientific research, it was not long before those who did the research came equally into the focus of the criticism. The uproar among university students in the United States turned, after a short delay, onto the Institutes of Defense Analysis. Within the universities some scientists espoused the critical attitude of the students. The bonds between universities and the government and particularly the United States Department of Defense were subjected to the most stringent and embittered criticism. University administrators and scientists who had unreservedly accepted the existing relationship now turned angrily or prudently against it. Various movements were initiated to prohibit academic scientists from engaging in research which could have military applications; the simplest form was a demand that universities prohibit 'classified' research from being conducted in university buildings; a more advanced form was the demand for the classified research of university staff to be prohibited wherever it is conducted. Consultative services by academics for governmental bodies have likewise come under the fire of criticism.

The consequences of the revulsion against the technological application of scientific discovery have now spread beyond industry and warfare into other fields of scientific research. The progress of the life or biomedical sciences has also agitated the sentiments which underlie the 'anti-science' movement. The prospect of genetic engineering and the actuality of organ transplantation continue to generate alarm and arouse fantasies about scientists like Dr Moreau, malevolently creating monsters out of sheer scientific curiosity or a desire to pre-empt divine powers. The ultimate ethical postulate of medical technology is on the way to being questioned when the great growth of population through the reduction in infant mortality and through the successful application of public health and sanitary measures is considered. The prolongation of life by the application of the discoveries of medical science which has always been an absolutely unquestioned postulate of research and practice in medicine is now beginning to come under the shadow of a doubt. The 'population explosion' is not viewed by anyone nowadays in western countries as a blessing—quite the contrary. In consequence, the advances of medical science have begun to take on a little of the coloration of the 'disaster' which their application has made possible.

The tremendous technological achievements of space-exploration have added to the scepticism about the value of the technological application of science. To many sensitive persons the great publicity for space-flights and landings on the moon has only helped to raise doubts about the value of technology. Whereas it was once believed that every new technological possibility was automatically and inevitably beneficial, the great achievements in outer space have helped to dim the light once cast by technological progress.

Science, engineering and technology have all become amalgamated into a single entity which is conceived of as a source of damage and a costly waste. The research workers, engineers, military men, industrialists and politicians are seen as a homogeneous group, with each section pursuing its own advantage at the expense of the rest of society.

Since about 1967 it has been downhill all the way and very bumpily too. From time to time there are reports that, because they fear evil applications might follow, certain scientists have decided to discontinue particular lines of research they had pursued with distinction. One also hears or sees remarks to the effect that certain lines of research might have to be prohibited because of their potentially dangerous consequences.* The latest development is Dr Bronowski's call for the 'disestablishment of science', by which he means the cutting of all ties between government and science—except of course for the flow of financial resources from government to science.[1]

Yet this determination to break all ties—except the one-way flow of financial support—which connect scientists and government is not a counsel of withdrawal to the 'ivory tower'. The refusal to allow the products of scientific research to be used by government or industry except under the control of scientists—and the refusal to allow them to be used at all by the military—is not tantamount to an indifference to society. On the contrary, the anger against the technological application of the results of scientific research is addressed only to the negative consequences of technological application. In principle it accepts the technological application of the results of research exactly as did the tradition which it rejects. A significant difference is that whereas the hitherto prevailing tradition saw only beneficial consequences for the national society flowing from the application of research, the new 'anti-science' standpoint sees negative consequences and it is up in arms against those. The acceptance of the primary value of science as technological or utilitarian is common to the traditional scientism and to the recent anti-science views. But whereas the former could not imagine negative consequences flowing from science, the latter is more realistic. It is however realistic only up to a point. It believes that the evil technological consequences of science came from its association with authority and power—with government, industry and the military. If scientific research could escape from the application of its results by these groups, then the traditional conception of the exclusively benign consequences of scientific research would be reinstated.

Anarchism and a belief in the uncorrupted virtue of scientists—once they are free of the servitude of civil obligation—are the postulates of this theme of anti-science. As in the case of the first front of anti-science—the financial one—there is no doubt, in the minds of those who believe that science is in a

---

* For example, Prof. Lawrence Tribe has written '... the alternative might be to push the regulatory process back to the earliest stages of research and development, cutting off such lines of enquiry as seem most likely to lead to the bio-medical intervention we fear. One may recognize that the suppression of a particular avenue of enquiry need not mean the suppression of free enquiry generally and indeed that selective suppression may operate to forestall an unselective counteraction of a graver sort, while still regretting the inroads on a principle begun by such a step'.[2]

crisis as a result of the deeds of non-scientists, that science is entitled to continuing financial support on a grand scale as in the decade preceding its crisis. It is believed too that this support should come from government.

Critique of the scientific establishment

Science has been censured by anti-science, ultimately for its political connections. Scientists are blamed for subservience to the military-industrial complex and that alleged subservience is indeed seen as the cause of the negative consequences of science. Not all scientists however are regarded as equally guilty. Some are charged with being more involved with the political-industrial-military triangle than others. The most guilty of scientists are the scientific 'establishment', i.e. those who have given advice to government on scientific matters or on non-scientific matters in which science is involved; the establishment includes those who administer large-scale award-granting bodies and those who serve on advisory panels. The highest officers of national scientific associations and academics are also part of the establishment. They are charged by the bearers of anti-science—who include both scientists and non-scientists: academic, political and publicistic—with the subjugation of science to those who were acting injuriously towards human welfare.

Some resentment had been accumulating for some time against the great lords of science who influenced decisions as to which fields of science were to be cultivated, which institutions and individuals were to receive grants, etc. They were thought of as corrupt and contaminated. But as long as the benefits were widely distributed, there was no large-scale hostility towards them. When, however, governmentally supported science came to be equated with military science, they were subjected to much hostile criticism. As hostility towards political authority increased, the 'scientific establishment' which was its confidante was rendered even more abhorrent.

In all this, a significant part was played by a subprofession which had grown up around the wider scientific institutional system, namely the scientific publicists or, as Dr Weinberg has called them, the 'scientific muckrakers'. Some of these were intimate with the internal life of the wider institutional system of science. What they said about the self-serving propensities of scientists seemed authoritative.

The critique of the scientific establishment is part of the larger rejection of authority. Authority is charged with indifference and even malevolence towards what is essential in human existence: spontaneity, freedom from institutional restraints, freedom from the burden of the past. Individuality is the highest good and anything which curbs it or disciplines it is wicked.

The anti-science movement within the scientific community has not gone so far. Within the scientific sector of the movement, the postulate of the technological value of scientific research is still accepted; the value of scientific knowledge is still affirmed. It is only among the non-scientific sector of the movement that anti-science reaches its fullest extension and depth.

Will the crisis become serious?

Now, to what extent is science really in a crisis? How strong is the anti-science movement? How unified is it? And how justified are its arguments?

In my view, the crisis is not serious because the anti-science movement is not unified. The support is heterogeneous, although the various groups of its supporters overlap. For example, some politicians charge scientists with neglect of their social responsibilities and are especially critical of the scientific establishment, but most of the politicians who are the agents of the restriction of financial support for science are not anti-science in any other sense. There is a wide and fundamental difference between the two main anti-science groups—the anti-science scientists and the romantic anarchist wing of the new left. They are united in their opposition to scientists in government, and in their criticism of the 'negative' technological applications of science in military, industrial and agricultural fields. While the anti-science scientists are not against science as an intellectual activity, the romantic anarchistic anti-science movement is against science as such because it is institutionalized in universities and because it is disciplined and detached.

Let us look a little more closely at the financial side which many scientists interpret as evidence of the power of the wave of anti-science sentiment. For one thing it is, as I have said before, largely the work of politicians and administrators who are not anti-science. They might be a little less enthusiastic about science than they were before but on the whole they are not antagonistic to science. Some of them want to diminish military expenditure, some of them are very antagonistic towards the military—for example the 'Mansfield Amendment' originated by Senator Fulbright. For the most part, however, their action has been a response to the great demand for increased expenditure on welfare services—health, education, urban problems, etc.

And how dangerous to science is this diminished rate of growth of expenditure, or even its slight decline? I venture to say: not very dangerous. The total sums appropriated for the support of science are still tremendous—far larger than in any of the other great periods in the history of science. They are, it is true, required on that scale because of the much larger numbers of scientists and the greatly increased cost of equipment, but the fact remains that the funds available for research are immeasurably greater than they were fifteen years ago, when there was no such apprehension as exists today among scientists.

The impact of the diminished rate of growth or slight decline must not be overestimated. It does mean, however, that given the number of qualified scientists available, scientific knowledge will not expand as rapidly as it might have done if all the available, properly qualified scientists were engaged in research of a type they are capable of doing. This means that for the time being certain lines of investigation which appear to be scientifically promising will not be as intensively cultivated as they might have been, or that they will be cultivated by scientists in other countries. Scientists, especially those whose research programmes are constricted by having smaller sums than they desire—even though these are often very large amounts of money—are inclined to say that the 'cutting off' of funds is doing irreparable damage to science, etc., but in fact all that is likely to happen, at least in the near future, is that somewhat less research will be done on problems which appear to be ready for fruitful investigation. Is there a 'normal' rate of scientific growth and is it the rate which has obtained in the past two decades?

There are other aspects to be considered. The stock of qualified scientists has been produced in a period of increasing rate of growth of financial support. Its members have been trained to do research and to expect to be able to obtain the financial support needed to do the research they wished to do, as long as their projects could meet a reasonable standard of scientific respectability. A diminished or stable scale of support is therefore bound to frustrate some of them. They will be forced to make do with less than they believe they are entitled to have. Being no longer assistants or doctoral candidates they are bound to expect to be supported on the scale of other independent scientists who were receiving support while they themselves were still juniors. In this respect, they are likely to be frustrated. They are also likely to be embittered. So are their patrons and sponsors who are already interpreting the reduction in funds for studentships and research assistantships as evidence of the hard times into which science has fallen.

Accompanying this will be a reduction in the number of graduates going on to do research for advanced degrees. In Great Britain there has already been a turning away from science among those coming up to university. A variety of explanations have been given for this. Among them are: young persons are becoming disillusioned with science and with its results in society; young persons do not believe that science is 'relevant' to the major problems faced by society or by themselves; they reject 'specialization' and 'narrowness' in scientific training and the scientific career. There is undoubtedly some substance in these interpretations but the events to which they point are not catastrophic. The interpretations also express the mood of those who offer them; the mood is a sense of being rejected.

If science were entering a situation like that of classics or theology in the present century, then there would be grounds for gloom. If the funds of the last few years were to continue more or less in the same downward direction, if there were a prospect that financial support and recruitment of talented young persons would continue to dwindle for one or two decades, then there would be a serious crisis. But science seems to be too rooted in modern culture, and the technological productivity of scientific research seems too incontrovertibly established to allow science to dwindle. Nor do I see any reason to believe that the hedonism which is a major characteristic of modern culture and which stands to gain so much from the positive application of science to technology is likely to diminish.

Scientists have entered the world of publicity. They have become used to seeing the names of their colleagues in newspapers and general periodicals which are not written for intellectual audiences. They have become sensitive to publicity and they have therefore come to believe in its reality. Some of them like to see their views in popular print and they have to some extent come to believe that the real world is accurately expressed by newspapers, writers, television commentators, speeches by politicians and their own more vocal academic colleagues. This is not the real world but many scientists think it is—alongside the more real world of their own investigations—and when it turns against them they think that the world has come to an end. The currents of belief in a society are deeper, more continuous and more stable than what is agitated on the surface. The intellectuals of our age—scientists among them, and especially those who like to mingle in science policy—have become like politicians and interpret a few straws in the wind as if entire haystacks are in movement.

The larger society is not withdrawing its support from science. Industry is committed to research; so are the armed forces, and government policies with regard to health and agriculture are firmly rooted. Likewise there is still a strong although exasperated attachment to higher education which has traditionally provided the locus and salary of senior investigators. The diminished flow of young persons into the natural sciences and mathematics certainly in itself and on the basis of the information available does not indicate anything like a total drying up of the flow of talented people into the natural sciences. It is only because expectations were exorbitant that the slight diminution has been disturbing.

The belief that science could go on expanding at the same rate as it had in the three decades since 1940 was an illusion, and the slowing down of the rate of growth in financial support and numbers of students is probably in many respects an advantage. After all, the reservoir of scientific talent is not indefinitely expansible and a restriction of numbers might well be accompanied by an increase in the proportion of the more highly talented scientists in the total body of scientists.

There is nonetheless something important to be learnt from the recent flurry of anti-science.

How firm is the position of science in our civilization?

It must be admitted that whatever the motivation for doing scientific research, the support for science depends on the beliefs of those who pay for it—politicians, administrators and ultimately the concerned citizenry which produces the revenue. The possible expansion of anti-science must be viewed in this light. Various of the excrescences of science and its technological applications might be very repugnant to many people but the matter-of-fact belief in regularities discoverable by systematic investigation is very widely accepted, as are the technological benefits of scientific research.

Science is also inseparably associated with education, which is the object of a very deep commitment in practically all modern cultures. There are numerous eccentricities, deficiencies and misconceptions in modern educational doctrine and practice but, whatever they are, instruction in science holds a firm position. As long as science continues to be taught in schools so that the interest of those with the capacity for it is aroused, and as long as there is a widespread desire for the benefits of technology and an acceptance of matter-of-fact empirical modes of thought, science will persist.

Of course anti-science makes some difference and it is desirable that such power as it has be diminished. This is desirable because much of it is repugnant to a reasonable ordering of social life. Some of these repugnant elements are endemic in human existence; many of them are exaggerations of valid moral and religious standpoints. The aggravation of anti-science in recent years is not entirely attributable to these. The aggravations are attributable to quite justifiable even if vastly exaggerated responses to excesses associated with the recent practice of science.

This does not mean that all the remedies proposed by anti-science in its various forms are correct or useful. For example, science cannot and will not be allowed to cut itself off from government unless its proponents really want to cripple it. It cannot be expected that scientists alone or with the aid of 'the community' which excludes government and industry should exclusively control the technological application of the results of scientific research.

The cure for the excesses of anti-science must lie in greater circumspection on the part of scientists. Granted that the future repercussions of scientific discoveries cannot be predicted with accuracy, still scientists should be more reflective about these matters—and their reflectiveness should be institutionalized and continuous instead of intermittent and apocalyptic. They must guard themselves against their own self-serving propensities. They must avoid striking promethean poses. They must learn to say 'no' in a discriminating way to all the opportunities which knowledge and research offer them. They must learn that 'more' is not necessarily better. They must distinguish the valid from the invalid in anti-science and they must mend their ways accordingly. Above all they must not yield to the temptations of the prophetic role.

Discussion

Thiemann: Can the so-called anti-science movement of today really be regarded as a normal historical development? The millions of people now involved in research and development are no longer the same kind of scientists as the older generation. They are employees and like any other employees are fighting for their own rights. They have become a distinct sociological group. Like the early socialist movement in the last century, they are afraid about their future. There is pressure for further exponential growth, but this will reach a limit—growth cannot go on indefinitely.

I recently saw a photograph of the sixty or seventy physicists who attended the Solvay Congress in Brussels in 1927 and every person there could be identified as having done outstanding work—the Braggs, Einstein and many others. Today a photograph of a Solvay Congress would not show many scientists we could identify with such outstanding results. Maybe this is because we now have quantity rather than quality of those doing science.

Bloch: This is another illustration of what I meant by increased specialization in science. Today those attending a Solvay Congress are all specialists in their own tiny field. They are well known to a small group of like specialists all over the world, but their relative anonymity to the rest of their colleagues indicates how segmented and split the scientific disciplines are today.

Toulmin: I am not sure that there is any disagreement between us here. I am always unhappy about the phrase 'the scientific community': it is clear from what Dr Thiemann says that we are concerned with a vast and internally heterogeneous social group. The sixty or seventy people at the Solvay meetings were all members of a common species, clearly enough; but one cannot regard all research workers today as members of a common 'scientific community'. First, they are not all people of the same kind doing commensurable work and, secondly—because of this—they no longer have clear common interests. The growth of scientific work has thus had consequences both of scale and quality: in particular, the vast and varied amount of research being done has blurred the boundary between what is 'scientific' work and what is not. The political and institutional issues raised by science are therefore much more subtle and complex than we can really do justice to, because we of our generation remember what is was like in earlier days.

Roche: Ortega y Gasset[3] wrote: 'Contemporary science, with its system and methods, can put blockheads [*tontos*] to good use'.

Medawar: One of the great achievements of modern science has been the democratization of learning. Anybody can be a scientist who is reasonably sensible and imaginative, so that learning and imaginative activities are now open to a very much greater population than ever before.

It may be worth emphasizing that the Royal Society's motto, *nullius in verba,* was not intended to imply that scientists would semaphore to each other or talk in symbols; rather it has the implication of a repudiation of authority, particularly Aristotle's authority. Also, the Royal Society as such does not advise the government and in this respect it differs from the National Academy of Sciences in the United States. Of course individual Fellows of the Royal Society can advise the government if they are asked to, but the Royal Society is not a governmental agency at all.

Long: The label of 'anti-science' implies to some degree an opposing organization, with a structure, journals and so on, but I see instead a very chaotic set of countervailing pressures and directions, some of which are covered by the term Arcadian. This is not so much anti-science as non-science. In the United States, at least, the people who set up communes in the most distant parts of New Mexico are not really rebelling against science but against a particular view of the world. Similarly there is an understandable irritation with the consequences of science and technology in a number of areas, including the military, as another piece of this rather confused picture. But these confused sets of pressures are hard to recognize as an anti-science movement.

Toulmin: We are here talking about a widespread public feeling which has been having a political influence, and Dr Shils underlined the effect this has had on the less generous support being provided for science. The politicians can cut down the support, because they know there isn't a very strong pro-science feeling in the community: science is no longer the great white hope. So there is no need for an 'anti-science' *organization,* with journals and so on.

Bullock: Do you distinguish this from the much more general phenomenon, among the public and in parliament, of disillusionment with universities and disillusionment with all institutes of higher education? Everything that you say about science is surely true of social science. The disillusionment with science is nothing compared to the disillusion with economics, with all forms of social science and with university work in general. The cuts in the science budget are nothing to the cuts in the social sciences budget.

Toulmin: True; and the answer is that today—as in Blake's day—the anti-science attitude goes hand-in-hand with a broader romantic anti-intellectualism and anti-authoritarianism.

Medawar: Blake's notorious anti-scientism was really just anti-intellectualism. His words were, in effect, 'I come in the grandeur of inspiration to abolish ratiocination'.

Toulmin: But there was a certain amount of Arcadianism about Blake as well.

Weinberg: When I have to dismiss two hundred people a year from the Oak Ridge National Laboratory, I appreciate Dr Shils's reassurance that this is all illusion and not really a reflection of anything very serious. To me it is very serious indeed. On the university campuses I find that the young people are in fact turning away from science. This is not a figment of the imagination.

Bloch: If you have to dismiss two hundred people a year, is this surprising?

Weinberg: It is a question of cause and effect. This anti-scientific ambiance is not an invention. The real size of the scientific establishment is in fact diminishing.

I was surprised at Dr Bullock's observation that the social sciences are also suffering. My impression is that otherwise very able and highly endowed young people who in the past would have gone into a field like physics or chemistry now go into sociology.

Bullock: Are we talking about funds or are we talking about the young voting with their feet? In England the Social Science Research Council is likely to be cut back much more than the other research councils, and people in parliament will still speak up for science whereas nobody will speak up for social science.

Weinberg: For me personally the most important thing is how many dollars I have with which to pay salaries. But with regard to what happens in the next ten or fifteen years, the attitudes we see among young people at the universities are really the significant thing.

Shils: Opinions about science and technology have certainly changed in the last six or seven years. The financial setback has occurred more recently than animosity against science. But we must try to keep a perspective on the matter and bear in mind the foundations on which science rests in our civilization. Basically it rests on our hedonism, on the fact that persons want to live longer, live more comfortably and labour less painfully. They believe that technology can improve their situation. They don't know much about the relations of science and technology but they have seen the improvements as well as the costs and they think some of the improvements are attributable to science. This feeling is very widespread in both advanced and underdeveloped countries. The man on the street still holds many of the beliefs which some sophisticated persons assert are illusions, and he is still uncritical in many respects about these matters. Many of the old attitudes which supported science are still there. Governments attempted to gratify their constituents or gratify their own prejudices. Present-day governments are also hedonistic in their outlook: they believe they can remain in power, whether they govern in a dictatorship or in a democracy, by gratifying the populace in one way or another, and that that means gratifying them with material goods; and they believe that technological and scientific research will lead to increased supplies of material goods, to better health, etc.

The second leg of the tripod on which the commitment to science rests in our civilization is a deeply rooted disposition to think empirically or, in other words, in terms of cause and effect. People don't believe much in miracles, although these might be desirable if they were the right kind. They don't believe so much in prayer as in science. There has become established quite widely in our advanced societies a belief that man's existence is governed by laws which science can disclose. Even believers in God do not believe in the likelihood of miracles. There has occurred something like a transformation, as far as ordinary people are concerned, in the conception of the structure of reality. It is true that there are fallings-away into astrology, magic and so on in contemporary society but they are not widespread and seem to me to be utterly unlikely to make deep inroads into the naturalistic conception of reality. This naturalistic state of mind is very widespread among people in advanced countries, and probably, for better or for worse, increasingly so in underdeveloped countries.

The third leg of the tripod on which science rests is the commitment of our civilization to education. People don't know much about how it happens but they know that if they are educated they are better off. They think they will enter into a new state of existence by virtue of being literate. They will share in a higher culture and become human beings rather than sub-human beings. Education offers that opportunity for ascent into a more elevated form of existence and I think it will always continue to offer that, even if education is 'oversold' today. As long as educational reformers do not expunge science from the school curriculum, it will be possible for intelligent young people with the inclination for science to have their passion aroused by it, and I don't think the flow of scientists will dry up. Even if all the places provided for students of science by the University Grants Committee in the United Kingdom are not taken up, that is not a great danger to science. All it means is that persons on the periphery who are not seriously interested do not enter science. Perhaps a potential scientific genius may fall away because of the slight turning against science, but we shall never know that. On the whole we can think of science in terms of a series of concentric circles with the most talented, most dedicated scientists at the centre and around them those less talented and less dedicated; the least talented and the least passionately committed are at the outer fringe and they are the ones who fall away. The cut in funds is of course a tragedy for the two hundred persons Dr Weinberg has to dismiss, and they should be dealt with constructively and compassionately, but it cannot be said that their departure from science would necessarily be a severe loss to science.

Pelletier: As far as I can see, scientists have become not aristocrats but clergymen. The aristocrat is a man who has power and the outward signs of power; the clergy were people who knew what others didn't know and were wrapped in mystery. There is no anti-science movement but a loss of faith. People lose faith in their clergy when that faith is eroded by the 'acids of the new modernity', as it were, now that the criticism of science occurs which didn't exist many years ago. We all took the pronouncements of scientists as the pure truth and the failure of universities as modern institutions adapted to modern times is obvious even to the man in the street. The realization has spread that the priest of science can be wrong and do wrong. The whole question of pollution proves that to anyone. Whether the tie-in between pollution and science and technology is real or not, people believe it is so. Einstein is dead. There is no Pope any more, and there is a shortage of archbishops.

In this crisis we should look at the kinds of crises the churches have gone through. Some of science requires an act of faith on the part of the laymen and there are bound to be variations in any faith.

Thiemann: I believe that there is an anti-science movement but that it is mainly a criticism about quality. If people see no achievements, they don't believe that scientists are doing anything worth while. For example, a politician told me that in his constituency in Switzerland they were very proud to allocate money to a nuclear research institute because they felt our society should allow young scientists to do interesting work. But when the post of professor of physics for a secondary school became vacant, to his great astonishment many of the employees of the nuclear research institute applied for it.

This politician was really shocked because he and his colleagues had generously allowed the young the opportunity to develop something new and then they discovered that these people were all unhappy and wanted a teaching job with a secure future. The same is seen now in the universities where because of the tremendous pressure of young people coming in we have to create many new professorships. There is a dogma that research and teaching have to go together (although its validity has recently been questioned by Lord Bowden[1]). If this dogma were maintained, we should see a tremendous increase in research activities, since every university chair would like to create its own research institute. Young people prefer to stay on at university because they are afraid of the responsibilities of other positions where they will not have the security of being government employees. We do not know where the limit for such growth will be reached and by what correcting actions. The politician doesn't know what percentage of the gross national product should be devoted to research and development. He has no rational criteria for such decisions.

Mathur: The trend away from science to other disciplines might be due to the manpower requirements of society rather than to any disillusionment with science. In India students are changing over from engineering courses to the faculties of commerce and management, not because they are disillusioned with building bridges or because trade and accounting offer greater inspiration, but because sixty thousand or so engineering graduates and diploma holders are unemployed, whereas people can more easily find jobs in management and business.

The disillusionment with science is due to its very success. The scientist has been successful in the theoretical as well as in the material and practical fields; he has created the concepts and their simulated models which society hoped for from applied basic research and technology, and all this is visible to society. It is the undesirable side-effects of the benefits that science has provided that have led to the present disillusionment.

The reason for the disillusionment with the social sciences is just the opposite: when opportunities have been given to social scientists to help in improving the condition of man, their prescriptions have not worked. The state of development of the various branches of social sciences is such that the advice which social scientists can give is based upon simplified models. It can miss by a wide margin the really active variables which govern the complex reality of a situation. Over the last fifty years, the social sciences have been neglected and they are not yet capable of dealing with the difficult problems of human behaviour in the same way as science with its well-developed methodology can deal with its objective material, matter and energy—both subject to simple and invariable laws.

Roche: Scientists are taught to use control groups so we might ask whether people who have had no science are well off. In Latin America and Spain there is the feeling, justifiable or not, that their state of material backwardness and economic dependency is due chiefly to the lack of science and technology. No one in Latin America is very happy about the situation. In the past ten or fifteen years people have become disappointed with literature and the humanities and they are shifting over to science. As always, we are thirty years behind, but this time it is a good thing, since we still trust science. In the University of Havana the percentages of students in the different faculties have changed as follows:[4]

	1957 %	1969 %
Humanities*	37.3	6.0
Science	7.2	16.0
Technology†	5.0	26.0

* Includes law, political sciences, history, literature, art, and journalism.
† Includes engineering and architecture.

In Venezuela the same general trend holds. Many secondary schools no longer have a humanities section. Many young people feel that these subjects are useless and that they have to get away from a tradition of literature in order to get on in the world. I don't agree with this, but it is the trend.

A civilization interested in the use of science must be basically hedonistic, as Dr Shils said (p. 47, 52). We in the Spanish civilization are not traditionally a hedonistic people, or rather we have believed strongly in an eternal hedonism, in another world. Lewis Feuer[2] divided humanity into two large groups: the hedonistic libertarians, who developed science, and the ascetic authoritarians, who did not. The Spaniards are in the latter group. Such generalizations are dangerous but this one fits a number of facts.

Rathenau: If in the West the number of students in science as a whole is decreasing, is this true of biology as well as of physics and chemistry? In molecular biology the numbers are still increasing, and this is an area of science which is developing rapidly.

Bloch: In Switzerland, and I think in other countries, the number of students interested in molecular biology and biochemistry is still increasing rapidly while interest in chemistry, for example, is waning. This development is disturbing, because very soon there will not be sufficient job opportunities for molecular biologists to work and make a living in their chosen profession, while on the other hand there is a demand for trained chemists to fill the many vacancies. It would seem natural for there to be a reasonable relationship between the number of applicants and the number of openings. Although traditionally it is not the concern of the universities to provide jobs for their graduates, it cannot be their task either to train the future unemployed.

Rathenau: I understand that one reason why the United States government will not give subsidies to universities is that they say reasonable thinking is absent when rebellious students want to overturn society and use undemocratic methods in their attempts to do so. How far is this true?

Long: The arguments used by the United States government have many elements and the really important thing may be the general ambiance and not the stated arguments. The stated arguments have two interesting components. One concerns the increasing unemployment in science and engineering and the resulting feeling that federal money should not be used to expand the number of students in science. Secondly, and curiously, an argument used by the present administration is that money should not be given to institutions but to people—that is, to students and individual research workers, not to the university itself. The argument that money shouldn't be given to universities because students are being outrageous is certainly brought up on occasion, but it has no official position.

Brock: I agree with the view that the apparent movement against science today is only part of a much wider movement against intellectualism or the scholarly approach to life. I think this has focused most heavily on science because science has produced the most troublesome results. Through technology science has produced destructive weapons and the pollution of which everybody is very conscious at present, and it is apparently failing to produce what people want. In the last decade there has, for example, been a striking movement against medical science and in favour of medical practice. The medical profession is said to pursue scientific investigation for its own benefit while failing to supply medical services. This reaction has been most obvious in the United States and it has extended to other countries, especially those with a Western outlook. If I understand people correctly they want happiness or what I would prefer to call satisfaction, or a sense of meaning in life. They feel that intellectualism is not reaching that goal and in particular that science is failing to reach it but instead is reaching other undesirable goals such as pollution. The need for satisfaction is a very deep instinct in human beings. Being a physician makes one a philosopher. The physician meets people when they are desperately sick or obviously at the end of their lives. At those times particularly they want satisfaction and to feel that life has a meaning for them personally. We will misjudge the movement against science unless we see it in that much broader context of a revolt against intellectualism and back towards the intuitive approach to truth—the approach of the artist, the musician and perhaps the priest.

Bourlière: In France there is not much anti-scientific feeling among the general public but many university undergraduates and graduates have this attitude. Students are objecting to the approach science teaching has taken in the last few decades. For instance, medical students or biology students point out that far too much emphasis is still put on those scientific disciplines in which they have to learn more and more about less and less. Not enough emphasis is given to actively developing fields such as molecular biology, behavioural sciences and also social sciences, broadly speaking, but seen from a more biological angle than is usually taken in the university. The same is true in the engineering schools, where very bright people are given only straightforward instruction in mathematics and physics, with nothing about biology or behaviour. What the young people ask for is not less emphasis on science but more emphasis on the aspects of science which might lead to a more sympathetic approach to human problems, not only now in the advanced countries but also in developing countries. At least in France, not enough emphasis is put on the new avenues of science which in the next ten years or so will probably change the attitude of many people towards scientific research.

Freeman: I certainly wouldn't underestimate the tremendous importance of science and technology in their contribution to economic growth and to the satisfaction of human needs through economic growth. But Professor Brock made an extremely important point when he suggested that the Benthamite type of utilitarian calculus of happiness or satisfaction is perhaps not quite enough for human beings and that they are demanding something more from science and technology. Both the humanities and science should really be concerned not just with happiness but with a life worthy of human beings.

Bullock: We are confronted here with something which is perhaps even wider than anti-intellectualism. Professor Brock says that people are turning from science towards the intuitive in the arts and in literature, but the main characteristic of the contemporary movement in the arts and literature is anti-art and anti-literature—the destruction or overthrow of all that we understood by the arts in the past. Surely this anti-intellectualism is a form of primitivism—rejection of the orderly and disciplined is not just rejection of the rational and scientific; the great musician or great artist also had to lead a life of discipline in the development of his art. Now this is rejected as well as the scientific. Perhaps a better term would be anti-cultural.

Medawar: I think Professor Brock somewhat underrates the benefits of medical science. There is no more deeply rooted instinct in human beings than the desire to be alive rather than dead. If we at this meeting had lived a hundred years ago we would have been dead by now! Yet people don't say how pleased they are to be alive because, as someone pointed out, there is no good control experiment. They don't know what it is like to be not alive. What is illustrated here is simply that we are conscious of the miscarriages of technology but not nearly conscious enough of the marvellous things it has done.

Bloch: Do medical research and medical care have to be in opposition to each other? If it is a matter of competition for funds, one may decide that more should go to one than the other, but the two are complementary and there would be no good medical care but for medical research. The two must go together.

Shils: There has certainly been an increase in hostility among intellectuals, including students, towards anything that is *given,* that is, inherited from the past, towards anything that is offered by institutions or by authority. There is a profound mood of anti-traditionality to which science has contributed to some extent but not very much. This anti-traditionality comes out of the tradition of romanticism, out of the tradition of prizing individuality, out of the appreciation of the spontaneously expressed self. This has been fostered by the very progress our society has made in enabling us, thanks to technological and medical progress, to avoid consideration of the limited powers of man. We have been fortunate to live in a society which has dispensed, for much of the population, with the need for heavy labour; we can, thanks to the extension of the lifespan, afford to disregard for a time the imminence of death. Our society, especially the educated part of it, permits itself to think that the determinants of existence from which mankind suffered for so long have been put away and that now there is, within relatively easy reach, the freedom of the self to expand indefinitely towards perfection, to have every sensation, to accomplish every possibility.

Now what is the situation for scientists? Scientists are intellectuals for better or for worse. Many of them are very specialized and very narrow-minded but they have been educated too. They live in this society, and they too acquire some of the antinomianism of the intellectuals; they acquire it by osmosis from all sides. They also get it from their own scientific traditions. As a result, even young scientists share passionately in this belief that all that man has done thus far is a grievous mistake. Many scientists who continue to do their science conscientiously and even at times creatively have fallen for this view. In doing so, they are eroding the moral and cultural foundations on which science rests. Like many other human beings, they want to run with the hares and hunt with the hounds. The late Professor Ronald Hargreaves, who was Nuffield Professor of Psychiatry at Leeds, said at a meeting of the Tavistock Clinic, when certain persons were misbehaving in a crisis of the institution, that he had heard of rats leaving a sinking ship but it was the first time he had come across rats actually sinking the ship. It is very important that scientists today should not be the rats who sink the ship. We are taking for granted all the accomplishments of science, all the great benefits which science and technology have conferred on human beings; we must not lose sight of them. There are negative by-products but we are not going to deal with them effectively by allowing ourselves to become hysterical and by frightening ourselves with Gothic tales of the iniquity of science. In the present situation scientists would do well to keep their cool.

Bibliography

1. BRONOWSKI, J. (1971) The disestablishment of science. In *The Social Impact of Modern Biology*, pp. 233–243. Ed. W. Fuller. London: Routledge & Kegan Paul.
2. TRIBE, L. H. (1971) Legal frameworks for assessment and control of technology. *Minerva, 9*, No. 2, pp. 243–255.

Discussion

1. BOWDEN, B. V. B. (1971) Science in crisis. *New Scientist*, p. 127, 21st January.
2. FEUER, L. S. (1963) *The Scientific Intellectual: the Psychological and Sociological Origins of Modern Science*. New York: Basic Books.
3. ORTEGA Y GASSET, J. (1958) *Obras Completas*, Vol. 6, p. 143. Madrid.
4. ROCHE, M. (1970) Notes on science in Cuba. *Science, 169*, 344–349.

The responsibility of scientists
to the community: a discussion

June Goodfield-Toulmin: We have already talked about the profession of
science and about science and the community. I shall refer here only to the
'central core' of scientists that Dr Shils mentioned, and not the peripheral
fringe of people who are being spun off.

I see the problem of the anti-scientific movement not so much as a reaction
against the actual, proper, ambitions and desires of scientists, but as a crisis
which affects us all because something has gone badly wrong with the
external relationships of the scientific community to the rest of society. What
we should perhaps be looking for are better ways of organizing the relationships between science and society at large. And I want to argue that the
profession is singularly ill-equipped to cope with these external attacks, and
it is equally ill-equipped to promote better relations with society at large
basically because it has rarely given the problem any thought! We should
be asking: should the solid core of scientists, as a community, therefore take
time out to look at the problems of their external relations, to argue about
questions which up to now have been considered as extraneous to their proper
role as scientists? Should scientists attempt to speak with a common viewpoint, so that the public know where the community of science stands on
genetic engineering, for example, in the same way as they know where the
American Medical Association stands on socialized medicine?

If these fundamental questions have to be brought within the activities of
science itself, certain institutions of science will have to change. Who then
will be—should be—the popes and archbishops, and where are they now?
How should the diverging viewpoints within the scientific community be
hammered into an agreed standpoint? Who should be the spokesmen? How
should they be chosen? At present, eminent and influential scientists become
eminent and influential through the existing patterns of authority, but are

these patterns appropriate when a man may be asked to pronounce, not on the intellectual merits of a theory, but on the social merits of genetic engineering? When I read that the Democratic Senator for South Dakota says we should no longer support the present regime in Saigon, I would be naive to think he was echoing the official doctrine of the Democratic Party. But years of neglect have done their work and for twenty-five years people at large have tended to treat the utterances of high priests of science as reported in the press as gospel. So when I read that Dr John Smith, Nobel Prize winner and President of the American Physical Society, says something equivalent, not only do I regard what he says as gospel, but I also tend to believe that he is the authoritative and chosen spokesman of the American Physical Society, making this pronouncement *on behalf* of his colleagues.

Over the last twenty-five years—the period during which science has been greatly in the public eye—the way in which the relationships between science and government have developed in the centres of political power, combined with the indifference of most professional scientists—summed up by the attitude 'If he wants to go to Washington, let him'—has made this public reaction inevitable. Vannevar Bush may emphasize[1] that the National Academy of Sciences never actually pronounces as a body but that statement is twenty years too late, and nothing has ever been done by the profession to educate me otherwise; moreover I suspect that some scientific entrepreneurs are quite happy to be regarded in this way as the 'voice of science'.

The history of the profession reveals how this state of affairs has come about. It is a young profession by historical standards—one hundred and twenty years old at the most—and probably without too much exaggeration we can say that never have so few people made so great an impact in so short a time. I suspect that the Newtons and the Darwins and the Maxwells, perhaps even T. H. Huxley himself, would have been appalled at the present ramifications—entanglements even—of the enterprise. Their reaction would be: 'This is not what we were meant to do. Our job is solely to push back the boundaries of knowledge'. So it is paradoxical, even quixotic, that the depth and extent of the impact which led to the present situation should result from science's own success. The profession quite deliberately withdrew from external affairs in order to concentrate single-mindedly on its proper intellectual concerns. The Royal Society specifically excluded religion and politics from its discussions. Yet the profession is now involved up to the hilt with all these extraneous matters. Name any contemporary problem and science touches it at some point. Perhaps it is the single-minded concentration by the scientists on the core of their endeavour—this fierce, self-centred critical methodology, to the exclusion of all else—which has been both the cause of their success and the reason for the present fumbling and uncertainty when it comes to dealing with external issues. One might say that whereas the profession has a strong methodological ethic forged by history and tempered by this very intensive self-scrutiny, by contrast the corresponding institutional ethic—by which I mean accepted patterns of behaviour—is extremely weak, if not totally absent.

The distinction between the methodological ethic and the institutional ethic was made by Joseph Harberer,[2] and I want to add a gloss on it by referring back to the problem of patterns of authority. The form of the methodological ethic of science is very well known. If I were Arthur Hugh Clough, I would write a new decalogue—the 'ten commandments' for science. We all probably know them, including 'Thou shalt not cheat'; 'Thou shalt make thy experimental results available in the form of data which can easily be confirmed', 'Thou shalt not covet thy neighbour's X-ray diagrams', or 'If thou dost covet them, thou shalt not acquire them', or 'If thou dost acquire them, thou shalt have the proper decency to keep quiet about it'! We know all about this; it is the core of the enterprise. Without commitment to this ethic, the enterprise would vanish entirely. Those influential and eminent men who temporarily hold authority within the various disciplines of the profession see it as their job not only to pronounce upon the various merits of the theoretical variants that may come into the science, but also to act as trustees and guardians of this ethic. The process by which those people become influential whose judgements and attitudes count is a very reasonable one, and is apparently accepted by the profession as a whole.

By contrast, or by default, there is a very weak institutional core in science, and there is no corresponding ethic, no corresponding accepted standard of behaviour, for dealing with the outside world. There is here a contrast between scientists and doctors. In science, a strong methodological ethic lies at the core of the enterprise, and doctors too have a strong methodology which is expressed in the way in which they make their diagnosis. But in medicine, a correspondingly strong institutional ethic lays down how doctors will behave, what their relationships are with patients, and so on. Nothing like this exists in science, and this is a fundamental weakness which leaves the profession almost naked in a crisis like the present one.

While the profession of science was only concerned with the problem of pushing back the frontiers of knowledge, this didn't really matter. The only thing that brought these people together was a commitment to a methodology, and any questions involving social or political order could be quietly pushed to one side as being no concern of science at all. But can scientists ever again push those questions away? And ultimately are scientists going to be allowed to push them away? I doubt it very much, for many reasons. If scientists do decide that they must be concerned with questions about their external relations and about the impact of their work, then, in the ensuing battles and debates, what weapons are in the profession's armoury? A well-developed methodology to which they are all committed, and that is about all. But what relevance does this methodology have to those areas where, willy-nilly, they are being drawn in? Absolutely none, I would say, or at the most, very little.

If the scientific community wished to forge an ethic and to take common attitudes, how would they select men who would be trustees for this? Does thirty years of distinguished service in the laboratory qualify a man to speak with authority and in the name of the profession? Or do we have to look for something else?

Clearly science cannot go on as if nothing had changed. The naive recipe of total withdrawal is not going to be possible. History is beginning to assert itself and questions about what kind of a profession science should now become, with what kind of concerns and with what kind of attitudes, are questions to which the members of the profession will have to devote considerable time. If as a result the discovery of the next quasar, or the next subatomic particle, is delayed by a decade or so, does it really matter when considered both in terms of historical time and against the gravity of the issues?

Bullock: I think the present disillusion with science is part of a larger movement of criticism and disillusionment with all our accepted forms of culture. As a historian, I tend to view these things as phases. I don't think that science is living through a crisis which is restricted to science. Like Dr Shils I think the word 'crisis' is a bad word. The present attitude is a mood or an atmosphere. Unless the whole of history is misleading, there will be a reaction against this, and a swing back. There are indeed parallels between certain phenomena today and in the early 19th century, as Stephen Toulmin mentioned. I don't think this bad patch will go on forever, though it may be uncomfortable while it lasts.

What June Goodfield-Toulmin has said seems, to one speaking as an outsider, to be a true description of the situation of science at the stage of development it has now reached as a profession and as a recognizable form of activity. The core of the enterprise is a methodology and the commitment to it. The real scientists are those who add to knowledge, not their auxiliaries. This is what brought them into the business and this is what still seems to them the sacred duty. Left to themselves, they would like to go on doing this, but they can't be left to themselves for several reasons which have already been mentioned. First, science costs money, and they have to get money to pursue their experiments. Secondly, the impact of science on our society, through technology, is such that it is impossible not to be concerned about it.

Science is in a painful dilemma, as anybody outside can see. The scientists really want to be allowed to pursue their science. They are uneasily aware of the fact that they have an impact on society, but basically most of them are only concerned about that in off-duty moments. While they are still active most of them resent being taken away from their work of adding to knowledge. Their dilemma is that to justify this activity and particularly the demands it makes for money and resources, scientists have had to act from a very early stage as propagandists for science. They suggested to people who were not scientists that the great justification of science was its usefulness, although in their heart of hearts this was not the justification they gave themselves. It is not merely the scientists who have fallen into this trap. In the university world most people, and not only the scientists, are doing what they want to do, they like doing it—it interests them. But they know they have to justify the rather pleasant lives they lead, the degree of autonomy they have, and all the rest of it. So they say: 'Higher education leads to economic growth', which is a very doubtful proposition. They don't really believe it much themselves. It is what might be called a second-order form of truth. What they may believe but hesitate to say is that the pursuit of knowledge is intrinsically important for its own sake.

Most people would agree that science can be useful to society. But the question is, who is to decide how and where the knowledge of science is to be applied? The disillusionment of many people with science arises largely because it has not been the scientists who have decided. They were willing to advise when asked questions, but the questions to be put and the use to be made of their knowledge was primarily something they were ready to leave to other people. Governments came to them, industry came to them, all sorts of people came to them and scientists became involved because they *advised*. Are scientists going to go a stage further than advice, which is a sort of reaction to demands and priorities established from outside? Are they going to say: 'You asked us about a space programme but what we really think is that any sane society would devote itself to the problems of poverty, malnutrition and bad housing'? Science is helping government to solve problems which government is posing, but science itself seldom points to the problems that need to be solved, or it points to them much less effectively.

The great involvement of science with defence or with the space programme, especially in the United States, has come in for much criticism, especially by the young but also by ordinary people who feel that the real problems in our society are social problems or economic problems, not the problems to which national governments often give top priority. If this is so, should the scientists try to intervene to alter the order of priorities? If they wish to alter the order of priorities, are they prepared not only to take time off but also to become effective politicians? A man can give advice and remain a scientist. If he takes the initiative and states priorities I suspect he is going further than most scientists are prepared to go in the demands on their time and in the nature of the activity in which they would have to take part. At that point, he is no longer speaking with the voice of authority but has to take his coat off and go in to fight.

Scientists who became politicians have in the past been scorned by their own profession. Maybe there will be a change but I don't see that science can assert any views on social responsibility unless it is prepared to be politically active. To many scientists this would seem to draw them away from what they have hitherto regarded as their central purpose. I am not sure they can avoid the problem; I think they are stuck with it for life. In most countries, especially the United States, scientists seem to be hovering on a sort of 'advisory' principle, and getting drawn towards the other but without accepting it and without organizing for it. Yet who can wonder that they draw back from it! Let us have no doubt, however, that in the last resort social responsibility means politics, and when you get into politics, you lose your immunity. You can get hit, you can get knifed and no holds are barred—that is politics. Scientists naturally enough draw back.

Todd: A dilemma then arises because the qualities that make a man go into science are not those that fit him for success in politics. I agree about the necessity for going into the political arena but you are asking a lot from people who are scientists in the first place, when you want them to go in for a political career.

Ashby: I would go further and say that being a scientist is a positive disqualification for politics, for a scientist is taught to deal with abstractions from reality, not reality itself. Politicians have to deal with reality as a whole.

One assumption which has pervaded this discussion so far is the idea that science is a profession; I do not believe it is. There are scientists teaching in universities, in the academic profession. There are scientists attached to government departments whose profession is the Civil Service. There are scientists who serve industry. Within those avocations the scientists do have some kind of ethic: a loyalty to students, or to government ministers, or to the directors of a firm. Indeed many teachers already think of their duty to their students almost as a Hippocratic oath, although few universities lay down rules about the number of hours to be spent with students as against doing research. So there are internal pressures of conscience to which a scientist already responds when he regards his duty to his students as well as to research. Similarly, if he is in the armaments section of a government department his job is to make weapons or defence materials which will either kill other people or prevent his own countrymen from being killed. So, although science itself is not a profession, scientists observe strong ethical principles towards the institutions which they serve.

All those characteristics mentioned by Stephen Toulmin, which anti-scientists regard as defects in scientists, are not peculiar to scientists: they would be equally evident among accountants. Accountants work objectively in figures; they show (apparently) no imagination, and their results are expressed in agreed patterns so that their balance sheets can be passed by the auditors. The significant fact is that scientists do their science according to a logic internal to science itself, just as chess- or oboe-players work within certain arbitrary rules and conventions. And the rules of science, chess, or oboe-playing have no relevance outside these disciplines.

What is confusing is that the scientist's loyalty is, and ought to be, not only to the inner logic of his subject but to the institution to which he is attached. But science differs from for instance, medicine, because a scientist, *qua* scientist, has no direct responsibility to the public; he has only a responsibility to his own standard of integrity and that of other scientists working in the same field. It is only when he becomes a university teacher or a civil servant or goes into industry that he begins to have a responsibility to other people for the consequences and implications of his work. A lot of the impatience of the young, when one really questions them about it, is because we in the academic professions do not define the limits of responsibility within which a specialist is expected to work. This is a weakness in the ethics of the academic profession. An engineer who designs a bridge uses techniques of mathematics in the same way as a mathematician uses them. But whereas the mathematician has *only* the intrinsic goal (to solve a problem in mathematics), the engineer has, as well, a clear *extrinsic* goal, namely to build a bridge which will not collapse. Now the young (stimulated by the instant visibility of social injustice in the world, seen on their television screens), are pressing the engineer to adopt a third goal: namely to take into account what the bridge is to be used for. If it is a bridge built between a black African state and South Africa, then its 'relevance' depends on whether it is going to be used to invade one side or the other. If it is, it is either immoral, or very moral, according to which way the army goes across the bridge!

When students talk about 'relevance' they are not expressing antagonism to science itself. They recognize pure science as something done with an intrinsic goal in view, contrasted with applied science which is directed by extrinsic goals. They are not as puzzled about this contrast as some of us at this meeting seem to be. What puzzles them is what attitude they should have towards goals of the next higher order: social and political goals. The answer has to be the one that Alan Bullock has given—that when it comes to goals of the next higher order, they have no special expertise. The scientist isn't capable of making political decisions nearly as well as someone who has spent his whole life in politics or in subjects which don't constrain the freedom of his thinking as science inevitably does.

Bullock: Yes, but there is no political expertise comparable to the scientific expertise—there is only experience.

Ashby: There is certainly a political expertise: it is the rare capacity to receive expert advice and to integrate it into what is considered to be policy for the public good. In this integration the relative weighting of evidence may change. A vivid recent example was the Roskill Commission's investigation of where London's third airport should be. The Commission spent a million pounds on an economic cost-benefit analysis, very sophisticated, leading to a fascinating and convincing argument about the 'right' site for the airport which became negligible when integrated into a political decision—not because of a strong lobby from the place where the airport didn't go, but because politicians realized that the cost-benefit analysis, for all its logic, was not a critical factor in determining policy for the public good.

Bullock: The politicians failed there to see what terms of reference the public wanted for the Roskill Commission.

Medawar: Both you and June Goodfield-Toulmin, Dr Bullock, underestimate the degree to which scientists already make pronouncements on matters of scientific interest which also embody moral judgements, and indirectly political judgements. For example, the National Academy of Sciences in the United States and the Medical Research Council in England have both produced very solid treatises on the hazards to man of ionizing irradiation. They stated that no dose of radiation could be regarded as harmless or salutary: it is a *bad* thing, and the message was that the pollution of the world with ionizing irradiation should be stopped.

Bullock: I don't regard that as a political intervention.

Medawar: It has political implications.

Bullock: It is only when scientists go further and say that priority in spending money should be given to this or that project that they are making political pronouncements. I realize that they make statements, but in a sense they are still speaking *ex cathedra*.

Medawar: These are both institutional statements but there is nothing to stop scientists getting together voluntarily and making such statements on matters of concern to the public. Before the Second World War, a number of Cambridge scientists did just that about air-raid precautions. Institutions may expedite the investigation of such matters and make everything more regular but institutional authority automatically attracts to itself repudiation or malicious criticism, simply because it *is* official and a pronouncement.

Bullock: Politics are not made by pronouncements.

Todd: A statement about radiation is based on scientific knowledge and scientific facts. The public will listen to the scientist when he makes such a statement because it is his business to know about radiation. Of course it has political implications as well. If, however, the scientist says: 'You can have your wars if you like, but cut out chemical weapons because these are in-human', he is expressing an opinion which is not a scientific opinion. Once people admit that war is acceptable, how they wage it seems to me totally irrelevant; and for the scientist to suggest that, because he is a scientist, his opinion on moral issues of this type is better than anyone else's is totally unacceptable.

Mathur: Then would scientists like you have justified the atom bomb?

Todd: No, I didn't approve of the atom bomb but I don't think that my opinion on the moral issues involved was necessarily better than other people's.

Mathur: But eminent scientists know more about the effects of the nuclear bombs than non-scientists like myself do. We expect the distinguished scientists to speak out about the likely consequences of using such weapons.

Bullock: They did speak out, but with two voices.

Toulmin: Nobody here is going to argue (I hope) that scientists as scientists have any special right to pronounce on political questions. What we are concerned with lies beyond that. It is not a question of creating new *institutions,* but of creating new institutional *arrangements:* that is to say, of how we should operate certain institutions that have to do with scientific affairs, or how certain institutions that already exist are to deal with new kinds of technical problems.

Sir Eric Ashby said that, aside from the methodological commitment, the only external duty of a scientist was that arising out of his position. But this is surely not the whole story. Special problems arise today because the consequences of the advice that scientists give, and of the way science is used in public life, are on a scale that affect other people's lives in all kinds of ways, more than ever before. The electorate—the public at large—are reacting because they feel that things are being *done to them* over which they have no influence or control, and that no machinery exists by which they can effectively influence these developments.

Around 1965 or 1966, some very promising discussions were going on in the United States between COSPUP (the Committee on Science and Public Policy) and the Daddario Sub-committee on Research and Development in Congress. It looked as though some effective channels of communication might be set up between the legislators (who are the electorate's representatives) and the scientists who could tell them the truth as they saw it, or give them a proper assessment of different problems as they saw them. We have the beginnings of this here in Britain, in the poverty-stricken Select Committee on Science and Technology of the House of Commons, which has far too little money and can get far too little research done.

We should all pay more attention to the question of how science is applied to solving problems whose prime impact is on the electorate at large, and more attention to how the advice which leads to the relevant political decisions is arrived at, so as to ensure that the interests of the political 'consumer' are protected. When the interests of the 'consumer' at the receiving end of a new dam, a new medical service, or a new transportation scheme, are automatically taken properly into account I think we shall be getting somewhere. In the resulting debate, the average man whose life is going to be affected as a result of some new scientific or technological development can feel that he has been involved, if only through his Member of Parliament or his Congressman. He can feel that his interests are being taken into account, that there has been adequate debate, that it hasn't all been over his head or behind his back, on a dark night with a cold chisel.

Ashby: The penetration of carbon dioxide through the stomata of leaves (to take a random example from plant physiology) is not a matter on which public opinion can be relevant. When an extrinsic, social, goal is added to the intrinsic goal of pure science, I agree that the public must immediately be involved. But until the scientist has himself a social goal, I don't think his work is any more relevant to social needs than that of the oboe-player.

Bullock: The enormous amount of money which goes into, say, high-energy physics is very important. In Great Britain the sums of money involved and the effect on other science are matters settled by bodies like the Science Research Council without the intervention of representatives of the public to open up the questions. The Science Research Council consists of scientists, who necessarily have particular views and interests to press, and government officials. Are these questions proper things to open up in this country?

Weinberg: In the United States this kind of thing is much discussed. In Great Britain I think scientists decided at one stage to support the CERN

300 GeV accelerator, but when this recommendation reached the Treasury and then the public they decided against it—although in the end Great Britain did support the CERN accelerator.

The issue hangs at least in part on an understanding of what science can do and what it cannot do. There are certain issues for which science is able to do something. Sir Peter Medawar calls science the 'art of the soluble', which is a marvellously apt phrase: science sets its problems in categories and languages which somehow are arranged so that the problems are soluble. When scientists speak about science they don't need any intervention from the public. They can use their internal ethic, and representatives of the public cannot help them very much. Some of the issues at the interface between science and politics, the issues that concern us here, are scientific issues, but most of them are not. I call these issues 'trans-scientific':[4] although they arise in science and can be stated in scientific or technological terms, they cannot really be answered within science. The question about whether 150 milliroentgens of radiation a year cause harm is a trans-scientific question, not a scientific question, because one cannot really prove it one way or the other within science.

Stephen Toulmin said that the anti-scientists object to the fact that science cannot predict events, that it deals in generalities or averages. Of course a characteristic of the social sciences is that they cannot predict the behaviour of specific individuals faced with specific events. Yet when science is used by policy-makers, they want to know what will happen if they follow such and such a policy. The scientists can't really answer that question. In dealing with these trans-scientific questions we must welcome intervention, and indeed we cannot avoid the intervention of the whole body politic. I rather welcome Ralph Nader's consumer movement in the United States, and all the subsidiary movements it has put in motion, such as the anti-pollution movements, despite the fact that they give me plenty of grey hairs because one of the things they are attacking is nuclear energy. But fundamentally they are right: they are asking questions, they are intervening in issues in which we scientists perhaps would not like them to intervene; but we must welcome the intervention because these are not questions that we as scientists can answer. We need all the wisdom we can get; and this includes the wisdom of the public.

In 1961 Frank Long and I were both members of the President's Science Advisory Committee (PSAC) and we shall never forget the extraordinary decision on the moonshot. President Kennedy had come into office and all of us knew that something was going on with the moon, but we were somehow kept out of the whole thing. Then one day, about half an hour before a meeting of PSAC was to end, when half the members had left to catch their aeroplanes, Jerome Wiesner, Mr Kennedy's Science Adviser, said 'Well, gentlemen, we have decided to go to the moon'. And that was the first official notice the President's Science Advisory Committee received of the moon decision. A book called *The Decision to Go to the Moon*³ provides a most illuminating discussion of this subject. The author says that the decision was not a scientific one—it involved science, but Mr Kennedy made the decision knowing full well that the scientists were opposed: and that is why he didn't ask them about it. He wanted to go to the moon for reasons other than science.

Bullock: What did the scientists do when he said that?

Weinberg: Some of us screamed loudly and bloodily. I was one of those who screamed loudly, but in retrospect I have to say that my self-righteous screams were not quite as justified as they seemed at the time.

June Goodfield-Toulmin: Sir Eric Ashby's attitude that science and science alone is the only proper concern of scientists is almost too pure to be true! It is classical 19th century. Alvin Weinberg's distinction between trans-scientific issues and strictly scientific issues is very helpful here. Possibly the difference is that Alvin Weinberg might say that these trans-scientific issues are the concern not only of scientists as people, but of scientists as scientists, whereas Sir Eric Ashby would say they are not the concern of scientists *qua* scientists at all. But this may be where the pressure from below is going to make society take a stand. Are you going to concern yourselves as scientists only with things which are, in the pure 19th century sense, strictly pushing back the boundaries of knowledge, or are you going to look at these trans-scientific issues as well and make them your concern too? Is it possible to take a stand *as scientists* on these?

Brock: Dr Goodfield-Toulmin made a plea that we should look at our public relations as scientists. But is there a profession of science? There is quite clearly a profession of medicine, and Sir Eric Ashby referred to the Hippocratic oath. I define my profession of medicine as an art or technique based on scientific knowledge. What makes us a profession seems to be that we serve the public. We have an elaborately set-up public relations organization and earlier it was suggested that science needs some organization publicly set up to govern its public relations.

June Goodfield-Toulmin: That is not exactly what I was suggesting.

Brock: But should scientists have any sort of public relations activity?

Bullock: What do you mean by public relations? Doctors have a lobby which is much more than a public relations organization. They don't wait to be questioned: they get into an act, and they get into an act politically. I am not criticizing them for that, but when they see something coming up, they get into it and they go to work politically.

Brock: Then is there a profession of science?

Medawar: Sir Eric Ashby says there isn't. I wish he would explain why he thinks that.

Ashby: For the reason you have just heard: a profession serves the public. Lawyers, clergy, doctors and dentists do this, but scientists do not by their training have to serve the general public.

Bullock: Dr Roche said earlier that after fundamental research has produced something it is then up to the public to use it for good or evil: it is their decision how they use it. If this attitude continues the public will say 'This is so much a Pandora's Box you are giving us, and it is so evident that it will be misused, that we had just better stop the fundamental research'. I can hear people saying: 'We just can't tolerate the problems that are going to be created by genetic engineering, and we will shut it down as a gift too destructive to the ordinary conventions and the ordinary *mores* of human life'. This is the dilemma, I think. I haven't got a solution to it, but Sir Eric seems to ignore it.

Ashby: If I ignored the dilemma I wouldn't be spending so much time on pollution of the environment as I do. This is what Alvin Weinberg would call one of the trans-scientific things where scientists have a contribution to make.

June Goodfield-Toulmin: They have a contribution to make, but I think you would insist that it was not as scientists, only as individuals. This is the issue between us.

Long: I have a great deal of sympathy with Sir Eric Ashby's position that science is not a profession in the sense that medicine is. But scientists are *professionals*.

Todd: The word profession is used in several ways. Perhaps the commonest meaning is a body of people who have particular qualifications recognized or registered by the state in which they operate, and that registration is intended to protect the public in the eyes of the state (examples are medicine and the law). At present science is *not* a profession in that sense.

Ashby: University teaching is a profession: in fact the original meaning of a degree is that it is 'the right to teach'.

Long: We don't remove the problem by definition. For example, chemists and other scientists speak of themselves somewhat casually as belonging to a 'professional society'. The inadequacy of our scientific institutions, which was Dr Goodfield-Toulmin's real point, is a fact, and it seems to me that one can ask, how are scientists responding to this fact and are we responding enough? Alvin Weinberg and I were recently on a committee of the U.S.

National Academy of Sciences which recommended a very substantial restructuring of the National Academy. Many of the recommended changes were to permit more effective responses in the ways we have been talking about. Our recommendations were shot down rather ignominiously by the Academy membership. Our report was 'accepted' and we were hastily dismissed. But only a year later, this same membership adopted several of our central ideas in slightly modified form. So, kicking and screaming, that rather august institution is moving with increased speed in the direction of building institutional capabilities to respond to societal concerns.

As another example, the American Chemical Society has established a Committee on Chemistry and Public Affairs and given its office an annual budget of $ 150 000. The committee's charter calls for it to become actively involved in such trans-science affairs as the development of public policy for the use of science.

In 1970 this Committee on Chemistry and Public Affairs persuaded the American Chemical Society to reverse its opposition to the United States Government signing the Geneva Protocol banning chemical weapons of war. The really interesting point is that the original position of the American Chemical Society, which clearly involved chemists mixing into public affairs, was taken in 1925. Hence, for at least fifty years the chemistry profession has been exerting itself in these broader societal problems.

The weakness of the present institutions is clear but movement towards changing them is evident. The question is, will they move far enough and fast enough?

Bullock: Lord Todd's phrase 'to protect the public' is a very strong reason why the public might think science ought to become a profession!

Todd: That was one of my reasons for using it. I am sure that hitherto that has been the real reason for setting up the so-called 'professions'. In England chemists have been battling for years to get chemistry recognized as a profession: they have never quite made it!

Roche: Would you exclude the creative writer or the artist from being a professional?

Todd: They would not be members of a 'profession' in the sense in which I have used the term, that is a registered group of people who have certain powers within the state. If you are not a registered medical practitioner, you have certain very grave restrictions on what you can do to your fellow human beings. If you do not have formal legal qualifications, you cannot perform certain legal functions.

Roche: That is far too legalistic and formal a view. A profession may exist without the state recognizing it. A profession is surely a group of people with common interests, ways of living and ethics based on consensus.

Bloch: Do you think scientists as such should be recognized as a profession, or each of the subdivisions of science?

Todd: It might be easier for science in bits rather than science as a whole to be given professional status. But at present scientists don't have that status at all. And none of them so far have institutions that appear to me strong enough ever to make them look like being a profession.

June Goodfield-Toulmin: Then Sir Peter Medawar has not been a member of a profession in his life, yet he feels he has been taking part in an activity which in some sense is a profession.

Medawar: To describe a man as a professional but not a member of a profession is like saying that somebody is not a Jew, just Jew*ish*.

Bullock: Don Price used the term 'the scientific estate' to try to avoid the word profession with its double meaning.

Long: One must give weight to the argument that scientists to a significant degree are coloured in their judgements by the character of their employers.

Toulmin: Now you've worried me badly! One could say that the way Hitler's doctors behaved was coloured by the fact that they were employed by Hitler. Fortunately, they were also members of the medical profession, and therefore had some countervailing ethical defence against being totally his servants. There is a strong argument for saying that scientists, too—in so far as they accept employment with different kinds of employers—should enter these employments with a sense of responsibility to the ideals of science, as well as to the demands of (say) chemical and biological warfare. The idea that one makes over one's external ethic to the requirements of one's employer *in toto* seems to me to be immoral.

Thiemann: This discussion about professions and professionalism indicates the different kinds of schizophrenia involved. We think we want to see science achieve stronger institutions, and this is probably because of a defensive attitude, but then we ask, what shall we use such institutions for? If the scientific community wants more money from governments, for instance, they could work as a lobby for that. This is already happening. Advancing civilization is a good reason for supporting the true scientists, the Michelangelos, but these are rather rare, although many scientists and university professors think they are Michelangelos. Professionalism is leading to its own organization; however society is only interested in supporting outstanding individuals in different cultural activities, including science.

Another dilemma is that we cannot define a clear need to do scientific research without some kind of policy. Governments, which pay for research, should see clearly the need for it and be able to judge its performance. The executive in a democratic government can only act when the legislators have made a decision, but the latter can only do so when backed by public opinion, because they do not want to lose the next election. Therefore science policy is very often a matter of politics. An example is the latest decision about the CERN accelerator. The public may not understand what high energy physics means, but they do understand that huge machines cannot be supported by a single nation. The scientist is already involved in politics.

Bullock: If you are already in politics, can you make your presence there more effective? At the moment it seems to me that science is reluctant, unwilling and half-hearted.

Weinberg: Scientists as politicians have a long and honoured history. Christopher Columbus was a geographer who 'politicked' in the court of King John of Portugal for eleven years trying to put over his views; when he didn't succeed there he went to Queen Isabella. Columbus was one of the first scientific politicians. When one examines how a big accelerator gets sold, one will find an enormously powerful scientific politician behind the project who has the energy, capacity, skill, and all the political paraphernalia that go along with success in politics.

Bloch: Lavoisier was a politician too, but it didn't become him very well.

June Goodfield-Toulmin: I get the impression from my own students that in the United States in the last few years, a high proportion of students who would otherwise have become research scientists in chemistry or physics have decided on careers in scientific administration and politics. This is new, and it may be a healthy sign.

Bibliography

1. BUSH, V. (1970) *Pieces of the Action*, p. 308. New York: Morrow.
2. HARBERER, J. (1969) *Politics and the Community of Science.* New York: Van Nostrand-Reinhold.
3. LOGSDON, J. M. (1970) *The Decision to Go to the Moon.* Cambridge, Mass., and London, England: M.I.T. Press.
4. WEINBERG, A. M. (1972) This volume, pp. 105–114.

Science: a consequence of science policy or an expression of civilization?

HUGO THIEMANN

The background to the problem

The difficulties of our time are mainly due to the rapid changes which are taking place, and which inspire feelings of insecurity about the future. In spite of the great achievements of science, there exists a certain disappointment with the performance of the scientific community. The cost of carrying this community has increased very rapidly, and as the problems only seem to become more complicated, there are doubts about its usefulness.

The scientific community is essentially associated with the university. Many new universities have been built and existing ones considerably expanded owing to the increasing number of students. However, it is not only the teaching load which is increasing. Research activities are also growing rapidly. Owing to the generally accepted and defended dogma that teaching has to be combined with research, most university professors are building up their own research institutes. This of course calls for personnel, operating budgets and high investment in buildings and equipment, which explains why the increasing number of teachers is causing an explosive increase in the costs of universities. More students feel inclined to stay on at university in the newly created positions and hesitate to jump into the cold water of a competitive entrepreneurial activity. At present there is no visible limit to such developments, and there seems to be an unlimited appetite for university research and teaching.

In consequence, society is becoming critical and is asking for the establishment of science policies in order to ensure that the scientific community does something useful and that its performance can be assessed. As the financial means are always limited, everybody is looking for criteria in order to rationalize the choices. It is paradoxical that many scientists who defend the freedom of science are also asking for science policies in order to get the necessary funds for their activities and to have a more secure future. We observe that in many cases professors are becoming fund-raisers rather than teachers and scientists.

This development may lead to a very dangerous situation, namely the opening of a gap between science and society. It is often forgotten that the real advances in science have always been due to a few outstanding scientists. However, these individuals, with a creative capacity similar to that of artists, do not need science policies to guide their work. They know better than anyone how to ask the essential question which forms the basis of a research programme. It is the same as with a good painter, who does not need instructions for what he has to paint. This ability is part of the nature of the individual as an expression of his culture, and a developed civilization should allow for the development of these individuals as real pioneers. This being so, we are faced with the problem of how to develop the necessary science policies without inhibiting the development of outstanding scientists. The difficulty is similar to that of drawing up a logical planning process which does not exclude intuitive decision, or of reconciling the conceptions of intellectuals with those of the mass of people.

The changing dynamics of the research and development community

When we talk of science, we usually mean research activity and sometimes also development. There is very often confusion concerning certain terms; for example, fundamental research may signify a scientific activity to some, whereas to others it is already applied work, depending on the long-range goals of those behind it. The scientist frequently feels that he is performing an independent scientific function, when to the one who pays for his activity it forms part of a puzzle with a very definite end in view. Science is knowledge, and the activity of obtaining new knowledge is research work. It is often very difficult to distinguish between research and development work, and it is therefore more realistic to talk of the total community of people involved in research and development (R & D) activity. In many cases, the development work and its difficulties give the scientist his inspiration in a new research area.

The structure of the R & D community has changed considerably in the course of the last twenty years. Ever since statistics became available, the growth rate has been such that the size of the community has doubled every twelve to fifteen years. Probably owing to the increasing sophistication of research tools, however, research costs have of recent years roughly tripled while the number of people has doubled. As the total number of R & D workers is no longer a negligible proportion of the working population in developed countries, the structure of the scientific community has altered. Instead of individuals following their own scientific lines, we have seen the creation of so-called 'big science projects', mainly financed by governments and motivated either by military or prestige goals. The scientist is nowadays surrounded by a large number of people who are needed to perform the experiments and to build the experimental equipment, and a large number of people therefore call themselves scientists who are really scientific workers without inspiration. One might speak of a kind of scientific proletarian.

Creativity in science manifests itself at different levels:

(1) The most difficult, which is the privilege of a very small number of scientists, is the search for questions to which the answer will bring about something essential for the future.

(2) The second level is thinking out the research programme, which means drawing up a kind of strategic plan. It calls for considerable experience. Nevertheless, quite a lot of people are capable of doing it.

(3) The third level of creativity is carrying out the research programme. The majority of scientists work at this level, particularly juniors.

In recent years creativity at the first level has become more and more important, and it is perhaps the critical element of future development. The share of those at the third level is developing rapidly owing to the big science projects and to the greater sophistication and automatization of research investigations, in particular in the analytical field. A sociological change is also becoming visible, namely that the majority of scientists are turning into employees working in a hierarchy. The individual's preoccupation with his future security of employment may become more important to him than research results.

The formulation of a good question relates to the goals of scientific activity. The rapid growth of the R & D community within the framework of the big science projects has led to large research and scientific missions, for example the space programme. The goals of many such missions have lost their appeal, and today we see many people in the research communities working without a clear enough aim. They look like becalmed sailing boats. This is particularly obvious within institutions belonging to governments or international bodies. The goal-setting process for such institutions is most difficult. It calls for strong personalities, because the individual in the research and scientific world is very conservative and does not like drastic changes. A scientist is generally inclined to dig deeper in the hole he has already started, and sometimes is not very interested in the question of why he is digging it. Often it appears that this kind of continuity is the easiest solution for the individual; it may become an escape from taking any responsibility with respect to the society which provides his funds.

The need for goal-setting

At present the scientific world is in general very well prepared and equipped to perform a given research programme. Those responsible know how research results can be obtained, and the individual research groups are very happy to build a sophisticated instrument—the particle accelerator, for example. They can define the work fairly well within the limits of a given research budget and within a given time. However, they are no longer concerned with the purpose of the research instrument and how it will be used. They feel that the mission is accomplished when the tool is in the hands of others who will be using it. But those who have this responsibility ought to understand the system. We are confronted with the paradoxical situation that the scientist who is best qualified to work in a system, and who could best grasp its complications, is very often not interested in the systems approach. He is therefore not much involved in deciding what to do, what choices should be made and what alternatives should be studied. This is a consequence of splitting a big job into small units compatible with an overall view. The work of the majority of the R & D community is organized in this way. As the size of the community—approximately two million in the United States and 1.6 million in Europe—is considerable, goals need to be set. Such goals should satisfy real long-term needs, but should also be a challenge to the younger generation to participate in a credible and important exercise.

How to set new goals

It is widely believed nowadays that research and development activity is a good thing independently of any goals, at least in the less developed countries. In Western industrialized countries, however, certain doubts have begun to emerge. But since research and development helped to produce the high degree of industrialization and higher standards of living in the West, people in the less developed countries find it difficult to understand these doubts about the rapid growth of R & D in the past.

Research problems may be posed by individual research workers using their own intuition, or they may simply appear and have to be solved. A glance at the statistics shows that the latter type account for by far the greater part of expenditure on R & D today. In view of the prevailing unhappiness about the use of these funds we can conclude either that the goals were not well chosen or defined, or that the R & D community was not capable of finding solutions. In certain fields, such as cancer research, there is a good deal of criticism about the speed of progress. In others, such as the space programmes or certain kinds of nuclear research, which are closer to development work, the achievement has been perfect. We must therefore conclude that the problem is linked less to performance than to how the goal-setting was done. The numerous industrial products of today are in themselves tremendous achievements. They fulfil many functions. The production of power, road transport, air travel and telecommunication have all become possible. Are there any new functions to be fulfilled? What kind of future is there for electronics companies now that most telecommunication and control problems have been solved?

The R & D industrial complex has not only brought us solutions but created many new problems and it seems likely that the solution of these should provide goals for R & D in the future. Existing products will need to be developed and improved, and this in itself will absorb part of the total R & D capacity. One of the key problems created by the modern way of life is the excessive growth of population, which is linked to industrial activity. The mechanism for continuous growth has been provided by the economy. Extrapolation of the present rate of growth shows us a disastrous picture of exponential growth, with a decreasing doubling time. This is true in many sectors, including mining, oil drilling, food supply, etc. For the first time during the evolution of mankind a limit is being imposed by the size of our planet. The situation becomes ever more complex as overcrowding intensifies the interdependence of the problems. The first great increase in population occurred when agriculture was invented and the world could suddenly support more people. The development of industry in modern times has made another explosive increase possible, but nobody knows how many people can finally be supported.

In setting new goals for R & D we should start with this new set of problems. Experience shows that there is always a considerable time between the grasping of a problem and its solution, and in view of the complexity of the problems with which we are now faced, a generation or more may be necessary. The present trend towards exponential growth shows that serious difficulties may already be experienced during this period, so that it is essential to start as soon as possible. The problems are no longer of a purely technical nature, such as solving the problem of making electricity from water power. Owing to their systematic interdependence, they affect even our institutions. The new goals cannot therefore be defined by natural scientists alone, who will need to collaborate with economists, sociologists and specialists in other 'soft' sciences.

The dilemmas

While it is becoming clearer how the important new R & D goals should be defined, it is much more difficult to see how to achieve them. We come up against the usual conflict between short-term expediencies and the long-term goals of our institutions and economies. Experience shows that as soon as economic conditions take a turn for the worse the noble long-term intentions and goals are thrown overboard. For example, copper will quite soon become a rare metal; steps should therefore be taken to recycle it more intensely and to look for substitutes. This, however, is against the interests of the industrial and commercial complex which deals in this metal and which may, on the contrary, try to promote higher consumption in order to make greater profits.

According to this logic the R & D effort may lead to the development of new industrial products in competition with existing ones. They will be a positive response to the new environmental boundary conditions which are necessary to avoid further deterioration of the world system, but such products are likely to be more expensive and to call for heavy capital investment in plant and processes. The present competitive industrial system may not introduce them unless government regulations are passed and enforced. Such laws may be against the economic interest of a country or of important industries, and the legislature may not care to enact them. Finally, therefore, it may become necessary to evolve new institutions in order to overcome this difficulty.

As the world becomes more and more closely interconnected, even national solutions are not sufficient. The obstacles to international control are primarily due to the human characteristic, whether on a private or a national scale, of preferring to let others make the long-term sacrifices while continuing oneself to profit from the existing situation.

It is thus clear that it will be very difficult to implement the necessary R & D policy. However, the R & D community is already very large, at least in the highly industrialized countries, and as it needs new goals for its survival and evolution, it is to be hoped that it will induce the needed changes itself in spite of all the obstacles. It is therefore of great importance for the community to agree upon a proper science policy in collaboration with those who fund the execution of projects. Recent declarations by the Organization for Economic Cooperation and Development that growth of gross national product should not be the only criterion of economic development for the next ten years could be a sign that new institutional solutions may not be out of the question.

The Michelangelos

The high proportion of scientific work which derives from science policy has been pointed out. But much knowledge also stems from the intuition of really creative scientists, whom I like to think of as the 'Michelangelos'. They represent the expression of a civilization in terms of science and are the source of new imaginative tools and knowledge on which science policies can later be built.

These outstanding scientists are only a small group of individuals working at the forefront of human exploration.

Many scientists believe that they are 'Michelangelos'. This makes it difficult to know what a science policy should be, and what support should be given to the real Michelangelos, who are difficult to detect in the early stages of development. Once they have made outstanding discoveries it usually becomes much easier, but not always. By their very nature, they are generally not inclined to work towards established goals. This is a difficulty today. As we have pointed out, the problems we face are becoming more and more complex, and it is necessary to think in terms of large systems, for which the present organization of science is not well adapted. We see this already at the university, which is organized into faculties with a whole encyclopaedia of science represented by the professorial chairs; we see it also in research laboratories belonging to industry, where the goals are very often in solid-state physics, theoretical physics, holography, plasma research, laser research, and such-like. The important goals such as new ways of converting energy, new and more efficient sources of light or industrial processes which do not disturb the environment, for the attainment of which these others are but tools, are often forgotten or not mentioned at the level of the research units.

The Michelangelos seem to remain aloof from these visible trends. They are capable of working along their own intuitive guidelines. Amid all the pressures of science policy today we have to ensure that our civilization leaves a place for the cultivation of this kind of intellectual expression.

There is a gap between this class of scientist and society, which is looking for practical solutions to problems. It seems that the ability to bridge this gap is characteristic of the degree of development of a country. Because of its mechanics, scientific work defined by science policy is much closer to public understanding. In some countries, however, it can be observed that a gap is created artificially to make a distinction between the scientist and society. There are excellent scientists working in the less developed countries but they are almost totally isolated from the problems of industry, economics or the community as a whole, so that the way of life of the average person is almost untouched by their work. Again, it is a difficult problem to distinguish the real Michelangelos from the others. For them the gap seems quite normal, and the need for science policy should not affect them. Owing to our own limitations, the rational approach is not a universal tool. We are learning from nature that there is a considerable element of redundancy in all creative processes, and in our management of creativity in advanced civilizations it will be well to bear this in mind.

Discussion

Weinberg: The obsolescence of large scientific institutions worries the scientific community in general and nuclear scientists in particular. Of course these institutions have a natural imperative to survive, as does any bureaucratic organization. If you were the boss of the Euratom laboratory at Ispra, for example, what would you do about this problem, Dr Thiemann?

Thiemann: I would probably get rid of many of the people in it. The decision to set up a laboratory of about three thousand people at Ispra was a political one, the idea being that it should be comparable in size to the Centre d'Etudes Nucléaires de Saclay in France. The community at Ispra had no clearly defined goal in the beginning. Certainly some very fine scientists work there, but they are like sailing boats with no wind.

Weinberg: But what do you visualize as the important issues for an institution like Ispra to tackle, once any necessary internal adjustments, such as getting rid of the less useful people, have been made?

Thiemann: One tremendous challenge would be to develop a nuclear power station with at least twice the present efficiency. That would mean removing the heat pollution front for another twenty years.

Another challenge would be to use the energy of the sun for useful processes. We could make an industrial forest that would convert the rapidly rising concentration of carbon dioxide in the atmosphere into carbon, using sunlight. Or, instead of solar energy, nuclear power could be used to convert carbon dioxide into hydrocarbons, which the whole world is geared to use.

Weinberg: This problem of the obsolescence of large institutions is in some sense one of the central structural problems of the scientific community, and it therefore affects the relations between science and society. The Oak Ridge National Laboratory in Tennessee has been very much concerned with this and we have redeployed to a fair extent. But it is very difficult to identify those issues that have sufficiently wide public implications to merit great public support and which are also at a stage of development where research can be done on them with some hope of getting real results.

For example, it would be wonderful if we could indeed use solar energy on a big scale. What is lacking is a really hot idea. Ideas such as that of enhancing the greenhouse effect with specially treated surfaces have nowhere near the crystalline beauty of the discovery of fusion. Once fusion was discovered, one had a clear idea of just where to move to exploit it.

There are certainly structural crises within the atomic energy establishments, either because they have been too successful, in which case they have worked themselves out of a job, or because they are not successful, in which case support is withdrawn. But actual redevelopment requires one to propose very definite things to do, not vague generalities.

Thiemann: I mentioned the institutional aspects; a passive person working on a project says it is up to someone else to decide what he does. When the project is over, whether it is successful or not, he is out of business. But one could also start ten years in advance to think that certain projects may end and to prepare new ideas.

Weinberg: This has been thought about at many institutions. The Atomic Energy Research Establishment at Harwell, for example, is in the process of redeploying.

Todd: Harwell had to do that because it was rapidly becoming a white elephant. The ruthless way is to say the mission is finished and disband the whole institution, but for various reasons this is not the sort of thing one can do. The permanent staffing of research institutions is where we make a big mistake. Redeployment is bad enough under any circumstances, but the permanent staffing of research institutions has given rise to much trouble. Finding big new tasks is a tremendous problem. One is starting at the wrong end: instead of finding something that one can work on, one is starting out with a set of facilities and people and trying to find a problem to match. Unless continually changing economic objectives can be found, research institutions die. The only way to carry on without economic objectives is in a university, where the reason for doing research is to train young people who keep moving on after a year or two and are continually replaced by new young workers.

Weinberg: Some redeployment is being done at Ispra; they are working now on the equivalent of an artificial forest.

Bloch: Isn't this the problem of every institution which doesn't by definition have a permanent task like a university has to train students? The human and the moral obligation, which results from the fact that an institution is there, that people have been hired to work there and cannot just be dismissed after ten years' employment, then becomes more or less an end in itself. In a purely economic set-up, the answer will come from the market place. But state institutions follow different laws because such institutions are not required to show a profit. They live on continuing government support. I think Dr Thiemann's view is too extreme and cannot be realized for purely human considerations.

Long: The economic or market-place approach cannot be dismissed so easily. Industry in general is certainly more ruthless about this kind of thing. If an industrial laboratory really becomes obsolete, it literally disappears. This sort of market-responsive treatment is presumably tolerable if it keeps overall employment at a high level, though there may be acute displacement of some people for a time. But if protection of outmoded laboratories leads to an ineffective economic system, the social loss could easily become the dominant consequence.

Rathenau: I would like to remove some of the suspicion about the ruthlessness of industry. Many industries keep their research laboratories young by shifting people as they get older into industrial positions with more responsibility. Where governments have scientists working for them, it might be a very good thing if senior people went into the appropriate ministry to advise the government on scientific matters.

Bloch: So scientists would become politicians.

Rathenau: Not necessarily politicians, but government advisers.

Freeman: In this whole question of the redeployment of government laboratories it is essential to bear in mind the experience of industry in making innovations. Innovation only succeeds where a need, a requirement of society, is clearly recognized. Simply to say 'Let's do environmental research' is quite insufficient. One needs to have a very clearly defined goal and, as Dr Weinberg said, one just can't get going on a vague and ill-defined objective. The kind of approach which might work in these circumstances is something the City Management Association is attempting in North America. This association obtained from five hundred cities lists of what they regarded as their most urgent environmental problems. These varied from dealing with fires, waste disposal or vermin to amenity problems. Altogether five hundred urgent problems for which cities were seeking technical help were listed. The association found that technical solutions already existed for one hundred and fifty of these and they were able simply to tell the people what the solutions were. They then recirculated a list of the remaining problems and asked the cities to rank them in order of urgency. On this basis they identified a short-list of urgent problems for which technical research could perhaps provide help. They are now working on these problems with the assistance of NASA which already has some expertise in some of the problem areas. This is the kind of thing required. One needs clearly defined goals in order to have missions which will be worth while from society's point of view.

Weinberg: A bill aimed at the establishment of national environmental laboratories will probably be brought before Congress within the next few months. The general idea is to establish large institutions, or perhaps a single large institution, which would look at environmental problems as a whole rather than in fragments.

I have in the past argued for development of what I call 'coherent doctrine' with respect to these difficult issues. The trend in the United States is for an agency to break up a problem into many little pieces and let out various separate contracts to many different institutions. Problems such as the environment get very badly fragmented; no one seems to look at the problem as a whole. *Coherent* doctrines are needed and I believe these are best developed in institutions that are themselves coherent. These big instrumentalities that the National Environmental Laboratory Bill would set up have the capacity to bring the whole together. At the Oak Ridge National Laboratory we are experimenting with the establishment on a small scale of a national environmental laboratory that looks at the environment coherently.

Thiemann: Without a certain number of entrepreneurs who can integrate this knowledge the whole scientific effort lacks life.

Weinberg: Every part of life needs entrepreneurs.

Thiemann: But some institutions in certain countries are killing the entrepreneurs.

The research scientists should not wait for problems to be given to them. Why don't they propose important subjects for investigation to the government? Someone has to raise the right questions and scientists have to be more aggressive in this respect.

Freeman: It is important to define 'entrepreneur' in this context. I agree with you completely, Dr Thiemann, if you are defining an entrepreneur as an individual whose responsibility it is to match the possibilities of scientific research and technology with the market or with the needs of society. But government entrepreneurs or people managing government laboratories need to have a much wider view of social needs and requirements. If an entrepreneur in this very broad sense interprets society's long-term needs, he is exactly the kind of person we want.

Science, technology and the political response

GERARD PELLETIER

We have gathered here to reflect on a common theme, 'Civilization and Science'. Although our approaches to this theme and our views on it certainly differ, I feel confident that we are all in agreement about its extent and complexity.

At first glance, I imagined—somewhat naively perhaps—that it would be easier to propose a preliminary definition of what is meant by 'science' than of what is meant by 'civilization'.

For the purposes of our symposium we shall certainly have no difficulty in admitting, for example, that biology is a science, but are we prepared to admit that a given type of behaviour makes man civilized, whereas another type marks him as uncivilized? Are we agreed to define civilization as: 'a set of characteristics peculiar to a specific society', or should we select another meaning of the term: 'the set of characteristics common to so-called advanced societies?' This is not merely a quarrel about semantics. The first definition would enable us to take a phenomenological approach to our subject, and to arrive at a sort of working consensus in order to study the nature of the relationships that obtain between science and a given state of civilization. The second would make immediate demands upon our individual value systems, our personal beliefs and our prejudices. It is not difficult to imagine the heat that might be generated, for example, by a comparison of the 'advances of science' and what the colonizers of yesteryear referred to as the 'benefits of civilization'.

Personally, I would not venture to define civilization in contrast with something called 'non-civilization'. I propose instead to consider here the dynamic process that links civilizations to one another, and to reflect on the influences which science and technology have exerted on such dynamics. Secondly, I shall draw a parallel between these influences and the attitudes of the politician to the role he is called upon to play in a modern society.

From the viewpoint of dynamics, then—that is, by approaching the concept of 'civilization' as a process of continual change—the history of humanity might be regarded as an irreversible transition from belief to knowledge, or more specifically from dogmatic belief to relativistic knowledge.

Dogmatic belief is the acceptance of a concept as absolute truth. Its characteristic dogmatism rejects and even fights against all doubt or challenge and —even more energetically—against any contradictory explanation. 'The earth is flat and the sun describes an arc from sunrise to sundown'. This is the typical dogmatic belief, which condemns as heresy Copernicus's theory of the universe. (Dogmatism here is an arbitrary extension of religious belief to things temporal, and an artificial reinforcement of our sense of security. It defends itself by exercising control over any information, beliefs and knowledge deemed to be heretical. The inquisition, the Index, censorship and segregation are all manifestations of this state of mind.)

The definition of relativistic knowledge, on the other hand, carries no implication of absolute truth. An idea is held to be accurate until it has been proved inaccurate. The mark of relativistic knowledge is its permanent acceptance of challenge. The scientific spirit is the very essence of relativism, because it not only accepts challenge but systematically encourages it.

This analysis of history as the transition from belief to knowledge does not, of course, explain the considerable differences that may exist at a given moment in history in the development of the various societies of the world, nor does it explain the decline of certain civilizations. However, when the evolution of any society is considered independently of others surrounding it at the same period, the same tendency towards relativistic knowledge is apparently always found, the differences involving only the rate of change.

At the extreme, there still exist today a few so-called primitive societies whose way of life has remained virtually unchanged for centuries. No doubt when we are agonizing over the 'advanced' state of civilization in which we live, we are inclined to think twice before affirming the superiority of our technological hardware over the incantations of the witch-doctor of some Amazon tribe. Nevertheless, if we analyse the way of life of such a tribe, we discover that its primitive nature is partly defined by a culture based on irrational beliefs, which are in fact magical and superstitious interpretations of natural phenomena.

As history has unfolded, this interpretation of natural phenomena has gradually given way to a rational explanation. Since the beginning of this century, however, science has become insistent, and has contributed to the acceleration of history discussed by the French philosopher Gaston Berger. Science is rushing contemporary mankind towards relativistic knowledge, and, through the development of communication facilities and the democratization of educational systems, this influence is being brought to bear on a growing number of countries and—within their different social strata—on a growing number of people.

Man today seems to be marking time while science and technology are advancing at an accelerated pace. More and more groups are offering passive or open resistance to scientific 'progress'. This trend is particularly strong among a certain segment of the young, who might normally have been expected to look the most favourably on scientific breakthroughs and on the spectacular achievements which they have made possible.

In his aphorism: 'Science without conscience is but the ruin of the soul', François Rabelais offers a key to partial understanding of this phenomenon. Contemporary man has reached a saturation point where knowledge is concerned. If salt is poured into a glass of water, a time comes when the solution is saturated and the salt will not dissolve, but merely forms into lumps. Similarly, the time comes when man is incapable of assimilating new knowledge. Although he is doubtless able to take in the new knowledge with his mind, he does not use it in solving life's problems, and it becomes parasitic in relation to his search for happiness. It is science without conscience, knowledge approached with the mental attitudes of dogmatism.

Our civilization—and this is true even of the most 'advanced' societies of which it is composed—rests on a mixed foundation of beliefs and knowledge. How many of those who followed the flight of Apollo 12 with such keen interest attributed the failure of the next Apollo shot to the malevolent influence of the number 13?

In truth, we have not yet recovered from the splitting up of humanistic studies in the mid-19th century, which put the sciences on one side and the so-called humanities on the other. Generally speaking, our educational systems have not yet abandoned the primacy of the *magister dixit:* the student learns ideas as revealed by a person in possession of knowledge; he does not learn experimentally, by trial and error. In most of the world's schools, error is still looked upon as immoral. Is it possible to conceive of a more inadequate preparation for 'mastering the unfamiliar', to borrow another expression from Rabelais?

Could not one cause of the sickness of civilization that we have heard so much about in the last few years be this surfeit of knowledge? Man is overburdened; from all sides, he is beset by a host of ideological solicitations. Science and the information media that popularize and convey it are destroying a good many ancestral taboos in the interests of a systematic relativism which is inevitably accompanied by considerable anguish. Part of the young generation—I am thinking in particular of everything encompassed by the hippy movement—reacts to this anguish by returning to a form of fundamentalism, and by turning away from the puritan condemnation of physical pleasure. This release is expressed in the longing for a simple, wandering life based on handicrafts, for a return to the soil, for a rediscovery of the physical senses, and so on.

For example, the fight against various forms of pollution has taken on very unusual proportions in the West in the last few years, with citizens of all persuasions and from all circles actively participating in it and feeling personally concerned by this question. Yet the threats that now hang over the environment are not new, and scientists did not wait until public opinion was mobilized before warning governments of the dangers inherent in pollution, in the aberrations of certain urban planners, and in the population increase.

If I were a psychoanalyst, I would ponder the significance of this sudden public interest in pollution problems and I would venture the following explanation: if the man in the street is increasingly concerned with the protection of his natural environment, is it not partly because his inner peace and order are threatened? Violence, fanaticism, intolerance and untruths are all forms of pollution of the mind which are not easy to combat. Viewed in this light, action to protect the external environment would be a necessary and beneficial catharsis.

McLuhan's global village links up with the idea of the planetary society dear to forecasters of the future and to writers of science fiction. In fact it would appear that, by eroding ideological dogmatisms, the near-instantaneous dissemination of news and the development of transport and communication facilities will hasten the advent of what might be called the 'interculture', that is of a widespread political and cultural consensus parallel to the different national and regional cultures.

I am not unaware that this notion is utopian indeed, and that in the present situation such a consensus could only be reached at the expense of cultures deprived of the scientific and technical support which makes it possible to resist assimilation and debasement. The interculture is not a form of cultural and ideological colonialism, any more than pluralism is a negation of the diversity of races, languages and life styles.

One cause of the unrest in Western civilization might therefore stem from a maladjustment between man's receptivity, the proliferation of knowledge and the diversification of pressures to learn. I am not referring here to man's capacity to understand or to learn, for I am convinced that this capacity is much greater than is commonly believed. On the other hand, he has not been prepared for this never-ending bombardment of sensory and intellectual stimuli; the evolution of man's innermost attitudes is no longer keeping pace with the development of his technology. Intellect and soul have parted company.

There may be many external causes for the decline of a civilization, but among the internally produced causes, one seems to me preponderant: it is the disintegration of the image a community has of itself, brought about by the impossibility of reconciling new knowledge with the set of dogmatic beliefs which form the cultural foundation of its civilization.

When I mention the importance of agreement between the proliferation of knowledge and man's capacity to integrate 'what has never been', I immediately think of the great geographical discoveries of the Renaissance and of the attitude of its explorers, who, unable to adapt to the unfamiliar, perceived the revelation of the unknown with the dogmatisms of the Middle Ages. Confronted with the difference, they knew no peace until they had destroyed it with a savagery that has become common knowledge. In Stanley Kubrick's film, *2001, A Space Odyssey*, we are shown the extension of this idea when a committee of international experts decides to conceal from the general public a scientific discovery—the existence of an intelligence in outer space—because they feel that people are not ready to cope with such a brutal revelation.

But is it even necessary to imagine anything as unusual as the presence of organized life on another planet in order to believe that man can be threatened by new knowledge? The My-Lai massacre, to take just one of a thousand examples, shattered the image that the American people had of themselves and —to pursue the idea I outlined earlier—I believe that the photographs of Vietnamese children gunned down by American soldiers and the fact that a group of New Yorkers decided to take brushes and pails and scrub the streets of their city are part of the same psychological continuity.

Young people who take drugs are not trying to forget the existence of the Martians; they are reacting to history here and now, which is something we share with them.

How will the politician react to the situation whose broad lines I have just described? To what extent are his acts and decisions subject to the influence of science and technology?

In the first place, I would say that the politician is the archetype of the overburdened man of whom I spoke earlier. Knowledge—in this case the influx of data—makes constant demands on him, while at the same time he is subject to political pressures of all kinds. The greatest danger threatening the quality of his judgement, and one which he does not always manage to avoid, is to substitute oversimplification for synthesis, to give certain data preference over others—not at the analytical stage, which would be legitimate, but *a priori*, at the collection stage. At times, political lobbying may also be considered as an element in the problem to be resolved, whereas in my view lobbying should not become a factor before the decision-making stage.

The overburdened man can obviously call upon advisers to help with the process of synthesis; he may rely on experts to carry out the preliminary study of a question in his stead. In reality, however, the efficacy of such cooperation is limited by the degree of urgency of the decisions to be made—all too often urgency provides the initial impetus for political decisions.

Nevertheless, I believe that science and technology are in the process of effecting profound changes in the conventional ground rules of politics, or to put it more accurately, I think the politician is going to find himself confronted by an ever more clearly defined choice: he must either adopt new approaches and methods in order to discharge his responsibilities (and his primary responsibility is to make decisions), or face what, for want of better terms, I might call the growing polymorphism of direct protests involving certain segments of the population, as distinct from Parliamentary opposition.

The role of tomorrow's politician will be more closely related to that of a cyberneticist than to the one he now performs with more or less ease. In order to flesh out this statement, I propose to reflect now on the process of decision-making in politics.

For all practical purposes, a political choice for a man, a group or a party in power consists first in establishing orders of priority among tasks of all kinds which, when taken all together, constitute the administration of the state's affairs. This choice is necessary, whatever the type of government. Be it capitalist or Marxist, rich or poor, strong or weak, it will have to fix orders of priority for carrying out the tasks entrusted to it. All cannot be equally urgent. Some problems must be declared more urgent than others.

This political choice is necessarily derived from a system of values, that is from an ideology. Once the choice of priorities has been made, the politician has to make a certain number of decisions regarding the means to be employed in order to meet the deadlines for the priorities so chosen.

It is at this point that a great many politicians, with varying degrees of awareness and complacency, seem uncertain about the real extent of their powers. Although people may believe that because of science and technology today's politician has a broad range of means at his disposal for achieving his objectives, a detailed analysis of the situation by experts will in fact reduce the selection to a few alternatives. What is more, these alternatives will not always be understood by the uninitiated.

Thus, when speaking of decision-making in politics, we are sometimes tempted to believe that there are as many options as there are means, whereas most of the time, when it comes to determining ways and means of acting, the politician's role is limited to forming a judgement on the worth and loyalty of the specialists on whose contribution his decisions are based. Moreover, his role is further diminished from the moment when the job of implementing the policies laid down by a government is handed over to its officials.

I admit that the outline I have drawn here is anything but encouraging, but this is surely not a reason for withholding it from you. This situation contains the root cause of an ambiguity against which more and more people are reacting. At one end of the process, the politician states his intentions; at the other, he is judged by the electorate on the measure of agreement between the objectives he has set and the achievements of his government. There is no question here of challenging this legitimate right of the electorate; on the contrary, it is a matter of showing that a politician who wants to assume his responsibilities in a modern society can no longer look upon his role as it was defined in the 19th century. I hasten to add, however, that any politician who set forth the nature and extent of his role exactly, without exaggeration, would run the risk of being ejected from politics by the very mechanisms of our democratic systems, characterized by universal suffrage and Parliamentary opposition.

As a rule, Parliamentary opposition forces even the most watchful of politicians to oversimplify, for it uses the weapons of dialectic argument and speculation against the complex administration of a modern state. However, power in a post-industrial society is exercised within such narrow margins that there is little room for manoeuvre, and although a change of government can effect a reshuffling of priorities, it can rarely do anything about redefining the means of meeting them. In fact, unless a frankly revolutionary approach is taken, the operational responses to such problems as inflation, unemployment, pollution, drugs or organized crime are few in number. However competent the specialists it hires, however ingenious its consultants, and however imaginative the government itself may be, there are no miraculous solutions—except perhaps in the minds of those who, removed from the centres of decision-making and not over-anxious to learn the exact nature of the issues which arise, settle the country's major problems by dialectic and speculative argument that is often completely divorced from reality.

Political choice in a democratic system entails the risk of being challenged by the majority of voters. We in Canada have had the example of a provincial government which carried out such a sweeping reform of its system of education that it was defeated in the next election, contrary to all predictions.

In the last ten years or so, however, the ratio of forces that I have just described has been upset by a form of opposition that is not conducted within the conventional rules of politics. This is the all-encompassing protest by what we may call the counter-culture, or alternative culture. Basically, the counter-culture does not seek to gain political power. Certain political ideologies naturally ride along with the counter-culture, but this strategy has been employed since the beginning of history. What is new is the outright rejection, the systematic non-participation, the political disengagement.

We are faced here with two closed systems: politics, in which adults are in the majority, and the counter-culture, which includes a great many young people. The meeting and partial interpenetration of these two systems is a human challenge infinitely more complex and delicate than, for example, the linking of two space vehicles. This is all the more evident in that the social and political control centres are no longer located in government offices—the press and the interest groups have their fingers on several of the buttons that control the weaponry for social change.

The role of the politician here is to coordinate the efforts of scientists and humanists, an action that can be viewed as comparable to that of the Soviet technicians when, from the earth, they supervised the docking of Soyuz II at the space laboratory Salyut.

I think it would be a mistake to consider the various manifestations of the counter-culture as a fleeting or superficial reaction. I believe these reflect the ambiguity that I mentioned earlier, and that they will be intensified if this ambiguity persists. In fact, one of the causes of the present withdrawal from politics or of the recourse to a more or less exotic form of anarchy seems to me to be the fragility of the symbols of authority and the difficulty of personifying responsibility.

The news media have made the symbols of authority essentially fragile and short-lived. Political idols are devoured almost as quickly as star pop singers. Furthermore, whatever they may claim, politicians no longer in fact succeed in personifying the responsibilities entrusted to them. I believe that this failure is not yet a widespread phenomenon, which is one reason for its taking us unawares.

I said earlier that the rules of the game compelled the politician to simplify. At the same time, I feel that the inroads made into the management of public affairs by science and technology force him to synthesize. To illustrate this viewpoint, I have chosen as an example a problem which is particularly acute in Canada: the dilemma of 'inflation and unemployment'. Because of her competitive position in world markets, Canada is very vulnerable during inflationary periods. Rising costs and prices can lead to the loss of foreign markets, which is reflected in a loss of the jobs to which these markets give rise. In order to regain the markets, we would have to devalue the dollar, but then we would be unable to pay for our imports.

Naturally, a high rate of unemployment impairs a country's social and political climate. The opposition movements, whose role it is, will attack the government, using binary or dipole dialectics. That is, in this instance, the Parliamentary opposition will claim that the unfavourable economic situation should be attributed to the errors of the government in office, and that if the opposition were in power the situation would be rapidly corrected.

These are acceptable tactics and Canadian politics certainly has no monopoly on them. However, this binary dialectics has the secondary effect of forcing the government to defend its position by using the same language, that is by simplifying the facts to the point of distortion.

In fact, the relationship between inflation and unemployment is not a binary one, and no government ever has a choice between inflation *or* unemployment. The alternative is quite different: allow the inflation to continue—which would aggravate residual unemployment—or curb the rate of inflation; but this restriction will obviously not help to reduce unemployment, at least in the short run.

The simplifying process here consists in exaggerating out of all proportion the influence of the authorities over a phenomenon of this nature.

I also said that the invasion of the field of management of public affairs by science and technology has forced the politician to synthesize. To return to my example, the government will learn at the same time as the opposition and the public at large what the increase in the unemployment rate has been over the last three months. Furthermore, this information will be published by a quasi-governmental agency, financed from public funds.

A simplifier despite himself, and a cyberneticist by calling, the politician has to reconcile the defence of his objectives with the facts as they appear. He has to master science and technology, but he cannot do this alone. It is urgent that scientists communicate with politicians and that, together, they seek means of processing these facts for assimilation by the political authorities in their synthesizing operations and in their decision-making.

We all remember the first attempts by the United States to put a satellite into earth orbit. These attempts had been preceded by so much publicity that each new failure increased the humiliation of the Americans, and we recall that even certain dignitaries who had a reputation for liberalism wondered at the time about the advisability of informing the public of a satellite launching before it had proved successful.

This question still has significance, and it covers another more basic question concerning the organic relationships that obtain between science and politics in a modern society. I do not think that I have answered it at all, but I hope I have succeeded in making you aware of the problems that I encounter daily in performing my duties as a servant of the public, and I am looking forward with much interest to the reaction of the scientists.

Discussion

Long: I take it that you agree that, since science will continue to contribute new ideas to technology, the general impact of science and technology can only increase in intensity. Furthermore, I gather that you as a politician think that the rate of social change caused by this impact is getting near to saturation point. What does one do then? Political responses are normally made not by revolution but by evolutionary changes of the existing system, most commonly by successive introduction of several small steps. Could not a series of such steps be taken to increase the assimilability of technology and enhance the rate of social change? One can imagine the use of a variety of communication systems, with public television centrally involved, to develop a more rapid and more reasoned public response. Must we sit and watch this tide creep over us? What is Canada doing in response to this great social problem?

Pelletier: We have tried to provide systematic information to the public about what the government is doing, and to get a feedback. While this government has been in power (3¹/₂ years) we have not advanced far with this, but it is very important. Generally people can assimilate only a certain amount of what comes their way and they then revert to belief instead of understanding. I think this is the limit of participatory democracy if participatory only means that people understand what is going on. The dialogue between the government and the people outside the known circuits of information is just beginning to develop. However, if we master the techniques of communication in a democracy, we politicians will be accused of dealing in propaganda. How do you draw the line between propaganda and information, between telling people about what you are trying to do and being accused of peddling your own programme with the taxpayer's money? There is no simple solution and all we can do is take a lot of initiative over the years.

Scientists in both the social sciences and the physical sciences could help the politicians by getting together across the boundaries of their various disciplines and trying to discover how to change the intellectual attitudes of people as fast as society changes itself through the impact of technology. Very little has been done in that direction yet. Technology is so much in advance that man cannot adapt to it, so he develops neuroses. As politicians we are concerned not so much with neurosis as with misunderstanding, but this is a basic problem we meet every day, not a theoretical one.

Toda: In my opinion nothing short of obtaining a new science that enables us to predict the future reasonably accurately will solve that problem. The task of obtaining such a science, however, should not be left to social scientists alone. It can be accomplished only with the support of all branches of science, and the importance of creating this new science must be realized by all scientists. Scientists today are so powerful, with so many research tools, that I think there is a fair hope of achieving this task, once scientists make a concerted effort across disciplines.

Thiemann: Your remarks make it clear that politicians have to make choices and define certain problems, Mr Pelletier. You mentioned the financial situation and the unemployment in Canada. Although scientific discoveries have been made in many different areas we know surprisingly little about this economic problem, which affects everyone. A year ago the Minister of Finance in Switzerland said that he would not revalue the franc because he could not predict the consequences of such a decision. He took advice from the national bank and from experts all over the world and concluded that although he didn't understand all the consequences, neither did they. Isn't there a challenge here for the scientific community? We should try to understand such a fundamental problem.

Pelletier: Part of the answer is that although politicians are always asking for accurate predictions of the future, scientists cannot provide these yet.

Thiemann: The Council of Churches in Geneva has been discussing man and technology. The churches are very concerned about what they should do in the future. They have asked scientists to tell them what scientific developments can be expected in the future, so that they can adapt themselves to the changes. But scientists are also human beings and we cannot predict what science will do. Science is largely a function of the problems it is asked to deal with, not an independent force.

Weinberg: In thinking about the relation between science and society and between science and politics, scientists must be sensitive to the intrinsic limitations of science. The scientific paradigm which has been so enormously proficient and successful in the physical sciences just isn't so applicable to these more difficult situations that involve classes with infinite variability. Physical scientists are so powerful in making predictions because they deal with homogeneous classes: every electron is the same as every other electron. Further away from the physical sciences, first in the biological sciences and then in the social sciences, the individuals themselves display great variability. Therefore one cannot expect to make the same kind of predictions about particular events as in the physical sciences. Scientists would do well to remind politicians that science in principle cannot perform miracles of this sort. I am a physical scientist, and my impressions of the social sciences and their limitations are strongly coloured by my own experiences. Do the social scientists generally believe this or do they think that in another hundred years they will do better? The social sciences are not so new any more, but fundamentally it is a different and trans-scientific question.

Shils: The social sciences are very uneven in their development. The most advanced branch is economics. Sociology and anthropology are the subjects I know something about and they are intellectually extremely difficult. The difficulty may lie in the fact that the physical sciences, and mathematics particularly, attract more intelligent people than sociology does, although of course the two groups overlap. Similarly those studying economics and those studying education show a difference in intellectual gifts. It isn't that economics is more important than education but somehow the flow of superior intelligence is into the former field. Economics has now reached a state where it is both more satisfying and more challenging to young people of high intellectual capacity; they respond to it with greater zest and they therefore find it more attractive. But this is only one aspect of a very complicated problem.

Johnson: I think we have to take a broader sociological view of the nature of the attractions and the disadvantages of various kinds of careers. Our society is quite prepared to have people pursue knowledge for its own sake, providing it is knowledge about things that are not human. People get interested in subjects like economics, anthropology and so forth mostly because they come from some part of society which makes them worried about the nature of society; but society itself imposes limitations on how far they can use their minds. It is possible to be a brilliant mathematician, a conformist and a member of a church. It is not really possible to be a good economist and a conformist at the same time. In the social sciences you are therefore faced with the problem of compromising between where your brains are taking you and where your society wants you to end up. That is one reason why there are more brilliant mathematicians than economists. Economists in a way are self-limited by their sociological origins. I observe this particularly in relation to the status of mathematics as compared to economics in two countries, India on the one hand and Japan on the other. Both of those societies are terribly confused as societies. They don't know what they are about. It is possible to be a brilliant mathematician in either of them because that doesn't challenge the nature of that society. It is very difficult to be a good social scientist in those countries because that involves trying to make sense of what is completely senseless. We have to consider scientists themselves as part of the socio-logical process, with a selection process and a reward system. Some kinds of science are highly rewarded and people in them can go where they like. Other kinds are greatly limited by the society they come from and to be good in them you have somehow to transcend your own society. But we don't train people to transcend their societies; we train them to conform.

Weinberg: If a society is senseless, how can it be an object of scientific enquiry?

Johnson: It can be an object of scientific enquiry in terms of some theory of what society is about. Professor Ely Devons used to make the point that if we did discover anthropological and sociological rules for society these would be about things we couldn't do anything about. The problem is that the de-mands made to social scientists are for solutions of immediate problems defined by the society itself. It is like having a hive of bees and asking one of the bees how to increase the honey output. The answer may be: 'I wouldn't start with bees'. The other bees wouldn't accept that answer.

Weinberg: The engineer does answer that kind of question. If he is asked to build a bridge, he can do so.

Johnson: He can build a bridge, but if you ask him how can human beings cross that river in a way conformable with their religion and their beliefs about science he couldn't answer that so easily. Building a bridge is an impersonal objective thing and nobody cares much what the bridge looks like, so long as it serves its purpose.

Weinberg: That is the point. Presumably where the politicians want the social scientists to help them is on the difficult questions of inflation and so on.

Johnson: Those are easy questions. The answer is that they have created the problem themselves and have to put up with it.

Weinberg: I gather that the politicians would like to have some kind of magical answer that makes it easy for them.

Johnson: They are asking people to build a bridge without using any raw materials. The social scientists get sucked into the idea that one can build a bridge without any materials and without any knowledge, that somehow there is a way of casting a spell which will put a bridge across that river. The poli-ticians keep asking us for impossibilities: they ask for solutions to problems which we know are insoluble because they are created by the public and their politicians themselves. In Canada, the United Kingdom and the United States there is inflation because for five years there has been expansion of demand on the assumption that there could be full employment without inflation. Eco-nomics tells you that there is a long lag but eventually you will have the in-flation. Then you try to stop the inflation by having unemployment and you find it takes more unemployment than you want. Then you are high in the sky again, trying to build a bridge without any materials.

Jean Medawar: Mr Pelletier, you referred to the difficulties that responsible people in government, who are trying to find solutions, have in communicating with young people who are protesting and who reject reason. The Canadian government has begun the experiment of offering money to these young people for their own projects. Is there a ray of hope here, if the protesters are asked to take responsibility? Has this worked out well? When they were given a bit of responsibility and a bit of money did they have any better ideas than older people?

Pelletier: They have had remarkable ideas. The response has been tremendous. It was very difficult for government circles to abandon the bureaucratic approach and there was much scepticism about going directly to the young people. Quite surprisingly to the sceptics, we were flooded with projects, all except a very small percentage of which were excellent. The suggestions were not at all what one would think would come from youth as described and perceived by adults. Young people are supposed to be interested in themselves alone but eighty per cent of these projects are of a social nature: they want to help older people, the disinherited and the kids in large cities, to record textbooks on tape for blind students, and so on—there is a tremendous variety. It remains to be seen whether they can administer and manage these projects and get results. The initial result, of course, is that the opposition party and even some of my own party are asking for my resignation for having saddled them with this scheme. This is our first experiment of this kind and it is on quite a large scale. The projects are just starting now and there don't seem to be too many difficulties. We have more difficulties with adults than with the kids. Some civil servants don't like it either; they think it is very unorthodox and shouldn't be done. The initial response certainly indicates that the kids were waiting for something like this. We were literally flooded—we had fourteen thousand projects and we could finance about three thousand.

Toulmin: The complex relationship you spoke about in your paper, Mr Pelletier, contains a number of terms. One was that politicians are faced with making decisions which are much narrower than outsiders are inclined to think. Then you and Dr Long were talking about how to keep the general public informed and in sympathy with the nature of these choices. But there are also the scientists themselves, the people to whom you turn for discussions of how various possible choices might be implemented.

The relationship between the politicians and the scientists has in fact changed very much over the last fifty years. Even during the Second World War, when I was working in a government radar research establishment, I recall being struck by an obvious ambiguity in the phrases 'scientific adviser' and 'scientific advice'. In the early days, the picture was always of the politician as the man who *first* formulated for himself questions about the political options, about the choices he had to make: on this view, he *subsequently* turned to people called 'technical advisers' and asked them how to do this or that, how much each option would cost, and so on. A lot of people still see the relationship between the scientist or technologist and the politician on this model—which one might call the 'Tizard model'. This was often an extraordinarily powerful and fruitful relationship, but even during the war scientists were being transformed into people who could very often see a fresh range of policy options *before* the politicians could. Again and again, for example, we would have to tell the Air Force people that their whole range of options was transformed because we could now give night-fighters ways of tracking their targets in the dark—or whatever it might be.

To some extent, the institutional relationships between politics and science have not yet caught up with this change. So one might envisage a situation in which perhaps, within each functional department, there were clearer channels by which the people with political authority could debate with outside scientists the range of options which should be considered at any given time. This debate would not necessarily alter the real political decision when the Minister himself finally confronted it—but it might.

This is, of course, quite different from saying that the scientists and technologists are in any better position than the politicians to answer the questions formulated. They are not, and Lord Todd is quite right in saying that the scientist and technologist can only *help* to formulate the options. It takes a politician to understand what is involved in making the choice afterwards. The actual problem is one of getting together to see where better arrangements are needed to ensure that the politician is informed of the full range of available options.

Todd: There should be better machinery for doing this but *some* machinery has been there for a long time and during the last fifteen years this has been used more and more often.

Toulmin: But scientists themselves don't see it as part of their professional duty to contribute to this. Neither politicians nor scientists are sufficiently aware of the extent to which these channels exist, nor are they sufficiently given to using them.

Science and trans-science

ALVIN M. WEINBERG

Much has been written about the responsibility of the scientist in resolving conflicts that arise from the interaction between science and society. Ordinarily the assumption is made that a particular issue at the interface between science and society—whether or not to build a supersonic transport (SST) or whether or not to proceed with the trip to the moon—can be neatly divided into two rather separate sub-issues—one scientific, the other political. Thus the scientist is expected to say whether a trip to the moon is feasible or whether the SST will cause additional skin cancer. The politician, or some other representative of the people, is then expected to say whether society ought to proceed in one direction or another. The scientist and science provide the means; the politician and politics decide the ends.

This view of the role of the scientist, and indeed of science itself, is of course oversimplified, in particular because even where there are clear scientific answers to the scientific components of a public issue, ends and means are hardly separable. The scientist and the politician must interact and react with each other.

Here I shall be concerned with a somewhat different aspect of the relation between science and society. Many of the issues that arise from the interaction between science or technology and society—the deleterious side-effects of technology, or the attempts to deal with social problems through the methodology of science, for example—hang on the answers to questions that can be asked of science and yet *which cannot be answered by science*. I propose the term trans-scientific for these questions since, though they may arise in or around science, and can be stated in the language of science, they are unanswerable by science—that is, they transcend science. In so far as public policy depends on trans-scientific rather than scientific issues, the role of the scientist in developing such policy must differ from his role when the issues can be answered by science. It will be my purpose to examine this role of the scientist, and particularly to explore the interaction between the public and the scientist where trans-scientific questions bear on public policy.

I begin with a few examples of trans-scientific questions; several are taken from my own field of nuclear energy.

Biological effects of low-level radiation insults

Consider the biological effects of low-level radiation insults to the environment, in particular the genetic effects in mice of low levels of radiation. Experiments performed at high radiation levels show that the dose required to double the spontaneous mutation rate in mice is 30 roentgens of X-rays. Thus, if the genetic response to X-radiation is linear, then a dose of 150 millirems (mrem; rem: *r*oentgen *e*quivalent *m*an) would increase the spontaneous mutation rate in mice by 0.5 per cent. This is a matter of importance to public policy since the various standard-setting bodies had decided that a yearly dose of about 150 mrem to a suitably chosen segment of the population was acceptable. Now, to determine by a direct experiment whether 150 mrem will increase the mutation rate by 0.5 per cent requires around eight thousand million mice! Of course this number falls if one reduces the confidence level; at 60 per cent confidence level, the number is 195 million. Nevertheless, the number is so staggeringly large that, as a practical matter, the question is unanswerable directly.*

This kind of dilemma is not confined to radiation. No matter what the environmental insult, to measure an effect at extremely low levels usually requires impossibly large protocols. Moreover, no matter how large the experiment, even if *no* effect is observed, one can still only say there is a certain probability that in fact there is no effect. One can never, with any finite experiment, prove that any environmental factor is totally harmless. This elementary point unfortunately has been lost in much of the public discussion of environmental hazards.

---

* To be sure, indirect evidence as to the shape of the dose-response curve for X-rays at very low dose can be inferred from experiments that measure the relative biological effectiveness of highly ionizing radiation and X-rays. Such experiments suggest that the dose-response curve for X-rays at low dose is quadratic, not linear. However, these experiments are suggestive, not definitive: they still represent extrapolations to very low doses of radiation of the observations taken at high dose.

The probability of extremely improbable events

Another trans-scientific question is the probability of extremely unlikely events—as, for example, a catastrophic reactor accident, or a devastating earthquake that would, say, destroy Hoover Dam and thereby wash out parts of the Imperial Valley of California. Probabilities for such events are sometimes calculated—for example, for a catastrophic reactor accident, one constructs plausible accident trees, each branch of which is triggered by the failure of a particular component. Statistics as to the reliability of each component are often known, since many components of the type under consideration—ion chambers, transistors, control rod bearings—have been tested. But the calculations are obviously suspect, first because the total probability obtained by such estimates is so extraordinarily small—say 10^{-9}/reactor each year, or one chance in a thousand million—and second because there is no proof that every conceivable mode of failure has been identified. Because the probability is so small, there is no practical possibility of determining this failure rate directly —by building, say, a million reactors, operating them for a thousand years and tabulating their operating histories.

These two examples illustrate questions that are trans-scientific because, though they conceivably could be answered if enough time and money were spent on them, to do so would be impractical.

Trans-scientific questions in the social sciences

In the social sciences trans-scientific questions arise frequently. One often hears social scientists categorize questions as being researchable or not researchable. In the former category presumably are questions that, at least in the estimate of the social scientist, can be attacked with some hope of success. In the latter category are those that cannot.

What makes a question in the social sciences non-researchable or transscientific? Before the advent of the large computer, I suppose many questions in social science were simply too large to undertake. Obviously the computer has changed this. But there remain two kinds of seemingly socio-scientific questions that will always be in the realm of trans-science.

The first is the behaviour of a particular individual. In physics, if we know the initial position and velocity of a specific macroscopic object, and the forces acting upon it, we can predict its trajectory—not the trajectories on the average of many objects like this one, but the specific trajectory of this object. Thus the physical sciences are capable of predicting specific events from the laws of nature and from the initial conditions. This enormous proficiency is attributed by W. M. Elsasser [3] to the homogeneity of the class of objects of discourse in physics—every hydrogen atom is the same as every other hydrogen atom, and statistical variability can itself be predicted. In contrast, the social sciences deal with classes displaying wide variability. In so far as the social sciences can predict behaviour, it is behaviour *on the average* of large classes. To expect the social sciences to predict individual behaviour, or even individual events, is generally asking too much.

A second sort of trans-scientific question in the social sciences arises where there is feedback between the act of measuring or studying a social phenomenon itself. This sort of social 'uncertainty principle' has been described by Harvey Brooks [2]: for example, the act of polling a population by straw vote may itself influence the outcome of the actual election since many people prefer to vote for the candidate they think will win.

Related to this are scientific questions whose very investigation might evoke strong negative social reaction. One such question is being put perennially to the U. S. National Academy of Sciences by Nobel Laureate William Shockley: is race an important determinant of intelligence? The mere investigation of this matter would undoubtedly cause strong resentment among black people, especially since the context in which the question is presented seems to involve a prejudgement on Dr Shockley's part as to the outcome of such a study. At least one Academy committee appointed to study the matter has judged the question itself to be trans-scientific on the grounds that each race represents too wide a range of genetic traits to allow a meaningful study to be performed.

Axiology of science as trans-science

Still a third class of trans-scientific questions constitutes what I call the axiology of science—that is, questions of scientific value. These include the problem of establishing priorities within science (the so-called criteria for scientific choice), as well as the relative valuation of different styles of science—pure versus applied, general versus particular, spectroscopy versus paradigm-breaking, search versus codification. All of these matters involve scientific values or taste rather than scientific truth. In so far as value judgements—that is, ultimate questions of *why* rather than proximate questions of *what*—can never be answered within the same universe of discourse as the one in which the question arose, these issues clearly transcend science even though they originate in science.

Increasingly, society is required to weigh the benefits of new technology against its risks. In such a balance, both scientific and trans-scientific questions must be asked. The strictly scientific issues—whether, say, a rocket engine with enough thrust to support a manned moon shot can be built—can in principle be settled by the usual mechanisms of science such as debate among the experts and critical review by peers. But what about the issues that go beyond science, on which the scientist has opinions that, however, do not carry the same weight as do his opinions on science? These issues are dealt with by two mechanisms: the ordinary political process, and adversary procedures.

As for the political process, I have little to say. Where the issue is allocation of resources and there is no market place, some version of a political process must come into play. The resources are then allocated by the interplay of competing political views. Those who want to build the SST exert political pressure; and this is resisted by those who dislike SSTs, for whatever reason. The purpose of the scholarly discussion of science policy is, in my view, to elevate and illuminate this political discussion, the give and take, at whatever level this occurs.

The other mechanism for weighing risks and benefits is the adversary procedure. This is a rather formal, quasi-legal proceeding at which representatives, both scientific and non-scientific, of opposing views are heard. For example, before a permit is granted for the construction of a nuclear reactor in the United States, the applicant must receive a licence from a licensing board. The board must find that the reactor can be operated 'with reasonable assurance that the health and safety of the public is maintained'.

The hearings before the board have a quasi-legal aspect. Those who oppose issuance of the licence, usually because they don't like what they believe are answers to the questions about the safety of nuclear reactors, appear as interveners. The procedure pits one adversary against another; out of this confrontation one resolves both the trans-scientific and scientific questions related to the side-effects of nuclear reactors.

The adversary procedure is likely to be used increasingly in our society's attempt to weigh the benefits and risks in modern technologies. For example, the U. S. Environmental Protection Agency now requires environmental quality statements from the promoters of any large technological enterprise that may have impact on the environment. These statements, if challenged, will undoubtedly lead to lengthy adversary procedures.

It is therefore important to examine the validity of adversary procedures for settling technological or semi-technological issues. Professor Harold P. Green of George Washington University Law School in Washington, D. C., has argued [4] that in adversary procedures representatives of the public are usually less knowledgeable than are representatives of the applicant. This places a heavy responsibility on the agency before which such adjudicative procedures are held to try to redress any such imbalance. To a great degree this now happens with respect to the U. S. Atomic Energy Commission's review of nuclear reactors. The regulatory staff of the Commission subjects every application for a nuclear reactor to a searching and highly informed technical scrutiny: the public adversary procedure is the culmination of a lengthy prior analysis by the staff of the Atomic Energy Commission. Professor Green contends that the regulatory staff of the Commission, at such hearings, bands together with the applicant against the public interveners. This is hardly the view of many applicants who are often distressed and frustrated by the painstaking and slow course that these reviews require.

Whether the adversary procedure is adequate or not seems to me to depend on whether the question at issue is scientific or trans-scientific. If the question is sharply scientific, then the methods of science rather than the methods of law are required for arriving at the truth. Ideally, one exhausts all of the *scientific* elements, one extracts all of the scientific juice from an issue, before dealing with the trans-scientific residue. Thus, with respect to the public hazard of the SST, the scientific evidence for the connexion between increased sunlight and skin cancer seems to me to be fairly unequivocal; on this I believe experts agree and this can be settled by the usual working of science. The effect of exhaust nitric oxide from SST engines on the ozone concentration in the stratosphere has less direct empirical evidence to support it, and therefore is more controversial: this part of the issue contains both scientific and trans-scientific elements and might be illuminated by adversary procedure. Finally, the question of whether or not to go ahead with the SST with the evidence at hand is an issue that involves primarily non-scientific questions—for example, the cost as compared to other competing activities; this must be decided by politics.

To anyone trained in law, rather formal and somewhat stylized adversary procedures seem to be a natural mechanism for arriving at truth—whether it be legal, trans-scientific or scientific. But to the scientist, adversary procedures seem foreign and inappropriate. To be sure, such procedures are useful in establishing the credibility of witnesses. In science, however, the issue is not a witness's credibility; it is his competence and this is not reliably established by an adversary procedure. On the other hand, in trans-science where matters of opinion, not fact, *are* the issue, credibility is at least as important as competence. Thus the adversary procedure undoubtedly has considerable merit for resolving trans-scientific issues where science and politics interact.

There is yet another possible way to resolve some of the unanswerable questions of public or environmental risk caused by the new technologies: this is to perfect the technology so as to minimize the risk. We say that there is a possibility (which we cannot quantitate) that low-level radiation insult will cause cancer. We can never eliminate these insults entirely—our technologies are too necessary for our survival to dismantle them, and it is idle to hope that we shall ever have technology with absolutely no risk.

To be sure, we shall always try, by improved technology, to reduce effluents and other unwanted by-products from any device. In some measure this is how the debate over the radioactive emission standards from nuclear reactors is being resolved. The original regulations of the U. S. Atomic Energy Commission permitted doses of up to an average of 170 mrem/year to groups of individuals in the vicinity of a nuclear installation. The heated controversy over these standards has been eliminated by technology: nuclear reactors can now be built that emit only one-hundredth or less of the original standards, and the standards are being lowered accordingly.

Even the residual risk, whose magnitude cannot really be determined by science, can be reduced if science can develop a cure for the untoward biological side-effects of the environmental insult. This line of argument has been suggested by H. I. Adler[1] of Oak Ridge National Laboratory, and I believe it deserves serious consideration. Suppose we developed a safe and simple method of immunization against cancer. That this is no longer a fantasy is believed at least by the panel that advised U. S. Senators Yarborough and Kennedy to launch a new cancer programme. Our whole attitude towards residual and unavoidable contamination of the environment would certainly be modified if we could somehow immunize ourselves against the side-effects about which we were concerned in the first place.

The possibility of genetic intervention and prophylactic abortion would also go very far towards eliminating the issue of residual contamination of the biosphere. At present there are twenty or more enzyme deficiencies, presumably of genetic origin, that can be picked up in the amniotic fluid surrounding the human foetus in its mother's womb. If science could, by amniotic analysis and abortion, reduce the risk of genetic abnormality by a large factor, I should think our attitude toward the trans-scientific question of low-level radiation insult would be greatly affected.

Science maintains its validity by the critical judgement of interacting scientific peers. The whole system is described by Michael Polanyi[6] very aptly as the 'Republic of Science'. To qualify for citizenship in the Republic of Science, one's scientific credentials must be acceptable. Only those with proper credentials are allowed to participate in the governance of science: only scientists are listened to in the mutual criticism that keeps science valid. What survives this criticism or, as Harvey Brooks puts it,[2] what has value in the Intellectual Market Place is incorporated in the corpus of science; all else is rejected.

The Republic of Science is elitist. Only scientists participate in its governance. On the other hand, where science and politics meet, issues can no longer be settled by scientists alone. The public, either directly or through articulate scientific pamphleteers, often engages in the debate. The issues affect everyone, not just the scientists, and therefore everyone, in some sense, has a right to be heard. A biologist with no credentials in quantum electrodynamics would never think of attending a scientific meeting on that subject: not only would he be unable to understand it, but his own scientific work would be untouched by it. By contrast, citizens galore now participate in debate on repositories for radioactive wastes in salt mines, the dangers of pesticides or the decision to build an SST. The obvious point is contained in the saying that he whose shoe pinches can tell the shoemaker something.

The Republic of Trans-science (if one can identify something so diffuse as a 'Republic') has elements of the Republic of Politics on the one hand, and the Republic of Science on the other. Its character must therefore reflect to a great extent the political structure of the society in which it operates. In the United States, where the political tradition is strongly democratic (some would say chaotic) and there is relatively little tradition for authority, the debates on trans-scientific issues are particularly noisy. By contrast, in the Soviet Union whatever debate occurs on such matters is far more subdued, far less open.

What are the advantages and the disadvantages of conducting the trans-scientific debate in a completely open manner, as is done in the United States? The disadvantages are clear, particularly to the experts. Often the line between scientific and trans-scientific issues is blurred: for example, some questions related to safety of nuclear reactors can be answered definitively by science. These aspects of the question, lying as they do in science, ought to be adjudicated by the methods of science—by the interaction of accredited experts. If the public becomes involved in the argument before the experts have thrashed the matter out, the scientific issues become diffused and blunted. It is hard to see how a public discussion about whether or not the emergency core cooling system in a pressurized water reactor will work as planned is likely to help the experts to arrive at a reliable answer to this important question.

That the public should have the right of access to trans-scientific debate on matters affecting itself seems clear. Should the public also have the right of access to *scientific* debates whose outcome will affect the public? The obvious difficulties are twofold: first, it is often hard to decide where trans-science ends and science begins; second, public access inhibits free discussion. For example, in discussing the possibility of a reactor accident (a question with both scientific and trans-scientific dimensions!), one will sometimes postulate an extremely improbable event—such as the simultaneous failure of all safety systems at a crucially important juncture. Such discussions are essential to the technical assessment of the reactor—yet, taken out of context, they can and sometimes do cause great confusion, if not panic. There develops an escalation of contingency: each unlikely event connected with a reactor, once it becomes a matter of public discussion, seems to acquire a plausibility that goes much beyond what was originally intended. In consequence, reactors now, at least in the United States, are loaded down with safety system after safety system— the safety and emergency systems dominate the whole technology.

By contrast, in the Soviet Union, where the public does not have automatic right of access to scientific and technical debate of this sort, the technology of reactors is rather less obviously centred around safety. Soviet reactors until recently had no containment shells, no emergency core cooling systems, no pressure suppression systems. The Soviet engineers insist that the primary systems are built so ruggedly that a catastrophic accident of the sort American designs are intended to deal with is entirely incredible. There was here a sharp divergence between the American and the Soviet view of how safe is safe enough. One cannot attribute these differences simply to the existence of the very influential Advisory Committee on Reactor Safety in the United States, since review mechanisms exist in the Soviet Union. I would rather attribute the contrast to the difference in degree of access of the public to the technological debate.

If the public becomes involved in debates that possess scientific as well as trans-scientific components, could this not tend to weaken the Republic of Science, where the constituency is rigorously certified? If the public has a right to debate the details of reactor designs, then why not extend that right to the debate on whether nuclear physics or high-energy physics should be supported more heavily? If it has the right to debate the use of pesticides in agriculture, then should it not have the right to debate whether or not we should do experiments that might lead to asexual reproduction, or cloning, by human beings or to a racial basis for intelligence? And if the unaccredited public becomes involved in debate on matters as close to the boundary between science and trans-science as the direction of biological research, is there some danger that the integrity of the Republic of Sciences will be eroded?

The danger of the public's involvement in 'scientific' debate is illustrated by the Velikovsky incident in 1950. To much of the public, I dare say, Velikovsky's treatment by the scientific community over the publication of his book, *Worlds in Collision,*[7] smacks of Galileo's treatment at the hands of the Inquisition. To a scientist, Velikovsky is not to be taken seriously because he did not conform to the rules of procedure of the Republic of Science; to the public, he is the victim of an arrogant elite. The public comes close, in the Velikovsky case, to demanding the right to pass judgement on scientific questions.

In the past, when science depended less completely on the public for its support, it perhaps was not so serious that the public's views on *scientific* questions were ignored by the scientists. Today, however, one wonders whether science can afford the loss in public confidence that the Velikovsky incident cost it. The Republic of Science can be destroyed more surely by withdrawal of public support for science than by intrusion of the public into its workings.

That the Republic of Science may be compromised by encroachment from the public is probably an exaggeration: there will always be a part of science that is so sharply in the realm of science, not trans-science, that it would be absurd to think of the uninitiated encroaching. But whether or not the Republic of Science is weakened is I believe a relatively trivial issue. In the final analysis, no matter what the disadvantages of public access to technological and trans-scientific debate, I believe we have no choice. In a democratic society, the public's right of access to the debate is as great as the public demands it to be. Especially where experts disagree, the public has little choice but to engage in the debate at an earlier stage than the experts themselves find convenient or comfortable.

Harold Laski was quoted by H. P. Green[5] in this connection: '.. special knowledge and the highly trained mind produce their own limitations .... *Expertise* . . . sacrifices the insight of common sense to intensity of experience. . . . It has . . . a certain caste-spirit about it, so that experts tend to neglect all evidence which does not . . . belong to their own ranks. . . . where human problems are concerned, the expert fails to see that every judgment he makes not purely factual in nature brings with it a scheme of values which has no special validity about it'.

We in the technological and scientific community value our Republic and its workings. But when what we do transcends science and when it impinges on the public, we have no choice but to welcome the public—even encourage the public to participate in the debate. Scientists have no monopoly on wisdom where trans-science is involved: they will have to accommodate to the will of the public. The Republic of Trans-science, bordering as it does on both the Republic of Politics and the Republic of Science, can be neither so pure as the latter nor so undisciplined as the former. The most science can do is to inject some discipline into the Republic of Trans-science; politics in an open society will surely keep it democratic.

Discussion

Bloch: Are your examples of what you call trans-science really trans-scientific according to your own terminology, Dr Weinberg? The 195 million mice needed to establish the biological effects of low-level radiation at a 60 per cent confidence level certainly represent a formidable figure. Those mice would weigh about four million kilogrammes and eat close to a million kilogrammes of feed every day! To carry out such an experiment would therefore be a big task, but not an impossible one. It is not a problem which cannot be solved by scientific methods.

Weinberg: That is only at the 60 per cent confidence level.

Bloch: If one were to perform that experiment, one would do it because of the assumption that extrapolation from the radiation response of mice to that of man is permissible. If similar extrapolations from the behaviour of micro-organisms to that of mice and men were possible, the problem would become simple and the millions of mice could be adequately replaced by a test tube full of microorganisms. These trans-scientific problems are just examples of where scientific knowledge has not advanced far enough to allow easily feasible solutions.

Another point concerns the average values the social sciences must be content with for making projections and predictions, as opposed to the more exact values with which the physical sciences operate. This is also true for biology which often has only average values to work with. Not all DNA molecules are identical chemically, even if their biological effects are indistinguishable. If genetically identical mice are immunized with the same batch of pure bovine serum albumin, a whole family of antibodies appear and each mouse produces antibodies slightly different from those of another mouse, in spite of the fact that all animals received the same treatment.

Weinberg: I agree, but as one moves from the physical sciences through the biological sciences to the social sciences, the individuals have a larger and larger intrinsic variability, and therefore the character of the science and the character of its predictions are different. The uncertainties increase, reaching a maximum in the social sciences. Therefore the usefulness of social science for policy decisions is somewhat limited.

Medawar: I agree with Professor Bloch that the distinction of principle between science and trans-science is not illustrated by those mice at all. What you are really saying, Dr Weinberg, is that there is no room for eight thousand megamice. If all the resources of the United States were diverted to keeping these mice, that problem is a soluble one! A real trans-scientific problem, from what you said, would be whether or not it matters very much if two thousand extra people die of cancer.

Weinberg: Eight thousand million mice are impractical, and will remain impractical for a long time. I will concede that a question which in my terminology is deemed to be trans-scientific at one stage may at a later stage turn out to be scientific.

Toulmin: The category of 'trans-scientific' issues is a mixed bag. One characteristic of some of them (for example, those connected with the emergency core-cooling systems for nuclear reactors) is that Dr Weinberg makes them look more scientific than they are. The question debated before the review board in such cases is: 'Will the emergency core-cooling system work with a sufficient degree of reliability to provide *reasonable and sufficient* protection for the public?' With phrases like 'reasonable and sufficient', this becomes a legal issue. That is just why adversary procedure is appropriate, because what has to be debated is whether, in the light of such investigations as it is practicable and economical to perform, the degree of protection which we can say with confidence will be provided is, or is not, reasonable and sufficient. This at once turns from being a scientific question—that is, a factual issue which we don't yet have the means of answering—to being a legal issue, which has of course to be determined *in the light* of our best factual knowledge, but which is not itself a scientific issue.

Freeman: One big difficulty here is that of defining the boundary line between science and technology, which, at least in the field of nuclear engineering, is becoming very blurred. Many questions of technology assessment are increasingly becoming questions of *science* assessment. If so, this has extremely important implications, not only in the military field, but also in the civil field.

The traditional attitude of historians is apparently that science and technology, both professionally and intellectually, have been relatively independent systems, and that technology has not changed very much as a result of the activity of scientists, but mainly as a result of the activities of practitioners, of people working with the technology, with very little intellectual contribution from science. There was interaction, but it was long-distance and remote, often divorced over time and space. This is substantiated by the 19th and early 20th century patent statistics, which show that independent inventors and ingenious mechanics made very great contributions to invention and innovation in manufacturing industry. But my own work on post-war innovations in a number of branches of industry suggests that this pattern has changed rather drastically in the last thirty or forty years. We find now that changes in the chemical industry and in electrical and mechanical engineering are attributable increasingly to scientific work. This means that there is a relative change in the position of the scientific profession and the engineering profession.

Of course there is the example of the atomic weapons work during the war. I have come to believe that this is not exceptional and that the whole relationship between science and technology has been profoundly changed in the last generation. If this is so, it has tremendous implications for society, and it also accounts for a good deal of the heart-searching confusion about the responsibilities of scientists. If scientists themselves, through this change in the historic positions of science and technology, are becoming increasingly involved in the immediate application of science, this means that the concern of the medical practitioner, for example, with the social implications of his work, must apply increasingly to the work of the scientist.

Todd: In fact the time-scale is longer. We are living in a second industrial revolution that started about 1850. Until then technology had little to do with science, but in the organic chemical industry which started in the second half of the 19th century the influence of science was present from the beginning. The whole development of the dyestuffs industry, from about 1860–1870 onwards, came through the scientists.

Freeman: What was the exception in the 19th century is now becoming the rule. Increasingly manufacturing industry is following the pattern of the chemical industry.

Bondi: Dr Weinberg mentioned small probabilities of disasters, but what does that mean? When the disasters are small enough and the probability high enough, we go to an insurance company. What we do for uninsurable risks is an interesting philosophical question, which it is really very difficult to pursue.

Secondly, where is science autonomous in the sense that it doesn't have to allow the public in, and where is this not so? My own answer is that when we go to the public for funds, as we always do, we go under two quite different hats. When we go for what is called small science we tell the public: 'It is good for your soul and for your culture'. We are like the Buddhist monk with his begging bowl. That is the autonomous part of science. But when we want to put a telescope into space or to accelerate particles to umpteen GeV, that costs a lot more, and it is not good enough for us to go to the public on general cultural grounds. Then we have to sell it, and the only way one can sell is to let the public in. Where the boundaries of big science and small science run is of course debatable, but this I think is the essential point.

Weinberg: Another class of questions which doesn't quite have that implication is, should the public be involved in the decision to go ahead or not go ahead with a scientific study of racial determinants of intelligence?

Long: That is also not trans-science, by your definition.

Weinberg: I was quoting the National Academy report that said it was trans-scientific, but I think they were copping out. It is a very important issue, and one that I think we shall increasingly be concerned with.

Brock: The amount of money involved is not the only question affecting autonomy. In medicine there are certain problems of ethics. It has long been the accepted practice and philosophy in the medical profession that it is legitimate to withhold life-prolonging treatment from people whose life is, in our subjective opinion, no longer bearable. I have never had any hesitation in this practice. In fact, the public are clamouring for us to go even further. They charge us with prolonging life unnecessarily. However, we have always made a very sharp distinction in medical ethics, and I think it is a sharp legal distinction also, that there is a world of difference between withholding action which would *prolong* life, and taking action to *terminate* life. We have now got ourselves into a very illogical position indeed, in which it is ethically and legally correct to terminate life before birth but incorrect to do this after birth. We can't go back, so some day we must go forward; in other words, euthanasia must come. I have never preached this doctrine, because I believe the public is not ready for it, but we can't go back, and we are in an utterly illogical position.

A similar position arises over heart transplantation. We have immense ethical problems now because Dr Barnard and others are waiting for a heart donation to save another man's life. I may have a possible donor patient in a brain-damaged state and may profoundly believe that he will never recover, but he is being kept alive by artificial respiration; if that donor heart is to go into a recipient patient, somebody has to turn off the respirator switch. However, this is a problem for the medical practitioner whereas the problem this symposium is trying to tackle is really why the public doesn't trust science. We physicians must also try to find out what action we can take to make ourselves, as scientists, appear trustworthy in the minds of the public.

June Goodfield-Toulmin: When it comes to the crunch, the one point at which the scientific profession puts its collective foot down firmly, not compromising its autonomy, will probably always turn out to be on this point of the methodological ethic. It will be a scientist who alone can say 'This is good science', or 'This is bad science', or 'This is a proven or unproven fact'. But as the relationship of science with society evolves I don't think it really matters if, that central core apart, public concern gets closer, and more identified with scientific enterprise. On the contrary: I think it would be a good thing.

Toda: I have the impression from our discussions that the natural scientists have a prejudice against the social and psychological sciences. I am certainly aware that the discovery of the laws of human behaviour is a terribly difficult task, but we are making discoveries, and in some limited situations we can even predict human behaviour fairly precisely. The psychological and the social sciences are developing, and I do not want to put the label of trans-science on these sciences!

The other point I want to make is about this hypothetical case of a low probability disaster. Because of the very fact that the estimated probability is low no one has measured it exactly, so we don't know its real size and the probability may even be high under certain conditions. The label of trans-science for that kind of event may prevent the investigation of the causes of the troubles, and that may have a rather dangerous effect.

Weinberg: I don't think it would suppress investigation of the causes of the trouble, but when one speaks of events of such low probability it isn't as simple as saying that if there are a hundred reactors, then once in a million years there will be an accident. Such a statement doesn't have much operational significance.

I didn't mean to include all of social science in what I shall continue to call trans-science. I am enormously impressed with much of what social science has achieved. I would repeat that, because the individuals with whom the social sciences deal have a much higher order of variability than the individuals one deals with in the physical sciences, the proficiency of social science in policy-making is less.

One always has to have much humility about these things. I believe you think that we can use history as a way of testing a science of civilization, Dr Toda, and I must say that you are a very brave social scientist. When I ask my friends in the political sciences why they don't go back and see whether their theories about political science could predict the French Revolution, they always have reasons why they don't want to do that, and I am therefore suspicious.

Bondi: The question of deciding between scientific or technological evidence, when the experts are of different opinions, is probably Alvin Weinberg's daily task, and it is in some ways my daily task. Richard Feynman once said to me that one holds a post of responsibility if one has to make decisions on matters one doesn't understand! But should this responsibility always be the responsibility of the ignorant? I don't think it is quite as dramatic as Alvin Weinberg put it.

Bloch: If it were, the world would be even worse off.

Weinberg: As so often happens, the drama is enacted in the United States more quickly than in other places. The involvement of the American public in the very difficult and serious environmental issues has become quite dramatic.

June Goodfield-Toulmin: What has been the practical effect of the adversary procedure in the United States with regard to nuclear reactors? Have the engineers ever been told to go away and make a better reactor?

Weinberg: The Columbia reactor, which is a small reactor, was denied a licence. There have been several other reactors where the adversary procedure wasn't quite used, but in anticipation of it changes were made.

Long: Those of us who are a little more sceptical of the beneficence of atomic energy than Alvin Weinberg welcome both the existence of adversary procedures and the participation of others than scientists and engineers in the decision-making.

Todd: One reason why the public doesn't always trust the scientists is that it doesn't hear one voice coming from them, but a lot of different and sometimes contradictory voices.

Bondi: Personally I would trust science a lot less if it only issued concerted statements like a big corporation.

Toulmin: Perhaps in this meeting we ought to have been asking not just why does the public distrust us, but also why do we distrust ourselves? If we trusted ourselves more, if we were more confident about our own role—and the honesty of our own role—in the present situation we should be less sheepish about making the claims which Dr Shils, speaking from outside science, has been the only one to make on our behalf. We do have guilty consciences about the part science has played in the last forty years, and it is these guilty consciences which help to prevent us from saying what we should always be ready to say first, and which Dr Shils has had to say for us.

During this period, we have been quite happy to milk the state for our own intellectual self-gratification, and this may have corrupted us more than we realize. I am deliberately putting the point harshly, because even Dr Bondi's dividing-line between where we ought to have a sense of public responsibility and where we need not is, as he stated it here (p. 117) slightly small-minded. Surely there are some lines of research that scientists should have scruples about undertaking, even if they do not ask for public funds to support them. And surely it should be made clear to the public, too, that scientists do have scruples about engaging in certain lines of research, even if they are not asking for public financial support for them. The public would distrust us less, and we would have less cause to distrust ourselves, if there were better—or even compulsory—opportunities for us to consider behaving as an authentic profession, as lawyers and doctors do. Then we should *have* to consider how far the interests of all our fellow-men, not just those in our own town or region or nation-state, are being properly borne in mind and protected in our choice of the work we do, and the way in which we do it.

Weinberg: No sensitive or even partly sensitive technologist today escapes this feeling of guilt, nor should we escape it. One of my colleagues asked me: 'What right does this generation have to make tons and tons of plutonium, probably the most poisonous material the world has ever known, without at the same time having a totally reliable and foolproof way of sequestering it forever, away from the biosphere?' This is one of those cosmic questions that bother one to death. The problem is that at the time we first unleashed nuclear energy this was the last kind of question that occurred to us. Could I thirty years ago possibly have thought that more than a quarter of a century later one of my colleagues would ask, what in hell have we wrought here? That is really the essence of the problem: we are only human beings and our crystal balls are dreadfully cloudy. Much as we should like to improve the mechanisms of technological assessment, they will probably never be much better than they are now, no matter how many boards and investigative groups we have.

I would propose that all of us, and certainly the technologists, should from now on make sure that we have a consensus of the whole public, and that the public know what we are doing. Then the entire society can share the guilt. We are always balancing a benefit versus a risk and the burden on the technologists is too great; they shouldn't be the ones to make the ultimate decision.

Toulmin: But we have to be prepared to let the public say 'No'.

Roche: It is very interesting to hear that people feel guilty in spite of the wonderful things that have been brought about by science. We in the developing countries are still backwards in that sense, since we feel no guilt! I am very much afraid, of course, that this sort of attitude will infect us and put a brake on the development of our science, which would be a bad thing for us.

Weinberg: Our justification for going ahead with nuclear energy is that we see no way of resolving the Malthusian dilemma except by creating an infinite source of energy.

June Goodfield-Toulmin: I think that Dr Weinberg has made an unanswerable case for involving the public in every possible way. This might help us with the problem of happiness, as defined in the spiritual sense. Somehow a gap has been left in the public mind by the replacement of dogmatic theology by science. Dogmatic theology did something for you. It told you where happiness was to be found—in the next world—and it had permanent answers to permanent questions. Our problem in this situation is to try to educate others, and ourselves, to grow to intellectual maturity, right up to the point of realizing that there are no permanent answers to any questions, even if they are recurring ones; and to derive a source of strength *from that very fact*. It is extraordinarily difficult to reach this point even for one's self. Science may have a very important role to play, because its history and the history of our civilization teach us that one can never look for immutable answers to problems which may be eternal. Each time we have to bring all our resources—both intellectual and humane—to bear afresh on the new situation as we find it, saying 'In certain respects this is an old situation, in certain respects it is totally new', and we must find our own answers within the context of our own time.

Mathur: One reason why science has begun to be distrusted in advanced countries is the wrong sense of priorities the younger generation thinks scientists have in their choice of projects. If Dr Weinberg were to include in his public response the people belonging to the poorer segments of the world community, some of the priorities in advanced countries would be readjusted. What is required from science is happiness and well-being, but whose well-being and whose happiness comes first is something for which priorities should be reallocated on the basis of the values of an integrated human society. Some of the feelings of guilt in advanced countries would then disappear, because it is just the guilt which any affluent society has about itself when it is encased in a crystal dome surrounded by a sea of poverty.

Jean Medawar: I hate to think of scientists working so hard yet feeling guilty. I am sure that is just part of the human condition. It is embodied in the legend of Pandora's box and even Eve's apple: knowledge brings terrific responsibilities. It is not science the public are frightened of, but too much knowledge too fast. There hasn't been time to make it clear how much science has done to push back the shadows. We have all been much too busy to realize and to remember that this is one of the glories of science. Probably the time has come for scientists to stress this, as well as to provide the new knowledge which people find so hard to digest when they are given too much too often.

Bibliography

1. ADLER, H. I., Private communication.
2. BROOKS, H. (1968) *Government of Science.* Cambridge, Mass.: M.I.T. Press.
3. ELSASSER, W. M. (1966) *Atom and Organism.* Princeton, N.J.: Princeton University Press.
4. GREEN, H. P. (1970) In *Nuclear Power and the Public,* p. 132, ed. H. Foreman. Minneapolis: University of Minnesota Press.
5. LASKI, H., Quoted by H. P. GREEN, Ref. 4, p. 136.
6. POLANYI, M. (1962) The Republic of Science—its political and economic theory. *Minerva, 1,* No. 1, 54–73.
7. VELIKOVSKY, I. (1950) *Worlds in Collision.* New York: Doubleday.

Science and the military

F. A. LONG

This paper is based on the following propositions about the relationship between science, technology and the military:

(1) Science has become a principal innovative force in the development of new technology; this recent and central role of science will almost surely continue.

(2) The innovative role of science in military technology became particularly evident during the Second World War and its effects have continued at an accelerated pace since then.

(3) There is increasing concern among the developed nations of the world about the social impacts of technology, arising especially from the rapid rate of social change brought about by science-based technology.

(4) These trends are particularly troublesome in the case of military technology, partly because of the special characteristics of military activities and the inadequacy of mechanisms for controlling them, and partly because of the comparatively low social benefits which come from modern military technology, added to the diversionary effect of allocating large sums of money for military research and development.

(5) Basic scientific research has been increasingly supported throughout the world by programmes of military and space research and development (R & D); this raises the twin dangers of a 'captive science' beholden to the military and of the development of an unduly influential scientific-technological elite.

These propositions, if accepted, strongly suggest the need for far better analyses of the application of science and technology to military affairs and also suggest that scientists must give particular and personal attention to this problem area. But before considering implications, it will be useful to reflect further on the propositions themselves.

Science as a generator of technology

Both science and technology have been with mankind for a very long time, science since the time of the Greeks and technology for many millennia more. Not until the last few hundred years, however, has science played a significant role in the development of technology. Indeed, it can be argued that in the early days of science the direction of influence was rather from technology towards science. As scientific information accumulated and as the study of science was systematized and extended, a gradual shift began to occur, ultimately leading to the great utilization of science for the development of technology which we now experience. A distinguished science historian put it this way:[4]

'... it is difficult to think of any scientific discovery made before the nineteenth century which radically altered man's diet, his health, his means of production, his transportation and communication, or even his methods of warfare. Today we are aware that the applications of new discoveries about the nature of the universe will be tomorrow the source of a new fabric, a new military weapon for offence or defence, a new means of controlling or preventing disease, or of founding an industry. Every major corporation in the United States now supports great research establishments; and the constant stream of new products and devices emphasizes the fecundating power of abstract science and its applications in altering the world. Yet this aspect of science is a characteristic of the last one hundred years only. Not until the middle of the nineteenth century did the applications of science begin to make themselves felt. Indeed, the organized research laboratory as a part of industry is hardly half a century old. Much of our bewilderment at the world in which we live may arise from the novelty of the revolutionary century at whose end we stand, and which itself was altered at its midpoint, about fifty years ago.'*

A particularly lucid analysis of the changing relations between science and technology was recently given by H. W. Bode.[2] Bode argues that the deliberate application of science to technology on a broad scale is an even more recent phenomenon than implied above, becoming important only during the Second World War. He lays particular stress on the very rapid development of science-based industries, as for example the chemical in-

---

* A specific example may be useful here. The central research laboratory of one of the largest oil companies of the world celebrated its fiftieth birthday only in 1969. This laboratory has expanded so far in this half century that it now employs roughly 2000 scientists and engineers and operates on a budget of several scores of million dollars a year.

dustry, the electronics industry and the computer industry. As Bode notes:
'The science-based industries naturally reflect, to some extent, the characteristics we have previously ascribed to modern science itself. For example, as modern science is becoming interdisciplinary, we may expect its applications to be even more interdisciplinary. Thus in many technological situations we may need substantial teams of scientists and engineers to encompass the required skills. As experimental procedures in a single science are increasingly likely to depend upon a mixture of tools and methods borrowed from other sciences, we can expect a corresponding hybridization of tools and methods in technology. The fact that science frequently takes long steps forward nowadays has its counterpart in the fact that technological projects are frequently quite ambitious'.

In sum, although the deliberate application of science to technology is relatively new, it is already very firmly established, and will inescapably deepen and expand. In doing so, it will modify both the ways in which technology is developed and the characteristics of the technologies themselves.

Science and the military

Understandably, most analyses of the increasing role of science in the military start with the development of the atom bomb in 1945. This was a remarkable event in the history of military technology, in that a major new scientific discovery, nuclear fission, was developed into a revolutionary military weapon during a single war. It can be additionally argued that the decade from 1945 to 1955 saw the advent of not one but three genuine revolutions in military technology: the atom bomb and its follow-on, the fusion bomb; the precision-guided intercontinental ballistic missile; and breakthrough developments in military communications and control. Science contributed fundamentally to the first of these and importantly to the other two, principally through the discovery of new solid-state electronic devices of which the transistor was the first. Major expenditure on science-based military technology has continued since these watershed days and the central role of new scientific information for the development of military technology is now very generally accepted. As a typical illustration, the chilling forecast of future directions of warfare entitled *Unless Peace Comes*[3] carries the subtitle *A Scientific Forecast of New Weapons,* and fully half the articles in the book relate to applications of recent science to military weapons or military strategies and tactics. We may safely conclude that scientific warfare is with us for the indefinite future. (See also Reference 6.)

Societal concern with science and technology

The developed nations of the world have exhibited a recent and rapid increase in concern with the impact of virtually all aspects of technology. These relate to the quality of life in general and the degradation of the environment in particular, the loss of privacy, and the fear of the impact of military technology. As a colleague of mine put it:[7]

'Too many of these [scientific] processes have effects which, though beneficial in many respects, often strike the average man as a threat to his individual autonomy. Too often science seems to be thrusting society as a whole in directions which it does not fully understand and which it certainly has not chosen'.

A similar but more extended analysis of the problem was given by Eugene Skolnikoff in a study of science, technology and foreign policy:[12]

'... the accretion of scientific knowledge continues to put ever more power under man's control, power with the potential of actual destruction of the human species or of alteration of the species and the environment in ways incommensurate with present values. The motivation can also be stated in more modest terms: scientific advances often lead to developments that increase the instability of power. Or, more precisely: the unpredictability of scientific advance implies that it is always a potentially destabilizing factor in international relations. The possibility of sudden developments that would make a new weapons system feasible, such as an effective missile defense or a discovery that reduces the cost and complexity of powerful weapons, thereby making them available to smaller countries, are cases in point.

'It is a platitude to observe that it is not science itself that is destabilizing and it is not science that is the direct agent for evil. It is, instead, man's technological application of scientific knowledge that should be the focus of attention. But the layman has the right to ask not only whether technology can be controlled but also whether the underlying science that made the technology possible can be controlled'.

Widespread as these concerns are for all kinds of technology and for the role of science in generating technology, there are ample reasons why concern should be particularly sharp for military technology. First, although military technology has an ancient and honourable history of application to civilian problems, in this recent period of science-based military technology the civilian utility of these efforts has become so much smaller that expenditure on military technology mainly diverts funds and technical manpower from civilian efforts. This change relates closely to the greatly increased sophistication and specialized character of military technology which the application of science has itself brought about. There remains substantial controversy over the precise amount of 'civilian spin-off' from military and space research and development. Certainly there is some spin-off, as witness the civilian jet aircraft which followed from the military aircraft developments of the 1940s and 1950s. But specialization has limited such spin-off, and a generous estimate is that perhaps 20 per cent of military and space R & D has significant civilian utility.

Another measure of the extent to which military technology competes with civilian-oriented efforts is the amount of trained manpower needed. One estimate is that about 40 per cent of R & D effort in the world has, in recent years, been for the military. This very approximate estimate can be roughly justified as follows. Military and space R & D in the United States is now about 43 per cent of the nation's total, although for the decade from 1957 to 1967 it was more than 50 per cent.[8] For the U.S.S.R.,[13] most estimates are well above 50 per cent, ranging up to one estimate of 80 per cent made by the Pentagon. If one lumps the U.S.A. and the U.S.S.R. together and estimates that half their total R & D work is for military and space purposes, an estimate of 40 per cent of the total for the entire world seems reasonable.

A crucial reason for being concerned about the role of science in the military is the open-ended character of the demands of the military for new science-based technology. The concept 'national security' turns out in normal practice to be given an almost entirely military interpretation. And the system of checks and balances normally used to establish social priorities in government expenditure turns out to work particularly poorly for military spending. A recent analysis by a United States Congressman, doubtless speaking from personal experience, put the difficulty in the following words:[1]

'The pressures from within the Pentagon for increased expenditures are enormous. They stem in part from traditional and still acute competition among the military services. In part, they are the natural result of increasing technologies; each new generation of weapons means greater complexity and sophistication, and the expense seems to rise by geometric rather than arithmetic progression ... The existence of a new technology seems to compel a new weapons system based on that technology; some of my ablest colleagues in the Congress believe that this process is inevitable with respect to MIRV [multiple independently targeted warheads], for example, and cannot be arrested by arms-limitation agreements or in any other way.

'To the experts in the Pentagon, the fear of what the other side may be doing is ever present. It is natural for the military man to try to achieve absolute security against any contingency that may arise, even though intellectually he may recognize that absolute security is unattainable, he is trained and paid to think this way. Thus, the military services will always and inevitably want more than they have. Their appetites are insatiable. And the industrial concerns that are ready and eager to undertake the required contracts will encourage them . . .

'The real trouble comes when those civilians in government who are supposed to see to it that the military's appetite is restrained are not capable of performing that function because they have come to share the military point of view'.

Further difficulties arise when one attempts to obtain an adequate *technology assessment* of military problems in circles which do not directly support the military. A serious difficulty for the public is the sophisticated and generally unfamiliar character of military technology. It is difficult enough to ask an intelligent layman for a thoughtful judgement on the environmental hazards of the supersonic transport; it is almost an order of magnitude more difficult to get an informed lay judgement on the technical utility or cost-effectiveness of a complex military system such as an anti-ballistic missile system.

Another difficulty results from the fact that most military technology is developed in secret. Even in comparatively 'open' societies like the United States and Great Britain, this greatly increases the problem of adequate civilian assessment. Consider, for example, the military technology of most recent political concern—multiple independently targeted warheads. The first public reference indicating the interest of the United States in this system was made by Defense Secretary McNamara in a wide-ranging article in *Life* magazine in late 1967.[11] This date, however, was so far along the road of the MIRV developmental effort that a decision to deploy was only months away. Clearly the time and information required for an adequate civilian assessment of MIRV had been precluded by the blanket of secrecy which covered its development.

What is the position of the scientist in all this? Scientists of many countries have become increasingly involved in disarmament studies, in analyses of national and international security, and in studies of the role of science in the development of military technology. The number of scientists whose research is supported by the military and space establishments has also grown greatly since the start of the Second World War in almost all the nations of the world. It is sobering to recall the prescient words of President Eisenhower in his 1961 Farewell Address.[5] After giving his famous warning against undue influence from the military-industrial complex, Eisenhower went on to say:

'Akin to and largely responsible for the sweeping changes in our industrial-military posture has been the technological revolution during recent decades. In this revolution research has become central; it also becomes more formalized, complex, and costly. A steadily increasing share is conducted for, by, or at the direction of the Federal Government.

'Today the solitary inventor, tinkering in his shop, has been overshadowed by task forces of scientists in laboratories and testing fields. In the same fashion the free university, historically the fountainhead of free ideas and scientific discovery, has experienced a revolution in the conduct of research. Partly because of the huge costs involved, a Government contract becomes virtually a substitute for intellectual curiosity. For every old blackboard there are now hundreds of new electronic computers.

'The prospect of domination of the Nation's scholars by Federal employment, project allocations, and the power of money is ever present and is gravely to be regarded.

'Yet, in holding scientific research and discovery in respect, as we should, we must also be alert to the equal and opposite danger that public policy could itself become the captive of a scientific and technological elite'.

Faced with this kind of concern, scientists have often argued that science itself is neutral and that the only problem is to control the technology for which science merely opens the door. But in view of massive governmental support for science, this is disingenuous to say the least. If we are to be concerned with military technology and with the role of science in generating it, then we cannot fail to be concerned with the character of the support for science itself and with the uses to which science is being put.

Responses

Supposing we accept as fact that science has become a major driving force for all technology and notably so for military technology, and further that adequate assessment and control of military technology is particularly difficult. Suppose we note further the world-wide tendency to give the phrases 'national' and 'international security' a military or quasi-military interpretation. What responses are indicated?

As a preliminary point, the very magnitude and gravity of the military problem puts it in a class by itself. This effort leads to the expenditure of $ 200 billion [$ 200 000 million] per year world-wide, an amount which largely diverts badly needed funds away from alleviation of the major social problems which face the world. Further, military R & D puts particularly large demands on the skilled manpower of the world, including notably the scientists and engineers. Finally, all of this occurs even though the appalling destructiveness of nuclear weapons makes it evident that major wars can no longer be 'won'.

If we are to respond effectively enough to counter the very considerable momentum of the military and of science-based military technology, we must operate simultaneously at several levels:

(1) There must be much more analysis, understanding and response from the citizens of the world.

(2) Governmental bodies, including national governments and the United Nations, must assume responsibility for more intensive analyses of national and international security and for the development of mechanisms which disseminate widely the results of these studies.

(3) The scholars of the world, and most notably the scientists and engineers, must assume a much more active role in these analyses, giving particular attention to the implications of their own studies in contributing to the military momentum.

(4) International, non-governmental meetings for study and exchange of views can help to overcome the sometimes xenophobic analyses of national security which make international agreements so difficult to obtain.

If the general public is to play a positive role in these analyses and in the decision-making processes, a critical need is for more dissemination of information about the military, about national and international security, and about the particular problems of military technology. Difficulties arising from secrecy and from the specialized character of military systems require an effort which goes far beyond the normal activities of news dissemination. A landmark in the development of major efforts to provide information on military problems was the campaign within the United States which arose in response to the proposed deployment of an antiballistic missile system. A consequence of the steady flow of articles, letters, speeches and books was that for the first time in the United States a broad segment of the general public was fairly well informed of the problems which would accompany the deployment of this particular military system. The continuing question then is, how can one develop procedures which will ensure that similar efforts to provide the public with information will accompany further developments in military technology? The United Nations has an important role here; its activities in the analysis and communication of military problems should be greatly expanded. So also should the work of national and international peace study societies and foreign policy analysis groups. It is, for example, a real tragedy for the United States that peace studies are fragmented between so many small, often barely viable, groups.

These attempts to provide the public with information must be supplemented by greatly expanded scholarly efforts to understand the problems of national and international security. These studies must give much greater stress than the military and their supporters are willing to give to the fundamentally new dimensions of warfare and security brought about by the advent of nuclear weapons and intercontinental ballistic missiles. One key question is, for how long should we be content to have nuclear deterrents as a principal element of national security when the implications are that in response to a military attack from an enemy country we shall destroy some tens of millions of innocent civilians living in our opponent's cities? What kind of world are we building if this sort of response is to be considered rational?

A principal centre and focus for study and communication should be within governments. Here in particular is the place where the concept 'national security' must be examined in a much broader context than that of the military. The dominance of defence ministries or committees such as the Congressional Armed Services Committee in decision-making on security must be shattered. A small but heartening sign in the United States is the development of a vigorous informal Congressional group called the Committee for Peace through Law. How much better it would be if such committees were formally established and had to place their recommendations alongside those which come from Armed Services Committees and Committees on Foreign Affairs.

A complicating problem is the suspicion, often bordering on xenophobia, which too frequently exists between nations and which supports and encourages the one-sided 'worst case' analyses which too often fuel the military arms races. The United Nations should play a role in minimizing these tendencies but too frequently the United Nations itself is paralysed by the competing national pressures.

Non-governmental international meetings offer an important avenue for increased international understanding. For example, the Pugwash meetings[10] which began in 1957 made it possible for scholars from East and West to exchange views on problems of peace and war at a time when almost no other openings existed. Clearly, ways must be found to increase these informal efforts towards international understanding.

In all of this, science and scientists have major roles which they *must* assume. In the face of the appallingly expensive military efforts and with clear evidence that science is a major innovating force for military technology, it simply will not do for science and scientists to plead neutrality. Science is being diverted into the development of technologies which are broadly diversionary and appallingly destructive.

What specifically can scientists do? First they must develop a greater sense of social responsibility for all aspects of the application of science to technology. This means that individual scientists must analyse the implications of their own work. It implies that there must be educational programmes to give scientists and engineers a firmer understanding of the potential impact of science and technology, as well as explicit practice in participating in the kinds of interdisciplinary technology assessments which are increasingly needed. The great scientific professional societies, the Royal Society in England and the National Academy of Sciences in the United States, for example, have an important role here in providing both a home for such analyses and a forum for their discussion. Surely there is a place in these societies for more explicit programmes of discussion of these problems, more sponsorship of study groups, and more provision of funds for such studies?

Scientists also have a major role to play in fostering international discussions of these grave problems. Given the international character of science it is not surprising that the international Pugwash movement[10] was started by scientists, brought together from many nations by the dreadful prospects of nuclear war. Pugwash has broadened greatly from those early days, but the role of scientists remains central in all its programmes of study and communication. But, effective as it is, Pugwash is only a single organization of mostly part-time participants. The world could use many more such efforts.

Above all, for all of these efforts, we need more scientific activists, more people sufficiently persuaded that these problems are so important that they personally must give much of their time to analysing them. It is almost impossible to over-estimate the importance to these efforts of a Hans Bethe, a Rudolph Peierls, an Igor Tamm, a Wolfgang Panofsky. What we clearly need is a nucleation technique which permits key people like these to catalyse the development of some scores of additional similar scientific activists. I know of no better way to underscore the problem and the need than to quote from one of these scientific activists, W. K. H. Panofsky:[9]

'Our knowledge of science will indeed increase continuously: the facts of nature are there to be explored, and they will not, and should not, remain hidden. But the process of going from science to military technology involves a protracted series of planned steps, including development, test, production and deployment. This chain extends over many years, or even decades, and it is up to man to decide through his political processes to undertake such steps or not to . . .

'I see no valid excuse why we should acquiesce in the development of weapons of ever-increasing lethality. If we subscribe to the belief that technology has a life of its own and that its progress in any direction, however antisocial, cannot be impeded, then it is indeed true that man has lost control over his own destiny'.

Discussion

Bondi: One point we should pay more attention to is the nature of foreign policy. None of our foreign ministries know how to make foreign policy except *against* somebody. Even at quiet times, say the early 1920s, foreign policy was a shapeless mess until there was some antagonism somewhere. Efforts in peace research are not negligible now, but the effort to define foreign policy except in antagonism has not been very great.

The secretiveness of the military is perhaps not unlike that of the medical profession. The military deal with matters of life and death, just like the medical profession, and they are afraid that if the uninitiated are too much involved, emotions will rise too high. It is all a very understandable defence mechanism. Some progress has been made in the last thirty years in making medicine a little less secretive. A little progress has been made with the military. A campaign is still needed to show the military their bread is buttered on the side of greater openness and more willingness to admit things they don't know.

Finally, we are not always aware how venerable a problem this is that we are discussing. Cook's great expedition to Tahiti in the 1760s had all the elements of the present complex: science, industry, the military and so on. The aim of observing the transit of Venus was scientific. The only hope of getting this done was to involve the Admiralty. The Admiralty responded magnificently by putting one of their best navigators, one of their best ships and a considerable number of men at the disposal of the enterprise. They gave Cook both his open instructions, that he was to establish a base for the astronomers, and his secret instructions, that he was to explore and take possession of such parts of the South Pacific as he could. As you know, he discovered the east coast of Australia and much else besides. This was big science, very much in the way we have it today: a few scientists needing to be supported by an army of other people regardless of cost. To get these large numbers of other people some military involvement seems to be unavoidable.

Long: What you are saying is that civilian spin-off existed even in those days. The percentage of spin-off was probably about the same as it is now. On the other hand, in the interplay between science and technology, the flow of creative ideas one hundred or two hundred years ago might have gone from technology towards science, in contrast to the present situation.

Johnson: Your paper is a cry from the heart, Dr Long, but where does it take us? The activists in science have been reacting against the disruption of civilization by the Second World War. If activists are worrying about the military use of science what should they do? What sort of world are they aiming for? You are asking scientists to exercise a lot of power on behalf of something you haven't specified, namely some concept of what the world should be like. I think the world ought to have one government and a war with Mars so that we could waste a lot of resources on that and all be happy and support a scientific establishment—and so far as we know there is nobody on Mars to fire back. The essential problem is that the world is divided into nation-states and into rather xenophobic cultures. I am not sure whether the scientists have a better view of what the world should be like than that. You say they should be more activist, but what are they going to be activist about and how are we going to know that their activism won't lead to betrayal or destruction of society?

Long: Fundamentally I don't understand you, Professor Johnson. Your position seems to be that if you cannot see a clear major goal, fully delineated, then there is no real purpose in doing anything at all. I was trying to argue that it was much more likely that progress is going to be made in many small steps, by many people. Equally I was trying to argue that scientists would probably only succeed in being useful if their contributions were made in a highly interactive way, in conjunction with people of many different talents. I was not trying to say what kind of major goal science alone should have.

Johnson: That is exactly what I object to. You talk in this emotive language of progress and activism without any definition of how you judge these things. Scientists may be very active and very progressive and yet submerge the world in disaster. The problem as I see it is that we have a world of nations and we have a lot of atavistic attitudes about those things. The question is, can one work within the world of the nation-state towards a world government, and do we know how to do it? It is no good saying we want to be progressive, activist and all those things unless we know how to do it. Essentially the scientist has been trying to modify the world of the nation-states and build bridges between them rather than tackling the major problem, which is that as long as there is a world of nation-states there is the possibility of war, and there will come a time when scientists, no matter what their own attitudes are, will have to cooperate in murdering other people. I don't see how you can face that on the basis of the kind of training scientists get, without facing the major problem, which is the world of nation-states itself.

Long: Edward Teller used to say, in effect, that the centre of all our military and political problems was secrecy. He argued that everything we do, starting at the military level, must be totally open and free of secrecy. However he would then add that until we got to this open state we must figuratively arm to the teeth and spend every dollar that the military ask for. The trouble with such an argument, and to some degree with your current ones, is that both are flawed by the fallacy of the excluded middle. In your case you seem to be saying that, until we eliminate the nation-state, we can do nothing.

Johnson: I am not sure that eliminating all secrecy will eliminate war.

Weinberg: One's attitude towards the involvement of the scientist with the military depends on one's perception of the world situation. Today the world is a polarized world, and the values by which others live are not the same as ours. In the world of tomorrow when the counter-culture, the young people and the hippies take over, these important differences in values may be submerged. But we can't prove that. The issue really is, who are the better guarantors of peace—people like Hans Bethe, Wolfgang Panofsky and the Pugwash group, or people like Edward Teller? That is extremely important with respect to the whole question of how society views science.

Last week I was a defence witness at an 'inquest on technology', complete with defence witnesses, prosecution witnesses, and defending and prosecuting lawyers. The question that came up over and over again was: 'What were you doing during the Manhattan Project, and how in the world could you justify your involvement with the manufacture of plutonium, and so on?' The answer I gave, an honest but not very clever answer, was that we were scared as hell of the Nazis. Then we were asked: 'How about the hydrogen bomb?' There the argument we use, and I believe many political theorists now concede this point, is that the existence of the hydrogen bomb has deterred truly large-scale war, though not Vietnam, Biafra, and so on. Therefore one can argue plausibly that it is indeed Edward Teller who is responsible for the kind of peace we have, more than my good friends who oppose nuclear weapons.

Scientists do have responsibilities as scientists to try to figure out means, technological means if you like, of imposing additional stability on this world of nation-states with their different values. To put a specific, concrete question: how can we arrive at a stable solution to the game of mutual deterrence when three, not two, states are involved? So far no one has shown how a three-party, offensive confrontation can be stabilized. I submit that the social responsibility of the military technologist in this case is to see whether there are some configurations, some kind of technology, some kind of strategy which would restore a kind of stability in a world twenty to thirty years from now when more than two major nuclear powers confront each other. Perhaps my concern can be summarized in the following question: do you think that Edward Teller is a good influence or a bad influence, Dr Long?

Long: I don't think I have to answer that. This is not a problem for scientists, as scientists, to make decisions about. It is entirely a political question. Nor was I arguing that people like Bethe, Panofsky or myself have any special competence in the decision-making. I simply say that science is making a major impact on military technology and will continue to do so. My further point is that, on the whole, in the decision-making about military systems the military have had more of a free ride than I like. The reasons have to do with the sophisticated character of weaponry, with secrecy, and with certain xenophobic attitudes which nation-states take. It is a major political problem to keep the pressure on to minimize the free-ride character of this decision-making. The scientists cannot do it alone. More emphasis on broad considerations of foreign policy would probably lead to a more reasonable assessment of what is true national security. Furthermore, I am not prepared to accept the position that as long as we have nation-states, all is effectively lost. Man is a much more rational animal than that, and we are going to be working in the context of nation-states for a long time.

Shils: Dr Long has made it clear that we are in a tragic situation. But the present situation also has elements of buffoonery and frivolity which attempt to deny some of the plain facts of life. One of these facts is that as long as we are alive, we live in societies. Our membership of them is at least a two-way relationship, not a one-way relationship. Many scientists, including some of the most vociferous, act as if it is a one-way relationship, as children do. Children, especially children of affluent families, feel entitled to have whatever they want from their parents but they don't think they owe anything to their parents and also they don't anticipate growing up. One reason why children misbehave so much is that they resist growing up. Some scientists nowadays are behaving like children and resisting growing up: they want to continue to get more and more so that they can go on doing whatever they wish to do. But scientists are citizens; they live in a society even while they pursue pure science for its own sake. Society supplies the financial support for that pursuit of pure science.

In my opinion, pure science is one of the highest forms of human activity, perhaps the highest available once one rejects traditional religion. Nonetheless scientists can't expect to have society give them, not just the inexpensive treats children desire or the bowl of rice Hindi *sadhus* beg for, but grants of millions of dollars simply because they are more spiritual and claim to be in contact with the laws of the universe. Other people have other interests in life and they think that scientists can help them to realize some of these interests. That is why they are willing to have so much of their money spent on scientists and the equipment and staff they need. Scientists do not have to take this employment; they can work as drivers of milk wagons, as shop assistants or as bus drivers. But scientists want to do science. Some of them are fortunate enough to be in universities, so they can do nearly anything they want, unless they want large amounts of money, when they have to persuade somebody else to give it to them. They have to meet the conditions of their employment whether they are in a socialist society or a capitalist society. A political philosopher can speculate freely on the obligations of man to obey or disobey the law but if he becomes a civil servant he is expected to do his job, whatever it involves. If he does not want to do the job, he shouldn't take it. But then he ought not to expect the salary and the powers of a civil servant. The same applies to scientists.

Scientists ought to recognize that they are citizens in a variety of senses. They ought to participate in the making of policy because they are citizens in a society; on particular subjects they know more than many other people know and they therefore have a special responsibility. They owe it to society as well as to themselves, to participate. It isn't just a matter of having a voice but also of doing a job. Scientist-activists, like the American atomic scientists at the end of the Second World War and the Pugwash group, are admirable but this kind of activity does not exhaust the obligations of scientists. An unwritten social contract binds them, whether they like it or not, to their fellow citizens. If they want money, the fruits of other people's labour, they must give the fruits of their particular kind of labour in exchange.

I respect the person who commits suicide if he doesn't want to continue to live; I respect the person who leaves science and becomes a baker's apprentice or something else because he believes that what he has done hitherto is iniquitous. What I do not like is the attitude prominent among scientists in the contemporary anti-science movement that they have two kinds of rights as citizens: a voice in what is being done in the political sphere and the possibility of unilateral denunciation of the social contract, while the other side, society, remains bound by the contract. I find it offensive when scientists who are willing to take the public's money say at the same time that they are unwilling to deal with the elected and legally constituted authority which pays out that money.

Toulmin: The sort of activism that Frank Long is calling for is not the activism of the people for whom Ed Shils feels distaste.

There is one woefully unhistorical thing underlying the whole of what Harry Johnson said. It is just not the case that the nation-state, as we now know it, is the only important fact about the modern world; nor that it is the only actual possible focus of loyalty and service; nor that it has except quite recently been the main focus of men's loyalty; nor that this is likely—so far as one can learn anything from history—to remain so for always. A man like Sakharov can continue to do his job for the Union of Socialist Republics, at the same time as playing a part in the international network of scientists.

Weinberg: He has lost his job.

Toulmin: Medvedev certainly lost his, but nation-states do not have absolute sovereignty, even now. The degree of xenophobia within existing nation-states is neither absolute nor immutable. The degree of xenophobia between Yorkshire and Lancashire used to be greater than the present degree of xenophobia between Switzerland and Austria, or even between France and Germany. And because of the internationally oriented activities of a whole lot of people like Jean Monnet, over the last fifty years, it is now very much less likely that there will be another Franco-German war. All that Frank Long and others are calling for—and rightly—is that the modern internationalism of scientists should be allowed the same legitimacy and scope as the attitudes of people like Jean Monnet. I do not see that one can (like Konrad Lorenz in his book *On Aggression*[1]) produce the nation-state as evidence of a genetically inherited aggressiveness in man, or as an immutable fact about the historical situation which determines the limits of all possible action. This is just not the case. Scientists are perfectly entitled to create an international network on the basis of their professional community of interests, without being accused of treason. This can eventually become politically influential, and may do something to modify the degree of xenophobia which at the moment is one of the major sources of political risk. The nation-state, as Harry Johnson talks about it, means that we have to accept permanent xenophobia as a basic fact of human existence, which it is unpatriotic—even treasonable—to seek to modify.

Johnson: I haven't made my point at all clear. It is not Jean Monnet who is responsible for the fact that there won't be another Franco-German war but the fact that both the French and the Germans know that the Russians and the Americans are far more powerful. They can either have a local war which nobody will care about or else they will be stopped. It is not goodwill. A large part of the argument is to build a Europe big enough to take on the Russians or the Americans if necessary.

I did not say that the nation-state was always with us. I said that if you want peace, if you want to end the waste of resources in war, the way to do it is to tackle the basic problem, which is the existence of the nation-state or groups of nation-states. One can try to do it through the fact that science constitutes an international elite of people who have had to divorce themselves to some extent from their own societies in order to be good scientists. Most of the scientists we have been talking about are like myself, immigrants from one country to another. They have had to escape from one culture and therefore they do think internationally because that is the only way they can survive. But to try to enlist this group of people in the effort to stop nation-states by some sort of conspiracy, to ask them to be activists and to reveal everything, is to ask them to violate their contract with the society they are working for. Two different questions are involved here. One is whether in fact scientists could do anything important to preserve peace, if nations don't want peace. The other is whether they have a legitimate right as scientists to contract out of society in the sense that they accept the responsibility to build atom bombs and then try to decide for themselves (and for society) whether those bombs should be used or not. They get the resources for that contract and accept them, and the nature of a contract is that there is obligation on both sides. They can't take the money and then refuse to do the job, or having done the job try to control how the results are used.

Mathur: Dr Bondi seems to have defended secrecy in defence research by making a puzzling analogy between the military and medicine as regards secrecy. But though they both deal with life and death these professions have opposite objectives. The military may have a deterrent which saves life, but it is an unreliable deterrent, giving an equilibrium no more stable than that of a tight-rope walker. As Professor Johnson said, if national sovereignty continues war is bound to happen some time or another. The obvious thing for the nations to do in order to survive is to give up national sovereignty. To say that only politicians can decide upon it and take initiative in the matter is to forget that sooner or later politicians have to follow public opinion; and then we may ask, who builds public opinion? If social scientists and scientists (who from their studies can clearly see the effects of various trends) do not take a lead in building up public opinion on this matter, through the press and other means, then how do we expect the politicians to take the responsibility for us?

Bondi: I only said that the doctor and the general had a characteristic in common, although in many other ways they are quite different.

It is quite true that national sovereignty gives us a tremendous amount of inertia. We know that reaching agreements between countries is an enormous

job. On the other hand we know that it is possible, when the political con-
stellation is favourable, to get over these difficulties. That is where the scientific activists come in. The partial test ban treaty came into being no doubt
because it suited the two super-powers, no doubt because it was from the
civilian and the military point of view the right moment. But I think that for
that moment there must be a lot of preparation—preparation inspired and to
some extent carried out by the activists. If work like that had not started
until the favourable moment had arrived, then by the time the necessary work
had been completed, the favourable opportunity might well have passed. So
I think we owe a great deal in peace to the activists and students.

Weinberg: You seem to make a distinction between what the scientists can
offer to the military and to the nation-states, and what the policy-makers can
do with what the scientists offer, Professor Johnson. Are you saying that the
scientists offer means and the nation-states and the politicians establish the
ends?

Johnson: I believe it is the responsibility of any intelligent and educated
man to work for world peace and for a better world. That cannot be left to
politicians only, but it is neither effective nor easy for scientists to conspire
among themselves to use their own particular expertise to try to impose on
the rest of society rules which the rest of society doesn't want.

Weinberg: The mere development of certain technologies pre-empts the
objectives and pre-empts the ends. Scientists who have a better appreciation
of these technological possibilities certainly have a responsibility to tell the
world what the unstated, unrecognized social implications of these military
technologies might be.

Johnson: Your paper made it sound as if you wanted to do this by setting
rules for the relation between science and society, Dr Long.

Long: If that is really what you got from my paper, there has been a
spectacular lack of communication.

Bibliography

1. BINGHAM, J. B. (1969) Controlling military spending. *Foreign Affairs, 48*, No. 1,
   51–66.
2. BODE, H. W. (1965) *Basic Research and National Goals.* A report of the National
   Academy of Sciences. Washington: Government Printing Office.
3. CALDER, N. (ed.) (1968) *Unless Peace Comes.* London: Allen Lane, The Penguin
   Press; New York: Viking Press.
4. COHEN, I. B. (1956) In *Frontiers of Knowledge*, p. 165, ed. L. White, Jr. New York:
   Harper & Brothers.

5. EISENHOWER, D. D. (1961) *Farewell Address.*
6. LONG, F. A. (1971) Growth characteristics of military research and development. In *Impact of New Technologies on the Arms Race*, pp. 271–303, ed. B. T. Feld. Cambridge, Mass.: M.I.T. Press.
7. MORISON, R. S. (1969) Science and social attitudes. *Science, 165,* 150–156.
8. NATIONAL SCIENCE FOUNDATION (1971) *National Patterns of R & D Resources— Funds and Manpower in the United States, 1953–1970.* Washington, D.C.: National Science Foundation.
9. PANOFSKY, W. K. H. (1971) Roots of the strategic arms race: ambiguity and ignorance. *Bulletin of the Atomic Scientists, 27,* No. 6, 15–20.
10. ROTBLAT, J. (1962) *Science and World Affairs: History of the Pugwash Conferences.* London: Dawsons.
11. SIDEY, H. (1967) McNamara goes. *Life,* 8th December, *63,* No. 23, 34–41.
12. SKOLNIKOFF, E. B. (1967) *Science, Technology and American Foreign Policy,* p. 307. Cambridge, Mass.: M.I.T. Press.
13. STOCKHOLM INTERNATIONAL PEACE RESEARCH INSTITUTE. *Yearbook 1969/70,* p. 288. Stockholm: SIPRI.

Discussion

1. LORENZ, K. (1966) *On Aggression.* London: Methuen.

Science in Spanish and Spanish American civilization

MARCEL ROCHE

Science does not come easily in Spain
PEDRO LAÍN ENTRALGO

Before we pass judgement on the possible ill effects of science on our civilization, I think it well to consider, as a control group, a civilization which is Western but in whose development science has played a relatively small role.

I am suggesting in the present essay that, although Spanish culture has been well gifted with many of the attributes which go to make up a civilization, it has been deficient in science—the systematic accumulation of new knowledge about nature and man. This singular lack, whose causes are briefly examined here, has contributed to the material backwardness and dependence of Spain and its area of influence.

In the late 15th and 16th centuries, Spanish culture flowered into a complete civilization. The sense of adventure, with the reconquest of the territory held by the Moors and the discovery of America, was overabundant, confidence was high and independence of foreign countries almost total. Art and beauty were plentiful and the search for truth had given rise to important contributions, particularly in the fields of geography, navigation and the science of war.[23]

Art and literature continued to flower after the 16th century, when the country was already politically decadent. Velázquez, Greco, Murillo, Zurbarán, Goya, and the religious wood-carvers were path-finders; the *Romancero* and the picaresque novel, Cervantes, the theatre of the Golden Age, Quevedo, Góngora and others made Spanish literature one of the three or four greatest in the Western World. In architecture, the Gothic and the Baroque styles were well represented in Spain, and such marvels as the Escorial by Juan de Herrera have few equivalents elsewhere. In all these aspects, Spain has been a weighty contributor to Western civilization.

However, in spite of its contribution in other spheres, Spain has produced no great names, no path-finders in science. The Spaniards themselves have been well aware of their country's deficiency, which has been termed *la cuestión científica,* the scientific problem. The Spanish historian Laín Entralgo [13] quotes the 18th century essayist Father Feijoó as writing wryly: 'Here, neither men nor women wish any other geometry but that which the tailor needs to take proper measurements'. Since Feijoó's gibe, many Spanish authors have elaborated on the point and the proof of this lies at hand in a recent 520-page anthology on the problem.[8]

The most prominent defender of Spanish science was Marcelino Menéndez y Pelayo who, during a celebrated controversy, was able to draw attention to the many Spanish men of science whose names at least he was familiar with.[18] But, as Laín Entralgo has pointed out[13], 'the many names of mediocre authors accumulated by the immense knowledge of Menéndez y Pelayo' could not conceal the fact that Spain 'had during the century and a half of its greatest glory not given a Kepler, a Galileo, a Fermat, or at least a Tartaglia or a Vieta'. The existence of later exceptions like Ramón y Cajal (Laín Entralgo calls him *ortus ex nihilo*—a garden out of nothingness!)[12] only serves to make the problem more evident.

It is not possible to review Spanish science here, but the following I believe serves to point out its real significance in a world context. In a short article on Spanish science,[13] Laín Entralgo mentions the names of 123 Spanish men of science, from the time of the Catholic Kings onwards. In a general book on the history of science, by the same author and López Piñero,[15] only 23 of these scientists are mentioned, 16 of them by name only, three (Pedro Nuñez, J. de la Cova, D. de Soto) followed by one line of text, and four (Ramón y Cajal, J. L. Vives, Félix de Azara, Miguel Serveto) by more than one line. In Spanish America, although there science has always been cultivated to some degree, the situation has been, if anything, worse.

In order for science to develop, there must be a social demand for it. This demand springs from two sources: a spiritual one, based on an appreciation of the joy of learning and discovery, and a material one, motivated by the capacity of science to satisfy the physical well-being of man. Neither demand existed to any degree until very recently in Spanish and Spanish American civilization. The reasons for this are enormously complex. It is my hypothesis, however, that they have a common denominator: the implicit choice by Spain, made early in its history, of a priority given to the after-life, to the detriment of commercial, industrial and scientific pursuit. As a result, Spain's best minds were attracted to other-worldly undertakings and its material prosperity suffered.[14] On this earth, war, often of a religious nature, was the other priority.

For the Spanish, through their protracted (711 to 1492) struggle against

Islam, religion became a particularly strong unifying cement, as it was to be for the Irish in their struggle against the English, or for the Greeks in their fight against the Turks. Religion, in fact, through contact with Islam, took on a fiercely intolerant character, which it was to maintain through many centuries.[4] When the Reformation came, Spain became the staunchest champion of orthodox Christianity; it closed its doors forcibly to foreign influence, through Philip II's famous edict of 1559 which forbade all Spaniards to study abroad.[27] In spite of a real, albeit modest, revival during the reign of Charles III in the 18th century, Spanish science never took on impetus.

Unamuno has shown[29] how the living belief in the immortality of the soul has given Spain a tragic sense of life—*sentimiento trágico de la vida*. This attitude makes material things appear unimportant and hinders the motivation towards disinterested scientific discovery—which has been the mainspring of scientific progress in the other important Western countries—and for the practical application of science. The greatest mystic of them all, Saint Teresa of Avila, could be a most formidable practical woman in her founding of convents, but this was always *ad magnam gloriam Dei*. Spaniards were interested, like everybody else, in practical and useful results. In fact, the exclusive insistence on the practical is given by some as one of the main causes for the lack of Spanish science.[18, 22, 23] But, as the novelist Pio Baroja has acutely remarked[1], 'religion for a Catholic, besides being true, is useful'. The chief concern of the Spaniards in economics, for a long time, was the business of salvation—*el negocio de la salvación*.

It may be significant that, in their painting, the Spanish classically have shown no interest in landscapes but concentrate on God and the Saints. Greco's severe landscape of Toledo, in the Metropolitan Museum in New York, is one of the few exceptions, and there is some portrayal of nature in Velázquez's backgrounds. But there is nothing of the loving landscapes of the Flemish or Dutch, or the studies of plants and nature of Leonardo or Dürer.

This dominance of an awesome and all-pervading religion was transmitted through an education in which authority was emphasized above all else. This character of education has been carried to our day into Latin American teaching, which puts great stress on memory and repetition of what the teacher or what the book says rather than on a critical examination of the evidence. 'A successful scientist must have a well-trained mind that will permit him to solve unforeseen problems. However, instead of training the minds of their students, many Latin American universities feed them with facts and information, trying to anticipate difficulties in detail by organizing courses to deal with them'.[20]

The main effect of this authoritarian teaching, coupled with repressive institutions and measures, was to stifle divergent thought. This may have been apparent in philosophy and theology as well. Unamuno did not think that the lack of science in Spain could be attributed to a preference for philosophy and theology. If this had been the case, he added, Spain would have given rise to great heresies, which it did not![30]

This does not imply that all Spaniards were religious-minded. There is another, liberal Spain, whose force appeared sporadically, as in the Cortes of 1812 or in the *Institución libre de enseñanza* in the 19th century. But this force has been regularly put down, as in 1814 by Ferdinand VII or in 1936 by the present regime.

There were many consequences, some of them of a highly practical nature, of this other-worldly priority, although looked at *sub specie aeternitatis* the choice was both logical and noble. The Inquisition was one result, and it is often mentioned as *the* cause of Spanish backwardness in science. In fact, the Inquisition was mostly concerned with Judaism and heresy (including Erasmianism) and not with science, at least not directly. In 1584, Diego de Zúñiga expounded and defended the system of Copernicus at Salamanca, and it was to Spain that Galileo thought of retiring, in 1612, when he was persecuted in Italy.[11]

In Spanish America, the chief crimes pursued by the Inquisition were bigamy, Judaism, solicitation and blasphemy.[16] The only brush, so far as I know, that a scientist had there with the Holy Tribunal was when the botanist Mutis in Colombia was reproved in the 19th century, although with no consequences, for teaching the Copernican doctrine.[16] The Inquisition, which was a generally accepted institution in Spain[11] and probably in Spanish America, was a symptom of the tendency to put down dissent rather than a direct cause of Spanish backwardness in science. 'Not a single important scientific book was ever placed on the Index, and the Inquisition only showed itself hostile to scholars who mingled theological speculation with their researches' writes Kamen in a book on the whole unfavourable to the Holy Tribunal.[11]

On the material side, the priority given to religion—saving one's soul—and to war—saving one's body—was a powerful instrument in the hands of the nobility in their struggle against the rising of the bourgeoisie. In the scientific countries—England, Germany, Holland, France—the growth of science was closely associated with that of capitalism.[2] It is possible that the 'Protestant ethic', especially of the Calvinistic variety, may have contributed to this process.[33] In Spain and Spanish America, the capitalist, scientific and industrial revolutions were inhibited, and the landed gentry remained in command, thus propagating a relative disdain for industry and for science.

The expulsion of the Moors and the persecution of the Jews, motivated again by a desire to maintain orthodoxy, also had grave practical consequences. The former had an ill effect on agriculture and the latter on commerce, industry and possibly science. Castro states unequivocally[4] that science was in the hands of Moors and Jews (especially the latter) and that the 'Spanish [*castizos*] christians . . . became accustomed to look at intellectual pursuit as proper of Jews, as deleterious [*nefanda* in the original] . . . This and none other was the cause of the cultural backwardness of the Spanish, visible still today in so many respects'.

The gaps left by the expulsion of the Jews were in large part filled by foreign immigrants who exploited rather than enriched Spain. Later, Charles V needed enormous sums of money for his foreign policy, which mortgaged the country's wealth to foreign hands.[6] The ready availability of Peruvian and Mexican silver caused local inventiveness and industry to deteriorate further. As an example, after 1600, there was an increasing dependence on foreign markets for such indispensable and strategic products as masts, hemp and sailcloth.[10] Even though some industries such as ceramics, leather, silk and Toledo blades continued to thrive, manufactured goods were mostly imported from abroad. Dependence on foreign capital and know-how was still widespread in the 19th century[28] and it will continue to be so as long as a native science and technology fails to develop vigorously.

As for Spanish America, it was physically and spiritually part of Spain until the 19th century. After Independence, in the early 19th century, through lack of confidence and creative originality and through the maintenance of an agrarian economy based on very large estates, the region was unable to

TABLE I

United States investments in Latin American manufacturing industries (millions of dollars)

	1950	1965	Percentage increase
Argentina	161	617	280
Brazil	285	722	153
Mexico	133	752	466
Chile	29	39	34
Colombia	25	160	540
Peru	16	79	393
Venezuela	24	248	933
Latin America as a whole	780	2741	251

Sources: *Survey of Current Business* 1966, quoted by Furtado,[7] p. 172.

develop an industry of its own; it became the easy prey, first of the British 'informal empire' and then of North American private investments. The progress of the latter has recently been outstanding, as shown in Table I.

This situation, although understandable in terms of the desire of the countries for rapid industrialization, is inimical to technological research. The entrepreneurs look for their know-how abroad and have no confidence in their compatriots' ability to do research.[25] The contemporary problem in Spain is somewhat similar, according to a recent report, which summarizes the situation in a terse phrase 'The intervention of foreign capital in our industry has been deleterious [*nefasta*] for our research, in most cases'.[21]

The acceptance of this lack of independence is symbolized by Unamuno's famous *boutade:* our trains run as well in Spain as in the countries where they were invented, our electricity works, we use logarithms, therefore 'let them invent!' [¡*Qué inventen ellos!*].[29] 'Graver still than an imperialist mentality in the developed countries is a colonialist mentality in the developing nations'.[3]

Thus scientific and technological research in Spain contrasts today sharply, in its penury, with that of neighbouring countries, and that of Latin America contrasts sharply with that of Anglo America. In this short discussion, we shall have to be content with bare facts which speak for themselves. Investment in science in Spain is of the order of 0.2 per cent of the gross national product (GNP) and it remained stagnant from 1936 to 1967.[21]

The proportion of the GNP invested in research and development (R & D) in the Latin American continent is not known exactly, but it is probably in general not above 0.2 to 0.3 per cent,[32] with the single exception of Cuba which invests 1.2 per cent.[24] For comparison's sake, investment in R & D in more developed countries, again in terms of GNP, is shown in Table II.

The number of personnel engaged in research and development is shown for Spain and neighbouring countries in Table III, and for the Americas in

TABLE II

Percentage of GNP invested in R & D in selected countries

Country	Investment in R & D (% GNP)	Year
United States	3.7	1963–64
France	1.9	1963
United Kingdom	2.6	1965–66
German Federal Republic	1.9	1964
Belgium	1.1	1963
The Netherlands	2.1	1964

Source [19].

TABLE III

Number of scientists and engineers in research and development in Europe

Country	Year	Total	Per million inhabitants
Belgium	1965	8 954	1093
France	1965	64 000	1307
German Federal Republic	1964	34 039	600
Italy	1967	27 755	531
United Kingdom	1965	53 825	990
U.S.S.R.	1967	770 013	3269
Spain	1967	3 842	120

Source: UNESCO.[31]

Table IV. In Latin America, only a few countries have given their data, and they are of a preliminary nature. Here again there is a profound gap between the magnitude of the effort in Spanish and Spanish American countries and those of the neighbouring more developed areas.

TABLE IV

Number of scientists and engineers in research and development in the Americas

Country	Year	Total	Per million inhabitants
United States [31]	1963	480 500	2468
Argentina [32]	1966	4 469	194
Brazil [32]	1968	6 000	70
Cuba [24]	1968	1 200	150
Chile [5]	1968	2 214	246
Mexico [26]	1968	2 611	57
Venezuela [9]	1968	1 644	179

The decadence of Spain, at least in a material sense, accelerated by her lack of science and technology, gave rise to a lack of confidence which is palpable in both Spain and Spanish America. The ordinary Spaniard, Mexican or Venezuelan who has studied history at school is just as strongly convinced as everybody else of the superiority of his country. But Spanish intellectuals such as Unamuno, Castro, Goytisolo, and Latin American writers such as Fuentes, Sabato and many others are full of doubts. In just two pages of a long preface [4] Américo Castro, describing the mood of Spain, uses the words 'discontent' [*descontento*], 'dark bitterness' [*sombría amargura*], 'to despair' [*desesperarse*], and 'discouragement' [*desánimo*].

There is no room for further quotations and the reader is referred to López Ibor's book on the Spanish inferiority complex.[17] Unamuno consoled himself with the glories of Spanish letters and art—'Santa Teresa is worth any

Institute, any Critique of Pure Reason'[30]—but Angel Ganivet and, I am sure, many others felt strongly that they would readily exchange the *Habanera* for the telephone!

Thus Spain and Spanish America provide a good control group to show what may be expected in the modern world in the absence of plentiful science and technology. Their civilization, in a Western sense, has been incomplete. They have failed to search for objective scientific truth and their material well-being has suffered accordingly. They are to this day insecure and dependent.

In the developed scientific countries there is a growing dissatisfaction with the ill effects of technology on man and the environment. It is all very well for these favoured countries to adopt this attitude. For the others to do so would be tantamount to the living skeletons one can see sleeping in the streets of some cities in India deciding that they should go on a reducing diet because there is a problem of overweight in the United States. We need insecticides on a large scale for malaria control and even polluting industries for our manufactures. We need to conserve for some time a naive attitude about progress and the bounties of science.

Indeed Spain and most Latin American nations are now engaged in a process of development based on economic expediency rather than on religious or spiritual considerations. In Spain, the National Research Council was founded by men many of whom belonged to the *Opus Dei* and the reins of a Government given to technocratic thinking are in the hands of such a group.[34] In Latin America, the Church no longer possesses intellectual dominance and all countries, whether Marxist like Cuba and Chile, rightist militaristic like Brazil and Argentina, or classical parliamentary like Colombia and Venezuela, have taken the road of material growth. Madrid's atmosphere is being polluted, a sure sign of prosperity, and the lovely mountains of Mexico City —Popocatepetl and Iztacihuatl—have disappeared from view, hidden by the gaseous excrements from motor car exhausts and industrial smoke stacks.

Yet the signs of a long history of a feckless attitude towards science and technology remain with us. Authoritarian memoristic teaching continues and our prosperity is not made at home but depends almost exclusively on foreign technology.

The remedies seem clear, although difficult to implement. A radical change in our education is necessary. We must take measures to limit the entry of international enterprises into our soft and yielding economy. In the long run this can only lead to a vigorous increase in our own science and technology, which will be better directed towards our needs and will not neglect disinterested research of the highest quality.

Discussion

Brock: This was a fascinating analysis of the lack of motivation towards science in Spain and Latin America. Some of the criticism that comes, at least from the younger members of the anti-science movement, is apparently based on suspicion of the motivation of science today. That motivation has much in common with motivation towards other fields of study such as music, art, sculpture—it derives from a creative instinct which must express itself particularly in the field of *why*, and to a lesser extent of *how*. What makes a man a successful scientist is this 'fire in the belly'. Is it just a form of curiosity or is it more than that?

The field of medical science is unique in that most of the financing for medical research comes from the belief among wealthy individuals, foundations and government agencies that advances in medical science will improve the lot of man. There has been a revulsion in the last five years against the inordinate pursuit of medical science to the virtual or partial neglect of medical practice or medical service. When we are recruiting for medical science we are recruiting people who have a competing motivation to provide service to the community. Some people are diverted into pure science and away from the patient, but those who become clinical scientists retain a direct concern for the patient. This concern brings out two qualities—sympathy, without which no one can face rows of sick patients in hospital wards, and humility, when we realize how much our patient has in common with us. This humility is very badly needed in science today. There is often a singular absence of humility in the statements of leading scientists and one reason why there is an anti-science movement may be a suspicion that those who represent science have no humility. If we are going to deal with this type of anti-science movement as expressed by our younger students, we have to satisfy those students that we have a sense of responsibility towards our patients on the one hand and towards students on the other. Students very quickly see through us if we want to escape all the time into the laboratory or away from teaching. They then become suspicious of our motivation.

Mathur: For a few centuries during the first half of this millennium Spain led the world in technology and science. Western science was introduced into Europe through Spain and Italy, which were the first recipients of the Eastern scientific tradition transmitted through the Arabs.

The lack of interest in science in Spain later on was not so much because more attention was paid to religion but because the Holy Inquisition existed to suppress free thought and heresies. This created a climate in which science could not flourish, for a certain degree of freedom of speculation and inquiry is a prerequisite for the advancement of scientific thought.

This holds a moral for us in the 20th century. Economists are increasingly taking to cost-benefit analysis in the advanced countries and in underdeveloped countries. I fear that functionaries who know neither the scope nor the limitations of cost-benefit analysis will set up committees to look at basic research projects on too narrow a basis, and that these committees will, in time, become a sort of Holy Inquisition for the scientists. It would be a sad day not only for science but for thought in general if every bit of basic research had to prove it was related to some directly foreseeable ulterior objective.

For instance, such a committee might ask whether goitre research should be encouraged if it does not increase productivity but only reduces unhappiness among those afflicted with the disease. In India, the Council for Scientific and Industrial Research is already under pressure to set up committees to look into the performance of basic research laboratories in terms of so-called economic costs and benefits. It is not difficult for cost-benefit economists to provide seemingly incontrovertible facts and calculations which tend to indicate that, as there is no immediate benefit, not even applied basic research need be undertaken. Applied industrial research can of course be evaluated and the determination of the type of applied research being undertaken is therefore important. But we must guard against narrow terms of reference and methods of evaluation by cost-benefit committees as far as basic research is concerned.

Long: Professor Roche commented that the difficulties of the Latin American countries in getting lively science and technology are to some degree associated with the characteristics of their educational institutions. Are we here simply discussing salary and other constraints which make it very hard to get the best minds into education or are there additional difficulties which make it very hard to get governments to give adequate support to education?

As a different point, the developing countries frequently pointed to as successful in leaping into science and technology are Asian countries such as Japan, Taiwan and South Korea. One of the characteristics they share is a substantial and well-respected educational system. If countries like these have been particularly successful in assimilating science and technology and bringing them into the development process, isn't there a need for a consortium of developing nations to permit them to work directly together? There is something seriously wrong when a developing nation feels it necessary to take its problems to a developed nation like France, Great Britain, the United States or the Soviet Union, which in turn must seek the answers from some other developing country. There ought to be another way to short-circuit this inefficient communication system.

Roche: The whole problem is indeed closely linked to the educational system, both quantitatively and qualitatively. The Spanish tradition of teaching is very authoritative and based on memorizing. I have heard Richard Feynman comment that science in Brazil and in Latin America is simply not taught; something else is taught: formulae for action, for doing thinghs, but not the art of creating knowledge. This is true not only of science but also of literature. In literature, in secondary schools, we don't read the original texts; rather we are taught the biographies of great men. This is part of the attitude of not seeking the original fact or the original text.

The need for integration is particularly true for Latin America. The situation is scandalous in that countries with a common language, a common culture and a common religion don't communicate with each other at all. We in Venezuela communicate with New York, London or Paris but not with Bogotá which is one hour away by air. We are politically, economically and scientifically separated. Something has to be done about this.

Todd: Dr Roche suggests that the problem for Spain was that it had risen to its peak of power before the time of the scientific revolution at the end of the 16th century. Spain was by far the strongest country of the Western world and had great possessions in America, with wealth flowing in from them. It built its educational system and its social system on the basis of this tremendous power. When the scientific revolution and later the industrial revolution arrived, there was apparently no need for Spain to worry. It had its huge colonial empire, the richest in the world, and it profited from everything that came through the country to the rest of Europe. By the time the Spanish American colonies broke away, however, significant changes had occurred. The industrial revolution was properly under way, notably in England, and on the score of industrialization Spain had missed the bus. The world had become sufficiently civilized for Spain not to get the treatment the Roman Empire had received: it wasn't immediately wiped out but it was left behind the Pyrenees to moulder on in its own way.

Unfortunately, by the time they broke away the Spanish American colonies had had the stamp of the educational and social systems of the decaying Spanish Empire put so firmly on them that they too missed the industrial revolution. Is this really the answer? If so, it might lead to depressing thoughts, because England is the country that took most advantage of the industrial revolution and developed an empire during that period. England developed at the same time an educational system in which science certainly played a part, but where it was treated in rather a dilettante fashion. We were on top of the pile and we didn't pay too much attention to technological education. One wonders at times if this is the real trouble with England. It is interesting that we imprinted our educational system on a lot of countries in the Commonwealth, including countries of the so-called white Commonwealth, such as Australia and New Zealand. Their pace of development has been slower than one might have expected, compared with the pace of development in North America. But, to return to my main point, if the discovery of America hadn't happened for another hundred or so years, Spain might have developed in quite a different direction.

Roche: I agree with much of your explanation but I still wonder why Spain and Spanish America never caught up with the bus after having missed it!

Thiemann: Gélinier has tried to correlate modern scientific industrial development with religious movements.[1] He suggested that the Roman Empire was killed by Christian philosophy and that the Catholic countries fell behind because of their attitude to the Reformation. The Reformation created a new ethic, the scientific industrial ethic, where intensive work was honoured. Work was not honoured by the Greeks: it was something done by slaves. The same happened in the Roman Empire and in Catholic countries before the Reformation. The Puritans had the new ethic that to do more work and better work ensures honour before God. When the Puritans came to New England they found the space and liberty to develop this ethic. Gélinier correlates it with the gross national product. The highest GNP per head today is in the United States; then come the Protestant countries of northern Europe, where it is about half as much as in the United States. Then come the Catholic countries of southern Europe with less than half the GNP of northern Europe; in South America the GNP is much less than in Spain. Gélinier concluded that there is no direct correlation between the GNP per head and natural resources. The high GNP is mainly a function of the outlook of the people and is therefore related to the Puritan ethic. The only exception seems to be in Japan.

Todd: Which is the chicken and which is the egg? Aren't these relationships simply due to that aspect of religion in which it is being used as a support for the state? Official religion has always had two functions: an ethical function and another in which it seeks to legitimize the state hierarchy.

Roche: Max Weber was, I think, the first to suggest that the Protestant ethic and the rise of capitalism went together.[5] Weber thought that it all derived from the Calvinist view of predestination. Calvinists ought to have been pessimistic about the future life and busy gaining eternal bliss through good works, but in fact they got the idea that worldly goods, particularly economic and industrial success, were outward signs of being chosen by God. This led to the development of an ethic of work and economic endeavour. The Dutch were the first to benefit from that in the 17th century.

Shils: Max Weber[5] claimed that the Protestant ethic, or the Calvinistic strand of Protestantism, particularly in the independent sects in England, brought about a situation in which the energy of man was directed to the transformation of the earth for the glorification of God. That entailed self-disciplined labour for the end of discovering evidence of whether one was saved for eternity or eternally damned. It was not just material wealth that men under the influence of this belief were seeking. They were seeking wealth by rationally self-disciplined exertion within the framework of religious conviction. Max Weber pointed out that in other civilizations too, men had sought to accumulate great riches. But only in the West was wealth sought through the rational organization of effort. Other civilizations also had striking accomplishments in technology as well as considerable accomplishments in empirical science. But only Western civilization, particularly the Protestant part of Western civilization, developed modern systematic science based on a rational theoretical scheme.

These two things—rational self-discipline for religious ends and rationally controlled scientific curiosity—are linked. The search to discover the intention of God, while recognizing that ultimately God's will is inscrutable, is integrally connected with the belief that it is man's responsibility to try to penetrate into it as far as he can. Weber quotes the passage from Leeuwenhoek in which he said that the will of God can be discerned in the anatomy of a louse: any part of nature, however humble, however degraded, however repugnant it might be, is a manifestation of God's will, and it is the task of man to discern God's will in all the various gradations of being. According to this line of interpretation, the motivation of scientific research lies in a universal curiosity to discern the fundamental scheme of existence and in the summoning of extraordinary powers of self-discipline to pursue that end.

Weber's original thesis has a great deal in it and Robert Merton[2] has given some additional statistics and observations which support this view. Obviously other factors are involved, such as educational opportunity, academic structure and traditions, and intellectual potentiality. But the capacity for self-discipline and a quasi-religious curiosity about the nature of the universe are two elements which have not been sufficiently stressed in discussions about the implantation of a scientific outlook in countries which do not yet have it. They are also overlooked in discussions about 'scientific manpower' in the scientifically advanced countries. We must cherish these qualities and not regard them simply as superfluous remnants of no longer accepted religious belief. There is a great wave of anti-puritanism now in the anti-science movement but we must not accredit it. We must not acknowledge it as being morally right. People now make statements to the effect that spontaneity, the gratification of impulse and realization of the self through allowing every impulse to come to the surface are the chief ends of existence. There is some truth in that, but those concerned with the intellectual well-being of mankind and ultimately the broader well-being of mankind should remember that without self-discipline, without willingness to forgo gratification, nothing will come of human exertion. It will be idle, wasted energy. Zealous self-discipline is a necessity for scientific accomplishment. We cannot maintain science and at the same time erode its moral foundations by denying the belief that man owes something to a higher transcendent realm outside himself. Put into less old-fashioned language, science needs a belief in the value of self-discipline as a path to objective truth which lies outside human will and desire. However valuable applied science is, it is in certain respects a derivative activity. Unless this moral-metaphysical belief and the psychological impetus accompanying it are maintained there will not be any pure science. Without pure science, there will also be no applied science either. I do not refer here to to what is called 'spin-off'.

We should also discuss here the view that there is plenty of technology in the world and the undeveloped countries have only to make use of it. However we must of course remember that they will not be able to do so unless they have a scientific sensibility, a scientific morale, a scientific capacity, and they only acquire these by doing pure science. Pure science is expensive and much of it produces no tangible results except papers in journals quoted by other scientists. Nevertheless, it has the very important consequence that it leads to a certain state of mind or disposition which I think is a precondition for doing good work in technology. This has not been sufficiently emphasized in our discussions. Many people speak about the material spin-off but there is also a moral spin-off, a psychological spin-off, from the spirit of pure science, which is really a generalized form of the Protestant ethic.

I should add that the generalized form of the Protestant ethic is no longer a monopoly of Protestants. Non-Protestants can have it, Hindus can have it, Moslems can have it; all peoples can have it if it is nurtured in them and if they exert themselves to acquire and practise it.

Bourlière: Science has failed to provide answers to many new ethical questions raised by recent developments in technology and in the biomedical sciences. People are becoming more aware of the individual and social implications of many new discoveries or research trends such as those for the control of population, control of some types of behaviour, biomedical engineering and genetic engineering. On the other hand, the influence of traditional religions and philosophies, including Marxism, is waning, particularly among the younger generation. These philosophies cannot provide answers to many of the new questions which appeared long after those philosophies were developed. The gap between philosophers and scientists has never been wider. No effort has been made to discover a rational basis, a new ethic or a new set of values. More and more people are therefore progressively inclined to distrust science, and to turn instead to irrational and more or less emotional answers to the problems of the last few decades. It is striking that out of thousands of new books appearing every year, very few deal with the necessity for mankind to build up new ethics. Jacques Monod's last book [3] touches on these questions but that is just a beginning. Is it impossible now to promote a new natural philosophy, as scientists in the 18th century did? This is a question that should be discussed at a symposium like this, because one of the reasons for anti-scientific attitudes now is the feeling that science is raising more problems than it is providing answers to either old or new questions.

Roche: In the last instance science and indeed civilization will be judged by their ability to provide happiness for humanity. The difficulty lies in defining happiness. It was probably one of the chief roles of religion to state clearly what happiness consisted of; religion may not have provided it in this world but at least it defined it, and people had guidelines and rules to go by. Probably happiness depends on a balance between the demands of people, their aspirations, and the availability of what is demanded. One can increase happiness through science, in theory, either by decreasing demands or by increasing the availability of goods, both physical and spiritual. For example, one could possibly decrease physical demands by controlling population. And obviously one can increase the availability of goods such as food. Whatever we do, whatever solutions we try to find in the future, science will be needed to increase availability of goods or to decrease demands; this would be its contribution to that very elusive thing called happiness.

Shils: In the 18th and 19th centuries, as Professor Bourlière pointed out, science was associated with the movement for the enlightenment of mankind and the improvement of the life of man through the eradication of superstition, through freeing the mind of man from the shadows, from the darknesses, from the fear of spooks and things of that sort. It was thought that a scientifically illuminated life would be a better life, not only materially, but a loftier life. There was an honour and a dignity of man which would be achieved when man understood his place in the universe, and his relationship to other human beings, to other living creatures and to other parts of nature.

This was a kind of secularized theology. In about 1848 Ernest Renan wrote a marvellous book, *L'Avenir de la Science*,[4] in which he said what a great thing science would be and what an extraordinary transformation in life there would be, not just a material transformation but a spiritual emancipation of mankind.

Today we are as fidgety as people who have sat down on an anthill. Although I am a social scientist, I am one of the few here who speaks about science as a spiritual undertaking, as the best we have in a sense to replace theology. None of the real scientists here have mentioned that point, although all of them are practising these religions in their own little chapels or laboratories. Nobody speaks any more about the transformation of life, the *éclaircissement*, the driving away of the shadows, yet I think these are good things. It is an improvement of life that men should face the fact that they are mortal —if that is what they believe—and scientists are neglecting their vocation when they fail to discuss such matters. In this regard science has much to contribute to a Montaignean humanism. But that is not all. The relationship between science, religion and ethics is not exhausted by discussion about euthanasia, experimentation on human beings, genetic engineering, and so on—important as all these are. These other matters seem to me to belong to a discussion of science and civilization.

Freeman: You pointed out (pp. 33-49) that really we are not faced with a crisis of science, Professor Shils, and I agree with you. Unfortunately, we don't have a fine enough measurement scale for this. On the meteorological scale, I would say we face something like a force 3 or force 4 situation, not a force 7 or force 8 gale. One of the difficulties with this terminology is that we argue about either a crisis or a revolution because we have no intermediate term. We have a ridiculous debate about whether there was an industrial revolution or not, because we don't have a proper scale of measurement.

The present situation, even though it is not a real crisis, is enough to cause concern. It would be a great pity if, in the metaphor quoted earlier, the rats weren't just leaving the ship because they thought it was sinking, but were actually participating in trying to sink it and in making the crisis worse. There are two ways in which the situation might be made worse than it really is through the inadvertent actions or attitudes of scientists themselves. One way would be if scientists were completely indifferent to the applications of their work. This would certainly cause young people everywhere to reject the whole thing, in my view quite rightly. A second way would be if the impression were to spread that scientists think they have the answers to questions when they haven't, and if scientists were to appear to be hostile to the whole tradition of the humanities and religion.

It is essential to be clear that what science has displaced is dogmatic theology. That is very different from replacing a vision of the universe that has been held by poets and people of religious inclinations through the millennia. It would be regrettable if, in drawing historical analogies as Professor Toulmin did (pp. 23-32), we were to see people like Blake or Goethe or Swift as simply the enemies of science. On the contrary, they have a great many affinities with science, and the affinities are more important than the differences. Certainly Blake was a mystic with a peculiar vision of the world, but he rebelled against a scholastic and pedantic tradition in education. So did Einstein. Blake rebelled against the inhuman conditions of people working in industrial situations. So did Einstein. Blake rebelled against a dogmatic interpretation of Newtonian physics. So did Einstein. Blake insisted on the importance of imagination and creativity. So did Einstein. The supposed antipathy between the arts and the sciences can be very much overdone. In many ways they are natural allies, and not opponents at all. I would like to see more emphasis on the commonality between the arts and the sciences. To my way of thinking there is a 'science of civilization' already: it is called the humanities.

Toulmin: I wasn't putting Blake and Goethe in genuine opposition to science: my remarks about this were in the nature of social and intellectual history. I was asking why people in general had occasionally thought that there *was* an opposition of this kind, whereas—like Dr Freeman—I would myself deny it.

Bibliography

1. BAROJA, P. (1961) *El Árbol de la Ciencia*. Barcelona: Editorial Planeta.
2. BERNAL, J. D. (1969) *Science in History*. Harmondsworth: Penguin Books (Pelican edition).
3. CALDERA, R. (1970) *Discourse before the Permanent Council of the Organization of American States*, 4 June. Caracas: Office of the President.
4. CASTRO, A. (1962) *La Realidad Histórica de España*. Mexico: Editorial Porrua.
5. CENTRO DE PLANEAMIENTO, UNIVERSIDAD DE CHILE (1969) *Bases para una Política de la Ciencia y la Tecnología en Chile*. Mimeographed document. Santiago: Universidad de Chile.
6. ELLIOTT, J. H. (1963) *Imperial Spain 1469-1716*. London: Arnold.
7. FURTADO, C. (1970) *Economic Development of Latin America*. London: Cambridge University Press.
8. GARCÍA CAMARERO, E. (ed.) (1970) *La Polémica de la Ciencia Española*. Madrid.
9. GASPARINI, O. (1969) *La Investigación en Venezuela*. Caracas: Publicaciones IVIC.
10. HAMILTON, E. J. (1937-38) The decline of Spain. *Economic History Review, 8*, 168-179.
11. KAMEN, H. (1965) *The Spanish Inquisition*. New York: New American Library.

12. Laín Entralgo, P. (1957) Estudios y apuntes sobre Ramón y Cajal. In *España como Problema*. Madrid: Aguilar.
13. Laín Entralgo, P. (1970) Breve sinopsis histórica de la ciencia española. In *Ciencia y Vida*. Madrid: Seminarios y Ediciones.
14. Laín Entralgo, P. (1970) La mente española y la ciencia. In *Ciencia y Vida*. Madrid: Seminarios y Ediciones.
15. Laín Entralgo, P. and López Piñero, J. M. (1963) *Panorama Histórico de la Ciencia Moderna*. Madrid: Ediciones Guadarrama.
16. Lea, H. C. (1908) *The Inquisition in the Spanish Dependencies*. New York: Macmillan Co.
17. López Ibor, J. J. (1958) *El Español y su Complejo de Inferioridad*. Madrid: Ediciones Rialp.
18. Menéndez y Pelayo, M. (1953) *La Ciencia Española*. Santander: Aldus.
19. Organization for Economic Cooperation and Development (1967) *The Overall Level and Structure of R and D Efforts in OECD Member Countries*. Paris: OECD.
20. Pan American Health Organization (1966) *Science Policy in Latin America*. Washington, D.C.: PAHO.
21. Presidencia del Gobierno (1967) *II Plan de Desarrollo Económico y Social*. Madrid: Comisión de investigación científica y técnica.
22. Ramón y Cajal, S. (1961) *Reglas y Consejos sobre Investigación Científica*. Madrid: Aguilar.
23. Rey Pastor, J. (1945) *La Ciencia y la Técnica en el Descubrimiento de América*. Buenos Aires: Espasa-Calpe Argentina.
24. Roche, M. (1970) Notes on science in Cuba. *Science, 169,* 344–349.
25. Roche, M. (1972) Dependence and the development of science in Latin America. *Cambridge Review, 93*, No. 2207.
26. Sala de Gomezgil, R. (1970) *Las Instituciones de Investigación de México*. México: Instituto de investigaciones sociales, UNAM.
27. Sánchez Albornoz, C. (1962) *España, un Enigma Histórico*. Buenos Aires: Editorial Suramérica.
28. Tuñón de Lara, M. (1968) *La España del Siglo XIX*. Paris: Librería española.
29. Unamuno, M. de (1970) El sentimiento trágico de la vida. Reprinted in *Ensayos*. Madrid: Aguilar.
30. Unamuno, M. de (1970) Sobre la lectura e interpretación del Quijote. Reprinted in *Ensayos*. Madrid: Aguilar.
31. Unesco (1969) *Statistical Yearbook*. Paris: UNESCO.
32. Unesco (1969) *La Política Científica en América Latina*. Paris: UNESCO.
33. Weber, M. (1970) *The Protestant Ethic and the Spirit of Capitalism*. London: Allen & Unwin.
34. Ynfante, J. (1970) *La Prodigiosa Aventura del Opus Dei*. Paris: Ruedo Ibérico.

Discussion

1. Gélinier, O. (1965) *Morale de l'Enterprise et Destin de la Nation*. Paris: Plon.
2. Merton, R. (1970) *Science, Technology and Society in Seventeenth Century England*. New York: Fertig.
3. Monod, J. (1970) *Le Hasard et la Nécessité. Essai sur la Philosophie Naturelle de la Biologie Moderne*. Paris: Le Seuil.
4. Renan, E. (1890) *L'Avenir de la Science*. [Written about 1848.]
5. Weber, M. (1970) *The Protestant Ethic and the Spirit of Capitalism*. London: Allen & Unwin [first English edition 1930].

Some economic aspects of science

HARRY G. JOHNSON

One fundamental reason why a conference on *Civilization and Science* should have been held at this time is an economic one: the simple fact that the vast bulk of scientific research and other scientific activities is supported at the public expense of the taxpayer. This makes it necessary for the scientists, on behalf of both their own search for facts and their economic livelihood, to justify themselves to the taxpaying public in terms that make sense politically to the public and at the same time scientifically or at least pseudo-scientifically to other scientists.

This linkage between science and civilization is a very modern invention indeed, and it may be dangerous ground for science to choose on which to debate its right to existence. For a civilization is not a static condition in which the value of every component is known and appreciated; it is a dynamic condition in which a useful balance has to be achieved between the forces working for conservation of what has been recognized to be valuable in existing society and the forces making for change in the whole structure of society. The problem for the human beings involved in a civilization is to preserve their faith in the stability of the structure while accepting and digesting the changes that make it dynamic and keep it alive and interesting.

In this context science has a very difficult political problem to face. In its own eyes and according to its own standards science is an arch-conservative force. Its function is to preserve, regularize and codify knowledge, to deepen that hard-won knowledge accumulated by past scientific endeavour, and to resist the addition to the common stock of knowledge of any new idea until it has passed the tests of scientific acceptability. But in the public eye science is the source of unexpected and often very uncomfortable change, precisely because its methods of testing new ideas are so effective that when a new idea is accepted it becomes adopted. This is what puts science in the role of a conservative in its own eyes and in that of a dynamic revolutionary force in the eyes of the public. Science is in the odd political position of both claiming and believing itself to be a servant of society when actually it is a revolutionary agent. Its acceptance depends on the extent to which the public is prepared to accept the idea of revolution and to live with it, and that belief varies over time.

In this respect science itself has been going through a highly disturbing—at least to scientists—cycle of public approbation and disapprobation over the past forty years. This cycle has been set against the general background of another major social change, namely the transfer of many functions that used to be private responsibilities to public responsibility, essentially to public funding. In the long historical past scientific enquiry has sometimes been popular and sometimes very unpopular indeed, to the point of the slaughter of the scientists concerned. It has until very recently been financed privately. It was financed either as a by-product of property ownership by people with lots of time on their hands, or else as a by-product of religious activity. In either case it was an indirect by-product of the economic process.

The important exceptions have occurred in times of war. It is only in war time that a society really feels compelled to change itself and make itself more efficient and effective. It has to change itself willy-nilly in order to survive and for that purpose it will pay handsomely those who can increase its effectiveness. So the problem that arises for science—and I believe we must consider the problem as a by-product of the Second World War—is that the public doesn't like either people with enquiring minds or professional soldiers except in times of war when these people are useful. Once the war is over they begin to question whether it is worth supporting scientists and soldiers at the level of reward offered in order to help win the war. The public feels it has to question whether resources sould be spent on this kind of activity instead of being devoted to the peaceful pursuit of private satisfaction. That I think is the essence of the problem concerning science at the present time. Science used to be a spare-time activity of people with a private income from somewhere else and it has become an activity paid for by the state which has to justify itself to the state and to public opinion.

The capacity for scientific activity became especially valuable to society in the Second World War, as the result of economic forces. The First World War was a matter of lining up your men against the other people's men and letting them slaughter each other: the country that had the most men would win. That technique of military enterprise became pretty loathsome. It therefore became important to try to save bodies by using science instead. England was particularly successful in this at the beginning of the Second World War and the United States later with the invention of the atomic bomb. But if science is valuable to society as a way of saving bodies that means it is closely related to warfare and the need for warfare.

Another factor is that in the European tradition people are trained to be ready to die for the sake of a principle, regardless of the hopelessness of their objective military situation; but American society has always rebelled against that notion and likes to rely on the comforting thought that it has superior technology. Europeans, and particularly the British, love to fight against overwhelming odds which guarantee that most of them will die in the process. Americans only like to fight if they have superior technology which will enable them to win without any loss of life. We see this in Vietnam at the present time. The Vietnam debacle is a result of the fact that one can't pull this trick off every time. When the belief in the superiority of American military technology breaks down there is a public revolt against it. There is no willingness on the part of the American public to see part of the population lost by attrition in the name of a principle.

The Second World War made the capacity for scientific endeavour a valuable international resource. That would probably have been a transitory phenomenon, and scientists, having been elevated into importance, would have returned to obscurity if it hadn't been for the 'cold war', and specifically for the launching of the Sputnik in 1957. We owe a great deal of contemporary science policy to the launching of the Sputnik, though one of my colleagues in Cambridge at that time suggested that the Sputnik was all a hoax. From an economic point of view, if there is a possibility of war, scientific research becomes important and valuable and worth supporting. But competition in scientific research leads to escalation of expenditure without necessarily leading to improvement in the results. That in turn leads the public to wonder whether the money is worth spending. Science policy, as we know, has certainly been beneficial to the scientists; but whether it has been beneficial to society is quite a different question.

There is also a natural and understandable confusion in the public's mind between politico-military survival and social welfare. Science has benefited from the notion that what is good in war is good in peace, an idea that won't stand up very long either. Essentially the public has begun to question whether science supported for the sake of potential military success is really good for the rest of us, and whether we need that much potential success. Escalation occurs and scientific expenditure becomes simply a matter of matching the expenditure of other countries without any demonstrable output. We get what is known in the language of the trade as the sophistication factor—which means you pay more money for less work.

The massive support of science has become an article of faith and policy in the major countries of the Western world. The scientists are naturally only too glad to welcome this even though some of them have been rather surprised by the fame they have achieved by riding on this particular bandwagon. Scientists have become accustomed to the idea that they are somehow socially important in a way they weren't when they started their careers. A scientific career used to be something that only a few strange people went in for and they had to get pretty tough about accepting the contumely that greeted them. Then they became advisers to presidents and things like that. Of course some of them got too used to that and they are now feeling the pinch of unpopularity.

Unfortunately for the scientists the cold war and the support for science policies that war generated have been rapidly receding into unimportance. People began to wonder whether the Russians and the Americans had reached some sort of an understanding that did not need all this massive effort to provide scientific military requirements. With that mounting doubt, there has been receding the idea that science is socially beneficial. That probably was a myth to begin with but it got attached to the bandwagon. If one loses faith in the necessity of military expenditure on science one can also lose one's faith that science is good for people in general.

Essentially what we are up against is that peace brings problems. In particular the expert in mayhem and murder becomes an uncomfortable neighbour once you decide to live in peace with the rest of your neighbours. He is uncomfortable to live with because he knows how to kill and you don't. The parallel with the Mafia is very clear. The Mafia used to be a protection for the immigrant in the United States and has since become a criminal syndicate. It is no longer welcomed for this protection; instead it is feared as a danger. People begin to question whether decent societies can afford to live side by side with murderers and then whether they can afford to live side by side with scientists. A society at peace hates to be reminded that it has been at war and may be at war again. As human beings always do, it wants to forget that possibility by eliminating the outward symbol of the possibility—the person who knows how to kill if that is what is needed. In addition a society at peace becomes very uneasy with itself. It is not only increasingly hostile to those who remind it of the possibility of war but it also begins to raise questions about itself.

The basic problem is that humanity has a long history of warfare. Warfare is what makes society, basically—warfare or the possibility of warfare. The trouble with peace is that you then begin to wonder what is the basis of society. It is very easy to blame dissatisfaction with society on those who are involved in the warfare side of it. We have the contemporary phenomenon that scientists are not only considered unnecessary any more for the waging of war but are deemed to be responsible for the evils of society, including both the possibility of war and the other defects that youth blames on society. This is the basic problem: peace breeds discontent and discontent seeks scapegoats.

The obvious scapegoats are the scientists who claim the responsibility for making our society successful. Scientific research has in the recent past been credited by scientists with the bulk of the benefits of modern society; and in the most recent past people have quite naturally come to blame it for the defects of modern society. In the past the benefits of the internal combustion engine, plastic containers, detergents, chemical fertilizers and a whole lot of other things have been claimed on behalf of science. Now we are beginning to realize that these things are not all that beneficial and to blame science for the bad effects.

The most socially awkward and embarrassing characteristic of the process of scientific activity is its myopic honesty. Honesty is a basic principle of science. Scientists were honest about telling people that detergents were good for them and now they are equally honest about telling them that detergents pollute the environment. Science itself gives hostages to fortune in the form of honest statements about what science has done to the public that the public often resents.

Another essential principle of scientific research is that all discoveries should be communicated to the public. This is not necessarily a good thing because the people who make those discoveries don't necessarily understand the full implications. The scientist could be honest twice—first in telling people that the detergent is better than soap and then next time round, and for the benefit of another generation of scientists, in telling them that detergents pollute their water. The problem of society is to arrive at some balance between the advantages and disadvantages. Science tends to have cycles of honesty about good things and honesty about bad things, and either may be deliberately misinforming the public. The honesty of science is not necessarily a good thing.

From the economist's point of view, science is a competition with certain rules and people win or lose according to their performance by those rules. The rules are set up so that they are beneficial from the standpoint of science but not to ensure that the results are socially beneficial. A scientific discovery announced to the world may win somebody a reputation or a Nobel Prize. The discovery of what was wrong with the last discovery may also win someone a Nobel Prize. What society really wants to know is not news but how to digest what is going on and how to live with it. There is nothing in the process of scientific research which guarantees that scientists have any responsibility whatsoever from that point of view. We have the problem that science is a competition like most other aspects of life, but the rules according to which the competition is rewarded or penalized are not rules that necessarily serve a social interest.

A whole batch of contemporary economic theory is concerned with problems of this kind, with the divergences between social and private benefits. The standard example that factories emit smoke was produced before the First World War and it was ridiculed at one time as the discovery that smoke is a nuisance! But smoke *is* a standard problem of pollution. Contemporary theory has reached the view that smoke is a social problem only to the extent that there is a failure of contract rights. If I have the right to sue the factory for putting out smoke then it must either stop putting out the smoke or compensate me for the damage it does. If on the other hand the factory has the right to put out smoke I have no right to object to the smoke. This really epitomizes much contemporary concern about the whole problem of pollution. Do factories or do they not have the right to put their waste into rivers? Is the river a common property resource which anyone can do what he likes with or do I as a citizen have the right to have the river clean enough to swim and fish in, even though I pay nothing to keep it clean and I am imposing on the factory owners and ultimately their customers the cost of keeping it clean for my benefit?

The process of scientific research is a market system in one sense and a non-market system in another. It is a market system in the sense that it is competitive; it is a non-market system in the sense that there are no contract rights by which I can sue a scientist who discovers something which is bad for me. This structure of competition and scientific endeavour is rewarded financially and in terms of social prestige according to scientific accomplishment, but it pays no attention to the benefits or the costs that that competition may impose on the rest of society.

I was on the Council for Scientific Policy in England for three years and I agree with scientists that this competition is probably the best way of improving science. There is honesty in it and that is very important because a lot of life is dishonest. There is success in it—it delivers. The problem is whether what it delivers is in the social interest. Some of the results probably are not in the social interest, because there is nothing in the reward and penalty system which asks the scientist whether what he discovered is to the social benefit or not. He simply produces the knowledge; there is nothing which makes him think whether the result is beneficial or not. This would not be a problem if our society was otherwise rational and intelligent: if the public, the manufacturers and the politicians who use science were themselves capable of assessing the results. There could be a competition in which people were simply competing to produce results and then somebody else assessed the results and decided how to use them. The trouble is that there is nothing in the political process to tell us whether the use of science is beneficial or not. The political process is interested in short-term results and the public certainly did not know that if it used detergents to make the housewife's lot easier it was also going to be polluting the rivers and imposing social costs.

There is nothing in the system which provides an outside check. Science has relied far too much on the assumption that there is an outside check when there isn't one. So we have the problem that our civilization rewards scientific endeavour without very much internal or external control over what the results of that endeavour will be. We cannot rely on the public being able to assess the benefits and costs of the results. We really have no concept in our society of what the use of science should be and what the checks should be on its social effects. Instead we alternate between welcoming science without asking that question and condemning science by asking that question before we ask ourselves what science has done for us recently.

I have talked about science as a competitive method of producing new knowledge and about the social problems this poses in principle. The next question is the problem of knowledge itself. This is a basic problem for economics, though the other social sciences are not worried about it much. We think of output or production of goods and services as having a functional relationship with the input of various kinds of productive resources. In particular, in the older style we thought of output as being a function of the input of capital, thought of as machinery and equipment, and of human labour. We have become much more sophisticated about that, and in particular we have become concerned in recent years with this functional relationship as a matter of knowledge which can be changed by investing in the acquisition of new knowledge. That is, we think of this functional relationship between input of labour and capital and output of product as a relationship determined by technology. Past work in economics tended to concentrate on the quantities of the inputs. Present work concentrates on the function itself and on what determines it, and considers that the function can be changed by research.

A major problem arises in this context. We think of inputs of labour and capital as isolated separable inputs which can be charged for. But when we think of the knowledge itself, it is what we economists describe as a public good. The simplest example of a public good is a park. Within limits anybody can walk in the park and look at the flowers, or at the animals if it has a zoo in it, and no one really gets in the way of anybody else walking in that park. The park is something which is not divided into individual pieces of property and it can't be so divided because enjoyment of it is not exclusive. I don't have to keep everybody else out of the park in order to enjoy it; similarly nobody else has to keep me out in order to enjoy it. We can all enjoy it. That means that the benefits are collective benefits and for efficiency these benefits have to be provided for by public expenditure. We usually do provide parks by public expenditure, though occasionally a park is provided by the generosity of some private individual who doesn't mind other people walking in his garden as long as they don't inflict their political views on his deer.

But if we charge for the use of the park we make it inefficient because it doesn't cost anything for somebody else to come in. If we charge him we deter him. The recent controversy in England about charging for entry to museums and art galleries raises exactly this principle—namely that somebody has to pay for the upkeep but once the pictures are on the wall it doesn't cost anybody anything for an extra person to look at them. That ignores questions of congestion on Sunday, of course, but generally speaking once the picture is on the wall it costs nothing for an extra person to look at it.

Knowledge is like this: once the knowledge is there everybody can use it and charging for it makes it inefficient. Some social processes in our society, such as patents, copyrights and so forth, do charge for the use of knowledge but these devices are least efficient in relation to the most important kinds of knowledge, which are not knowledge about how to make a better mousetrap than your neighbour but knowledge about the nature of the universe which couldn't possibly be patented—one wouldn't know how to describe it or how to prevent other people from using it.

Our society is based on knowledge and yet knowledge cannot be handled efficiently by the competitive system. In professional careers people are educated and then get a salary based roughly on the cost of their education. But knowledge cannot be charged for in this way. The major problem is how one allocates the use of knowledge once it has been obtained: how does one set up efficient mechanisms for developing it? One cannot rely on the market system to develop knowledge to the point where investments in knowledge production produce the same rate of return as other kinds of investments. Historically it has been a very hit-and-miss business. We relied on religious activities and private wealth to permit some people to support scientific research and enquiry. The results then became available and in fact were well advertised by those who discovered them. They were a by-product of the economy. It is only in the last twenty years or so that we have begun to think of knowledge as a basic public resource which requires public support in order to provide it on an adequate scale. But we don't know how to decide how much to provide. As I said, we have gone through a cycle in which we initially believed that any amount of money spent on science must be a good investment, up to the present period when some people question whether any money at all should be spent on science.

One of the problems for scientists is that having traded heavily on the previous period when they were universally regarded as public benefactors, they are still trying to do the same thing at a time when the public has become very suspicious of any argument on behalf of scientific knowledge. The public has begun to think about the adverse by-products of knowledge production rather than accepting an undemonstrated and unsupported claim that science must be good because of all it can do.

I have been engaged during my time on the Council for Scientific Policy in an attempt to try to provide some sort of quantitative measurement of the benefits of science. The idea that science must be good for you, and that therefore any amount of money the scientists claim as necessary should be provided, will no longer be accepted. So we have to find out what science does for society and particularly what benefits it confers. Many years ago I wrote a paper on this subject in which I distinguished sharply between science as a consumption good and science as a production good.[1] Much of the past argument for science was essentially that civilization needs science; scientific performance is a demonstration of civilization quality, therefore we should support science so that we will have scientists who will make discoveries that will be advertised to the world and show how good we are. The trouble with that argument is that one can say the same thing about the Olympic Games. Some countries have invested heavily in training Olympic stars simply because of the demonstration effect. The problem for science on that argument is that the vast mass of humanity can understand that some girls are more beautiful than others and if one of their girls wins a beauty competition this scores for their country, and if some of their men have longer legs than others they may win a race, and this also scores for them. But they have difficulty understanding intellectual competitions. It is pretty difficult to shift the competition from the purely physical, which everybody understands, to the mental, which is a very abstruse interest indeed. The argument for the support of science as a means of demonstrating cultural achievement is very weak and unlikely to gain much support.

We are left with the economic argument that science is beneficial because it improves the productive capacity of the economy. The major difficulty with that argument is that scientists don't understand economics. They want to claim the whole of the output as a contribution of science regardless of the cost of the capital equipment and the training of the people and so forth that is involved in producing it. The result is they look silly, not just to economists but to the public in general. The public knows that knowledge is only one part of the input—someone also has to do some work. They realize that the work costs something and that one should not claim for science the benefits of the work.

We have been trying in our research project to get at the question of the economic value of science. Obviously man has a higher standard of living now than when he was a nomad roaming the plains and surviving on raw meat and this is because of an increase in his knowledge. The question is how far the difference between us and primitive man is accounted for by more knowledge or by a certain amount of self-restraint in the matter of increasing the population. How much of the increase can we attribute to specifiable expenditure on science as we know it? People can get smarter and more able without any scientific help whatsoever. It is well known in economic history that productivity in agriculture roughly doubled between 1400 and 1600 without any new inventions at all. It was just that human beings by experience learned to do better. There was no scientist there enjoying a large grant and a high sophistication factor to tell them how to do it—they just learned by themselves.

What can we attribute to expenditure on science in its formal, organized, professional way? We don't know, for two reasons. The first reason lies in the nature of science itself. We have made quite a bit of progress on this problem, though it is a sort of sideways progress. Scientific knowledge is a pool; scientists keep throwing fish into it and other people keep trying to catch fish out of it which they can then eat in the form of applied research and development. The trouble is that one cannot identify who threw the fish in with a particular fish that somebody catches. Not only that, but fish are thrown in which die before anybody catches them and then they are no use to the world at all. Scientific discoveries made before their time simply die and have to be rediscovered. This characteristic of the results of scientific research as a general pool of knowledge makes it very difficult to say that certain research was done at this point and then forty years later an application was made, or that if only we could have had that discovery one year earlier the discovery of how to use it would have been made one year earlier and so society would have been better off. One just can't tell. Sometimes accelerating the discovery means waste because nobody wants it. There are famous stories in science about people toasting each other in champagne in the belief that what they discovered wouldn't be of any use to anybody ever, only to be refuted when the Americans made an atomic bomb out of it.

This first problem is that the nature of science is not a linear progression in which society receives specific economic benefit from a specific discovery, so that if it could only accelerate the discovery it would accelerate the benefit. If it were a linear progression, we could tell how much to spend on science by asking how much faster scientific discovery promoted by government support would lead us to eventual economic benefit.

A related question is one that is not understood by any national government I know. This is that because of the long time lag involved in the utilization of science there really is no reason why anybody should spend any money. Somebody else will spend the money and then you receive the benefit. The converse is that you may spend a lot of money on science and somebody else gets the benefit. That apparently is what usually happens to British science.

The other problem, the economic reason, is that precisely because of the nature of knowledge as a public good there is no place in the economy where one can obtain a measure of the benefit. In applied research, where a company spends money on a research and development project and then makes a bigger profit, one can relate the bigger profit to the expenditure. But for basic research one can't do this at all. This is partly because of the way we do our national income accounting. All government expenditure on scientific research is entered at cost, but there is no accounting of the benefit; one enters the salaries of the scientists, the cost of equipment and so forth but there is no measure of the benefit if there is any—which there may not be, of course. The only place where the benefits of expenditure on science show up is in the higher profits of companies, where the contribution of science is difficult to sort out from other reasons why there may be higher profits, and in royalties for patents and copyrights and so forth. Obviously this is a very small part of the total picture and it doesn't at all capture the benefit of basic research, which can't be captured in identifiable incomes but which contributes to the pool of knowledge in which people can fish.

The result of all this is that one can have a belief that somehow science is important to civilization economically but one has no method of measuring how important it is. That means that one has no method of coming to grips with the question of how much money the taxpayer should pay for this activity, given that he is not too keen on paying money to support his own scientific Olympic team. If he has to support it he has to believe somehow that it is going to increase his economic welfare. We can't really prove that it does, or at least we can't show how much it does. Consequently the thing becomes a matter of opinion and, as I said at the beginning, we face this cycle in which, from an excess of belief in the value of science to society, we have moved perhaps to an excess of disbelief. Either way we don't know where we are.

That is about the only message economics can give you: we are still confused, but we are confused at a much higher level of understanding.

Bibliography

1. JOHNSON, H. G. (1965) Federal support of basic research: some economic issues. In *Basic Research and National Goals*, pp. 20–34. Washington, D.C.: National Academy of Sciences Report to the Committee on Science and Astronautics, U.S. House of Representatives.

See pp. 183—190 for further discussion of points raised in this paper.

Scientific research and long-term economic growth

GAUTAM MATHUR

As an economist from a developing country I want to attempt to formulate certain guidelines which can be followed when resources are allocated for scientific research. In the long run these principles should enable the contribution of science to human welfare to be analysed. I shall briefly describe the economic background, with reference to the contribution of science to growth, and then suggest how resources should be distributed over the fields of science with reference to the needs of society. I shall also discuss the responsibility that scientists have of ensuring that no wide divergence from the ideal distribution takes place in practice.

Golden-age growth

The question of what science can best contribute to civilization can be answered only if we first determine what sort of society we want. A state of equilibrium has long been sought by economists, and may be used as a starting point.

Over the last hundred and fifty years classical economists have produced many different descriptions of equilibrium states of growth. But these were mostly dismal pictures of stationary states. In modern economics the equilibrium pertains to an economy in growth. A comprehensive concept of steady growth equilibrium called the Optimum Golden Age[6a] combines the elements of the von Neumann path, the natural rate of growth defined by Sir Roy Harrod[2] and the Golden Age analysed by Professor Joan Robinson.[9] This concept describes a long-term state in which, if all profits are invested and rates of growth of population and of neutral technical progress are kept constant, the distribution of labour between consumption and investment sectors remains unchanged, relative shares of wages and profits are maintained at the same level and wages rise at the same rate as technical progress takes place, while the rate of profit stays constant. With full employment, such a state has the highest consumption per person a society can provide while it remains in long-term equilibrium. It is a state in which the potential standard of living, with the latest available technology, is being fully achieved in each time span. In the golden age, of course, output consists not just of material goods but also of cultural activities, the products of which help individuals to relax and then to work and live better.

In my analysis of planned development, I have taken this golden age as the objective of all countries entering the field of economic development.[10] The type of growth seen in rapidly developing countries on the path towards this golden age is a form known for some time now as 'platinum-age growth', because it has a higher rate of growth (though at a lower wage level) than in the golden age with the relevant technology.[4] These two types of growth are the components of the modern theory of the approach towards—and, later, growth in—a state of economic growth-equilibrium.

This state of equilibrium is taken as referring to a closed and self-sufficient technological system. But when international trade is considered, all the trading sub-economies linked by the exchange of goods have to be regarded as constituting a single unified economy. In my opinion, the concept of the golden age as a desirable state is, therefore, fundamentally a concept of a unified humanity, and it will become meaningful only when we extend the theory to a real world in which humanity as a whole will be in that state.

Humanity as a living organism

In a unified and integrated society, the individual members must, in their own long-term self-interest, have the same aim as the society as a whole: survival of the economy as a whole as a social living organism. Like other living organisms, this one must convert intakes of matter and energy into outputs and try to survive with minimum human effort in the long run.[11] It would be in keeping with the aim of least average effort per unit time for human society to survive by changing its structure through new forms of production, the initial effort of investment for which would turn out to be very low when averaged over a long time.

A living organism operating in an unchanging environment does not immediately find it necessary to change its structure, and it survives with least effort through repetition of actions, routine and habit formation by its individual members. But it may then perish when the external environment unexpectedly changes. A society which can innovate, acquire new skills and hand them on through education to the next generation will survive changes in the environment by its ability to change its capital structure. Thus human society as a living organism must guide itself into a state of dynamic balance in which there is, on the one hand, repetition of actions and, on the other, action which keeps that society highly adaptable to a changing environment, through a continuous change of structure—that is, through innovations and through technical improvements which lead to higher output per person, or to higher quality of the output. This is partly expressed through an equilibrium state of golden-age growth with technical progress and partly through a sector where disequilibrium is purposely created to prevent human capacities from congealing to a condition of inertia in which the members of the society become attuned to life becoming ever easier. Hence the state of equilibrium with which we started the analysis has to be amended to a state of dynamic balance[5] as a model of ideal long-term growth in which steady growth equilibrium and purposive disequilibrium coexist.

The societies which can be called civilizations in the Toynbeean sense grew by adjusting to a changing environment. But in spite of technological adjustments they ceased to flourish when they could not reconcile their dissensions. Present civilizations face the threat of annihilation from another total war, and the balance now based on equality of arms is a very precarious one. These civilizations can ensure their own survival only by forming a supranational entity which will be the embodiment of human society as a living organism. This 'Central Subject'[1] will have mechanisms of effective checks and balances but not necessarily a system of totalitarian control. Nevertheless it must have an effective coordinating agency which will have supravening authority over many matters now under the jurisdiction of national governments.

The place of science

What can science do towards achieving the type of growth needed for the formation and survival of human society as a social living organism, a society in which the 'Central Subject' will have a mechanism whereby its components (which are themselves living organisms) coordinate their actions with that of others to grow in a state of dynamic balance?

First of all, we should observe that at present we have a conglomeration of nations and international institutions rather than the living organism of an international community. Social scientists and natural scientists will have to coordinate their research efforts into the methodology of creating this new living organism, though unfortunately the social sciences are themselves in a very uneven state of development and have to be restructured and developed to a state where they can perform the function imposed on them.

Secondly, in the world economy, disparities in living standards must be reduced if mankind is to form a living organism. No country can have a golden-age economy on its own, for unless the rest of the world has reached the same standard that economy will only be in a pseudo-golden age. The means of achieving equality may be subject to controversy, but we must accept that the goal is an egalitarian society.

Since, before a state of dynamic balance can be reached (and as a component of that state), the golden age has to be created for all and not just a few, national goals of science are irrelevant when allocations for research are determined: the goals must be international.

Further gains in advanced countries must therefore be sacrificed in favour of help for the developing countries. This help must not be merely material—the suggested contribution of one per cent of gross national product is in any case wholly inadequate: aid must also include higher-grade brainpower in advanced countries paying attention to the scientific and socioeconomic problems of the underdeveloped countries.

Having postulated the kind of society we want, we can now search for the kind of science that society needs.

Scientific research is usually classified as either applied research or basic research, but the latter may usefully be further subdivided into applied basic and pure basic research. Applied research has an immediate application in view, and its results can be assessed quantitatively. Applied basic research is theoretical or experimental work carried out without the thought of immediate or direct application, but with a view to solving some questions on which applied research would be based. Pure basic research, on the other hand, has no visible ulterior motive. It is conducted purely to satisfy human curiosity about the nature of the physical world. However, in practice an unknown percentage of pure basic research yields results which can be used either to help or to harm mankind.

In basic research the benefits of general productivity flow in the long run from efforts spread over many fields. But in applied research one may concentrate upon improvement in particular lines.

Optimum growth rate

The given resources available for applied research may be used to improve the physical productivity per man-equipment team in the equipment-producing sector. This is termed *capital-saving technical progress*. It increases the self-reproductivity of the machine-building sector and decreases its value in relation to consumption goods. This is one of the systems capable of giving a steady rate of growth. Alternatively, the available funds might be used to increase physical productivity per man-equipment team in the production of consumer goods. This is termed *neutral technical progress*. It leaves the self-reproductivity of the machine-building sector unaffected.

At a given wage rate, it is the technological matrices and the quantum of changes evoked in them by a given allocation of resources to applied research that determine whether the rate of growth obtained is higher through neutral technical progress or through capital-saving technical progress. Thus we can ascertain whether it is more worthwhile to use given resources for one type of technical progress or the other. We can determine the same thing for a given growth rate by looking for the method which yields a higher standard of living.

Next let us see what happens when the amount available for research can be varied. In golden-age growth the pace of growth at full employment is composed of the rates of growth of population and of output per person. The pace of technical progress thus governs the rate of growth of the economy, but technical progress itself depends on the particular type of applied research on which efforts are being concentrated. An optimum equilibrium for applied research can therefore be determined. In a model[6b] which combines the analytical technique of von Neumann and some ideas of Professor Joan Robinson and Professor Nicholas Kaldor,[3] I postulated that technical progress depends on how much is allocated to scientific research out of the surplus of the economy. A high rate of investment in physical and human capital requires a high rate of surplus out of which it can be maintained, given the propensity of entrepreneurs—both private and state—to invest out of profits. A high rate of surplus, on the other hand, is created by increases in productivity brought about by investment in research, both applied and basic. When the rate of increase of knowledge in terms of productivity increase equals the rate of actual increase of productivity through application, a state of equilibrium is achieved, on the basis of a given proportion of the surplus being spent on research. If this proportion is varied we get different equilibrium rates of growth, the maximum of which gives the optimum growth-rate in a golden age.

Research priorities and the scientist

The optimum growth of the golden age is likely to make the economy unfit to deal with sudden change, especially as people become less inclined to exert physical effort as standards of living rise. If a society is to survive, its sub-groups must therefore be kept adaptable by being made to undergo, in rotation, periods of intense constructive activity or disequilibrium. In a state of dynamic balance, scientific discoveries should help higher productivity to be obtained both in the areas of steady-growth equilibrium and in the areas of purposive disequilibrium. Resources used for the disequilibrium sector are not wasted, since it is in this sector that the technology of the remote future is to be built and manpower trained to deal with that technology. In periods of transition from one state of golden-age equilibrium to another at a higher level, the areas of intense exertion or disequilibrium would be relatively more important than those in equilibrium, and their rate of growth would be higher, an indication of a platinum age. Hence, in a dynamic-balance state, golden age and platinum age will not only coexist but will also alternate in importance according to whether the next technological leap is being taken or its fruits are being enjoyed.

However, the type of activity required for purposive disequilibrium by countries in a pseudo-golden age need not be highly capital-intensive. While there is poverty in the world around them, affluent societies can maintain a high degree of adaptability in their individual members by sending them to exercise their brainpower and undergo physical exertion in underdeveloped countries, so converting the limited golden age into a golden age for the whole of humanity. But the Sport of Kings—warfare—is far from being the ideal way to provide purposive disequilibrium. Nor is space exploration a meaningful adventure when so much remains to be done on this earth, although science policy-makers in the areas of affluence of the pseudo-golden age have tended to concentrate on such types of research, which show no regard for social priority for most of humanity. The scientist believes in the ideal of seeking Truth, but it can be sought equally well, and more usefully, in studies of the causes of cancer or the effects of protein mal-nutrition. When there are a million ways of seeking truth, and resources for only a few thousand, social priority for forming a human society out of dis-organized components must be the criterion.

An example of a socially useful platinum-age research project held up by lack of funds and badly allocated skills comes from the area called the Deccan trap in Southern India. Until the Koyna disaster a few years ago this plateau was thought to be relatively free of earthquakes, but now geophysicists think that if dams are built to provide essential hydroelectric supplies, the seepage from large masses of water may cause slippage of rocks affected by water and thus contribute to the occurrence of earthquakes in that region. Hydroengineers think otherwise. Geophysical and geological investigation is needed on a vast scale to locate safe sites for dams. The authorities issue reassuring statements but no decisive research is carried out; in the meantime either dam-building continues, with its attendant dangers, or the agricultural and industrial breakthrough is delayed for lack of water and electricity. Many thousands of such research projects can be found all over the world. In most cases the resources needed represent a minute fraction of the amounts already spent on some favoured fields in pseudo-golden-age science.

Useful results in scientific research with social priority can come either directly from research concentrated in a particular field, or indirectly, as the unplanned and unpredictable side-effects of effort in any field. Although the latter method is suitable for basic research, the former method gives quicker results when a particular problem has to be tackled and is the method which should be used for the many bottlenecks to growth in a platinum age. One of the arguments in support of space research is that the spin-off from it helps discoveries in random fields of direct human interest. This is a valid argument when used to support the balanced allocation of resources over a wide area for basic research, but here it is being used to justify concentrated research in a limited field. If one argues that money spent on research for space exploration might help terrestrial geophysics or wave mechanics or magnetism, then one can equally well say that spending on wave mechanics might help in random discoveries for the other three fields, and so the argument applies to expenditure on any other field. This supports the case for a balanced spread of investments.

On the other hand, if one argues that space research pays off in that field mainly, this favours the unbalanced distribution of funds, and the argument is not that it helps the other activities unexpectedly, but that research in that field helps itself, according to expectations. As concentrated spending on space research has indeed helped itself substantially, therefore, all that is proved is that any other activity towards which funds were to be directed in a massive programme would also have a fair chance of helping growth of that activity.

The distribution of research funds should depend on the engineering or technological background an economy already possesses and priorities should not, as suggested by Professor Polanyi,[8] be determined by the favourite fields of eminent scientists. The aim should be to enable the economy to reach the optimum rate of growth. In different countries this will be achieved by different types of investment, depending on local conditions. In some the choice will be capital-saving improvements in heavy machinery; in others neutral technical progress will give the best results.

But it may be emphasized that the long-term effect of any particular research activity on the economy as a whole is the only way to evaluate the benefit of expenditure on research. The ratio of immediate money benefit to cost of research in a particular field is a misleading criterion from the standpoint of social usefulness.[7]

Disparities in living standards must be reduced within countries as well as between countries. At present, in underdeveloped countries applied research is often used to help the more profitable industries which produce goods for the richer sectors of the population. The upper ten per cent or so of the population continue to receive benefits, while the rest fall further behind. Science policy-makers in these countries must ask themselves what kind of civilization they are trying to create and whom they want to help by their efforts. It is not enough to answer 'We are trying to develop industry'. The problems to be solved, if there is to be economic growth with social justice, are those dealing with the provision of basic necessities for the poverty-stricken masses. The techniques which will help this process in countries which have very large populations in relation to the available capital goods of superior efficiency are not necessarily those which are optimum for advanced countries.

To further the platinum age of transition, the scientists and science policy-makers should encourage proper and relevant fields of research. But we can observe that the motivation of scientists does not coincide with the idealism required for platinum-age science, and leadership is lacking to create the necessary enthusiasm. Young scientists prefer to turn to the science of the pseudo-golden age rather than face the truly challenging problems of platinum-age science. Labour is not scarce in developing countries, yet it is easier to have a costly labour-saving combine harvester devised than to have a cheap plough improved which would benefit more people at far lower real cost in terms of use of scarce types of capital, e.g. heavy equipment. Most capital equipment used in advanced countries no longer presents intellectual and scientific obstacles: it is the technologist and the high-grade mechanic who deal with the problems now. The challenges come from problems for which computers and other toys cannot be used. But sensational or well-paid projects are the ones which attract many scientists—who may therefore be classified not as seekers after Truth but on the same level as skilled wage-earners, best-selling authors or pop singers. Science of this kind cannot claim economic support on the grounds that it provides freedom of thought or enhances culture.

The scientist who does pure basic research sometimes claims exceedingly large support in terms of skills and materials just because he is virtuously inclined towards choosing to seek knowledge for its own sake. But more valid claims for pure basic research are based on the social criteria. Firstly, this research keeps alive habits of mind that society needs for long-term survival; secondly, some of the investment pays off unexpectedly in the form of benefits for society; and thirdly, the springs of knowledge will dry up but for this expenditure. However, humanity as a whole is not yet affluent enough to support 'science for the scientists' sake'.

As members of the community, scientists are responsible for examining the wider effects of their own activities, especially as they deal with materials and discoveries which change traditional patterns of activity. Many discoveries of science, even the useful ones, have had unfortunate side-effects and the layman blames science for all this. This is unfair, for it is the nature of the scientific process that some remedial actions produce side-effects which require further remedial action. Science grows out of this very process of having more problems to solve after they have been created by an earlier scientific advance. This is also how civilization itself grows, according to the challenge-and-response theory.

The essential aspect of the scientific system is that these further challenges must not be left unattended. The criticism of scientists as individuals is that, like operatives in other fields, many of them seek jobs where someone pays them a high salary to solve problems the employer chooses. They therefore tend to work in fields where the money is provided by organizations (both private and governmental agencies) interested in relatively short-terms gains. Here the system of further correction of side-effects does not work efficiently, because it is not in anyone's immediate interest to deal with these effects. The harmful effects then become an entrenched nuisance. This situation should not be allowed.

The expansion of defence research has produced a most unstable political balance in the world, and if this is upset at any time our civilization will cease to exist. Military scientists have found no way of collaborating with politicians and sociologists to stabilize this balance by making it rest on considerations other than the knife-edge of the nuclear deterrent and similar weapons. The safety factors in this balance are so small as to be unthinkable in any business or profession other than politics, yet defence scientists hand over lethal materials to authorities who themselves have no mechanism for firmly controlling the uses to which these will be put.

In these circumstances, further research on such weapons is not morally free from collective blame for scientists as a community. In the modern system of research, individuals cannot easily ensure the proper use of their work, especially if they are engaged in basic research whose side-effects are unpredictable. The only safe way to control the use of their work is for scientists and social scientists to form an international front and collectively withdraw their services from such work when any of their results are in danger of being applied in a way that could harm human society. This would effectively curb the misuse of science by political authorities; but the lack of support for international scientific organizations which stress moral issues rather than working conditions also seems to indicate that most scientists work for material motives rather than idealistic ones.

Conclusions

The rate of growth of the economy as a whole is the criterion to be used when one is assessing the allocations to be made for research in particular fields which are in a state of transition, or platinum-age growth, moving towards a state of dynamic balance. The beneficial effect of concentrated applied basic research and applied research, in particular sectors, is even more clearly visible here than in golden-age growth. Appropriate weight must therefore be given to research affecting such bottlenecks in the economy; but for pure basic research scientific resources should be spread out widely over many fields (which, however, does not necessarily imply that funds should be equally divided among all the existing industries).

In the platinum age, the creation of the living organism of humanity calls for the reduction of disparities among (and also within) different economic classes, nations and civilizations, and for closer integration of these sectors. In advanced countries technical progress in some rapidly advancing sectors must be slowed down in favour of technical progress which will help the production of goods needed by poorer countries. Technical aid is to be regarded neither as charity nor as a political inducement nor as a means of getting rid of unwanted goods, but as a means of creating the living organism of a world community where distinctions will no longer exist between rich and poor people, or developed and underdeveloped nations.

The true scientist, like the medical doctor, the artist or the priest, belongs to no nation other than the world community. His ultimate aim should be the establishment of an undivided and egalitarian society. If that aim is to be achieved without violence, scientific research must be given proper orientation and purpose, so that its goal can be reached peacefully and democratically. This is the contribution that natural and social scientists can make. Failure will mean disorderly transition between different economic states and international conflicts, with consequent distress and the danger that human society will disintegrate.

Discussion

Long: In your graph [not printed] showing scattered areas of affluence a large area at the bottom did not link up with the functional line, Professor Mathur. Does that mean you have no idea of what the function is?

Mathur: The functional line connected the superior techniques known to the world at various degrees of capital intensity and wage rates. The Y-axis referred to productivity per man employed and is termed the production function. Only the superior techniques of the production function need to be aimed at in a long-term production plan. The whole function rises upwards as technical progress takes place. A country which has achieved the golden age, with full employment and immediate utilization of the scientific knowledge available in any decade, would be at the upper limits.

The so-called advanced countries are nowhere near this ideal state, and only a small proportion of their economy has peaks of productivity which would be high up on the production function. Average Indian productivity is even lower down the scale. Some places in India are highly developed but these pockets do not represent the country as a whole. These are small areas in India which, on an ordinary definition of self-sustained growth, took off twenty to thirty years ago, but the rest of the country is still in a state of extreme underdevelopment. A fundamental difficulty about the Rostowian concept[3] of take-off is the unit of study. Is it the whole economy or one of its parts that has to be shown to have taken off? If we talk of the British economy having taken off, then Great Britain formed a minute portion of its Empire, like a high pyramid of productivity in a wilderness of underdevelopment. Where is the take-off of the Commonwealth as a whole? So on a proper definition of take-off the whole area at the bottom of such a scatter diagram has to get into self-sustained growth, and ultimately link up with the production function of superior techniques.

Weinberg: The problem of India, in a sense, epitomizes the problem of the entire world, but I think every scientist is basically hopeful that the problem of India can be solved. Do you believe this, and do you believe that somehow science will come to the rescue, Professor Mathur? That is a very big question, but in some sense it is the overriding question.

Mathur: As regards the purely technological problems we are quite hopeful for India. However, it is not scientific research in general but the type of scientific research which is most relevant. What is needed from research is a much improved type of technology which can be used on a small scale by the small operator in a mixed economy. Scientific and technological research used for an intermediate technology that conserves the scarce resources of heavy capital would be the most helpful in India. We also need applied basic research in science in order to sustain the applied technological research, and very much the same in the social sciences. Underdeveloped countries need much more aid for these purposes from advanced countries. Some favourite projects in advanced countries will have to be sacrificed if more research funds and the attention of top scientists are to be diverted to the problems of research in underdeveloped countries.

Roche: One of Professor Johnson's many *boutades* was to the effect that because of the lag in application there is no need to spend money on basic science and we should let somebody else do it. In fact we in Latin America and in many undeveloped countries have been following just that strategy. The results have not been particularly happy. We are consoled to some extent by the fact that we have a large harvest to reap, but we are rather tired of always being called countries of the future. We would like to be countries of the present. There must be some psychosocial relationship between doing science and applying it. Empirically it seems to work out that those countries that have created science have applied it.

Rathenau: Both Professor Mathur and Professor Johnson have cast some doubt on the immediately apparent usefulness of basic science. In industry nobody can immediately acquire useful power from basic science. It is better to start from some product or development and later on add some basic science. Professor Johnson asked how we know that if we put a fish in the pool of knowledge somebody else won't make use of it. I would say that if we don't have people who keep themselves busy with the fundamentals of science we shall not be able to understand the implications of fundamental findings in the literature. It is necessary to do some work yourself in order to understand that of others. You cannot catch the fish other people put in the pool if you are not familiar with fish from doing basic research yourself. I know that in my own firm the diversification of our interests is intimately connected with basic research.

Weinberg: Professor Johnson and I were on a committee some five years ago when I first realized the depth of his antipathy towards scientists, if not towards science. Sometimes I think he must have been frightened at an early age by a scientist! In his paper he implied that scientists are not much involved in bringing to the attention of the public what economists call the externalities of science and of scientific events. Yet my own belief is that although economists have talked about externalities it always made them very uncomfortable. It seems to me that the intense involvement today with externalities, with the side-effects of detergents, say, in fact does come from the scientific community. At the time the scientists were saying that detergents were a marvellous thing, the economists were saying the same thing.

Johnson: I wasn't frightened by a scientist at an early age, but at a much later age I was appalled at the ignorance of social science displayed by scientists, and the errors into which they fell when they discussed things they didn't understand.

The point I made was not that scientists didn't discuss externalities but that they, like everybody else, welcomed detergents when these were invented, then later they found out that these things had side-effects. We have no social mechanism which requires anyone to think about all the effects of a new result before he publishes it, or to say what they are. That would be an internal discipline. There might be an external discipline in which a body of experts looked at every new scientific discovery and thought about its social implications, but the structure of science is such that the internal discipline is lacking.

One exception to that is the whole question of the atomic bomb and nuclear physics, where scientists have been appalled by the results of their own discoveries. But society has more problems than the discovery of nuclear science every two hundred years. The questions are the grass-roots kind of problem rather than major ones. One could argue in relation to the atomic bomb that the politicians were right and the scientists were wrong: the atomic bomb has contributed to the pacification of the world in spite of the scientists' worry that it might be used for genocide and destruction of the whole globe.

My main point was that science rewards you for a discovery which is immediately obviously beneficial, without asking you to think about what the side-effects might be. And because of the nature of science, which is a change in the knowledge we have, we have no social or political processes capable of judging it.

In England twenty-five years ago there was a lot of talk about the proper role of the expert in relation to government. One of the stupid phrases coined then in place of thinking was that experts should be on tap and not on top. This assumes that politicians are able to evaluate the implications of science, and that just is not so. In my paper I certainly did not want to imply that scientists don't become aware of the externalities, but that the process of first rewarding you for discovering something and then rewarding you for finding adverse externalities is not necessarily the best way for society to digest information.

In reply to Professor Roche, I am very suspicious of the whole notion that science somehow is essential to economic growth. We have plenty of data on science policy and expenditure on science and there is an inverse correlation between expenditure on science and economic growth. I wouldn't want to push that too far. When people talk about economic development they usually don't know what they are talking about. That applies to both laymen and professional economists and I am not going to pretend I know any better. We have to distinguish very sharply in our own minds, as sociologists and anthropological observers, between real economic growth and a definition of economic growth which says 'I want my country to be as important as other countries so that I can be as important as the guys from other countries'. That is not economic growth at all but simply a claim for unwarranted status. Economic development as I understand it is a matter of people who start from nowhere being able to get somewhere, and not a matter of those in charge of a society aggrandizing themselves. When people in Canada talk about science policy what they mean is that Canadian scientists should be supported on the same lavish scale as American scientists are and that they should be supported across the board. I see no reason why doing that for them will do anything for the average citizen of Canada, other than give him a new master class in the universities and research organizations. When people call it economic development I just don't believe it. I believe it is a tax on the poor for the benefit of the rich. If they want to pursue scientific activities let them go somewhere else, as I have done, where the public is stupid enough or rich enough to be able to afford people like me.

Long: Do you really wish to stand on a position that there is no relationship between science and economic growth?

Johnson: There is no relationship between the amount of money a particular country spends on the support of science and economic growth. The reason is that other countries spend their money, and obtain results that you can use, while you may spend your money very imprudently, with results that neither you nor anyone else can use.

Todd: In the state of the world today a country which is developing must apply technical knowledge. It would be wrong, however, if only for educational reasons, to say that countries should concentrate solely on the applied side and leave out pure science. I don't believe research in educational institutions needs to be supported any further than is necessary to ensure a proper supply of trained manpower, but up to that point support is essential.

Johnson: That is something we are coming to in our work. There are many interesting questions and we have to remember that we have scientific establishments which have been created virtually in the last half century or less. We know that they are getting high incomes but we have no evidence that they actually do any good for us. If a country has a university system which trains scientists who will then go out and work for industry, how important is it to have a big research enterprise associated with the university? That is the really important question which Great Britain will have to face in the next five years. The cost of having big research in science is going to be very high indeed. The government wants to expand the university system without increasing expenditure any more than it has to. Is research needed as part of the training or not? There is evidence[2] from the United States that research has been in conflict with education, that people have been bribed to do research instead of teach. At the high point in the mid-60s some of my colleagues were saying that it was a fantastic world in which people were bribed not to teach so that they could do research for the government.

Todd: That is not a matter Great Britain is only having to face now. The last report of the Advisory Council on Scientific Policy in 1964 spelt it out in the same terms. But how do you quantify it? You say you can't see a direct relationship between the amount of science and economic growth. If you are talking about pure science—and many people are when they talk about scientific research—then, although I can't really quantify it, I think one should go as far as is needed to ensure the supply of the right kind of manpower to industry in the required amount. But after that it is a very difficult question how much research should be done.

Johnson: I am in favour of home and motherhood too. The question is to define who are good mothers and who arent't!

Bloch: Can you give an example of a country that enjoys a high standard of living and does no research?

Johnson: I can't, but that is not the question. The question is, how much research is needed? And countries with higher standards of living may not need to do the amount of research they actually do. They may simply be spending some of their income on the production of scientific prestige.

Bloch: Let me put the question differently. Is spending money on science a consequence of a high standard of living, or is it the other way round?

Johnson: There is something to be said both ways. To some extent research depends on the availability of finance and a rich country can spend more money on it than a poor one. The military influence is also tremendously important. The United States has spent enormous amounts of money on scientific research. I was associated with George Kistiakowsky in an investigation of French science policy and the French were telling us all about how they would give priority to this, that and the other thing, and how they couldn't possibly rival the United States but they were going to try. Kistiakowsky picked out one item after another on the American science policy programme as technological development and not science; the items he picked were the French priorities. Among other things he said that putting a man on the moon was not science but engineering. The only reason the United States adopted that objective was because President Kennedy was ashamed of the Bay of Pigs. Most of us got lots of pleasure out of watching those guys land but we didn't think much of having to pay for it. It is a difficult subject really, because culture is a consumption good as well as a production good. You may well find yourself in a rich country spending lots of money on science purely, as the French put it, so that your people will participate in conferences at the highest level.

Mathur: The balance between basic research and applied research is very important in finding out whether scientific research has paid off or not. We should remember the British and German examples[4] of what happens when too much or too little, respectively, is invested in basic research. A balance has to be found at the international level, because otherwise countries concentrating on applied basic research and applied research will flourish by making free use of pure basic research done elsewhere, and the latter countries will have an ever-worsening balance of payments—no royalties are payable for the products of the brainpower and equipment they use for basic research.

Long: With a title as all-encompassing as *Civilization and Science*, we might quite reasonably put a good deal more effort into this question of science and technology in developing nations. It is too easy for us to say that science and technology are essentially international, and that once discoveries have been made they are available to everyone. That is wrong. The kinds of technology needed by developing nations at this point are quite different from those now being used by the United States and the United Kingdom. There is a serious problem of how to utilize science and technology as well as how to educate technologists to do the applying. The urgency of this is made clear by the so-called Green Revolution. The Green Revolution is a technologically successful revolution; it is going to spread, and some major social consequences are being generated by it, consequences which may be particularly difficult for some developing nations to handle.

Brock: Over several decades I have been giving advice on how to improve nutrition in developing areas. We have known for decades how to abolish malnutrition and undernutrition, but nobody does anything about it, or at least what is done is quite incommensurate with what is required. My problem is, what does a scientist do when he is asked the same question again and again by governments but his answer is never put into effect? Does he become an activist or does he say, 'I have told you, and I'll tell you again'?

Long: Or does he look for a different technological solution more acceptable to the government than the one they refused?

Shils: The place of science in underdeveloped countries can be discussed much more fruitfully and less hypocritically now than when such discussion began ten or fifteen years ago. In those days the scientists flattered both themselves and the underdeveloped countries. The scientists talked about the power of conferring such great benefits, through the use of their great knowledge, on underdeveloped countries, and they also told the underdeveloped countries that there really was not much to it—it was just a question of doing the work. People are beginning to get a little more sophisticated about that. The report which Dr Freeman and others prepared for the United Nations Economic and Social Council in 1969 (later published in abridged form in *Minerva*[1]) represents a certain turning-point and a greater degree of realism although I think it is still a bit too optimistic. More tough-mindedness is required there, particularly about the linkage which we take for granted between scientific research and technological application. Not enough attention has been paid to the preconditions of pure scientific research, or the creation of what is called 'scientific manpower', which means the creation of a certain state of mind which is necessary for the assimilation and development of technological devices and processes.

Bibliography

1. AGAR, W. E. (1951) *A Contribution to the Theory of the Living Organism.* Melbourne: Melbourne University Press.
2. HARROD, R. F. (1939) An essay on dynamic theory. *Economic Journal*, March, pp. 14–33 (see Eqn 1).
3. KALDOR, N. (1961) Capital accumulation and economic growth. In *The Theory of Capital*, pp. 177–222, ed. F. A. Lutz and D. C. Hague. London: Macmillan.
4. LITTLE, I. M. D. (1957) Classical growth. In *Oxford Economic Papers, 9*, 152–177.
5. MATHUR, G. (1959) Economics of the living organisms. In *Science and Culture (Calcutta), 24*, 349–363.
6. MATHUR, G. (1965) *Planning for Steady Growth:* (a) pp. 182–184; (b) pp. 312–319. Oxford: Basil Blackwell.
7. MATHUR, G. (1970) Dangers of cost-benefit analysis in scientific research evaluation. Remarks in *Proceedings of the National Seminar on Management of Scientific Re-*

search Laboratories, ed. Jitendra Singh. Hyderabad: Administrative Staff College of India. Mimeographed; to be published in book form.

8. POLANYI, M. (1962) The Republic of Science: its political and economic theory. *Minerva, 1*, No. 1, 54–73.
9. ROBINSON, J. (1956) *The Accumulation of Capital*, p. 99. London: Macmillan.
10. ROSTOW, W. W. (ed.) (1963) *The Economics of Take-off into Sustained Growth*, p. 309. London: Macmillan.
11. ZIPF, G. K. (1949) *Human Behaviour and the Principle of Least Effort*. New York: Addison-Wesley.

Discussion

1. [INSTITUTE OF DEVELOPMENT STUDIES AND SCIENCE POLICY RESEARCH UNIT, UNIVERSITY OF SUSSEX] (1971) Science in underdeveloped countries: world plan of action for the application of science and technology to development. *Minerva, 9*, No. 1, 101–121.
2. MACHLUP, F. (1962) *Production and Distribution of Knowledge in the United States*. Princeton, N.J.: Princeton University Press.
3. ROSTOW, W. W. (ed.) (1963) *The Economics of Take-off into Sustained Growth*. London: Macmillan.
4. WILLIAMS, B. R. (1964) Research and economic growth—what should we expect? *Minerva, 3*, No. 1, 57–71.

The need for a science of civilization

MASANAO TODA

The fact that we need a science of civilization is so obvious that I hesitate to emphasize it here. Surely few would disagree with me. How wonderful it would be to develop such a science *if we could*. Such an assertion places me in the awkward position of advocating the obvious. However, it often serves a good end to have a persistent idiot keep mumbling 'The king is naked', particularly if winter is approaching and the king is likely to die of exposure or pneumonia unless he is properly clothed at once.

So you see that I am one of the pessimists, who characterize the future of civilization in black paint alone, who overkill mankind with all kinds of disasters—nuclear wars, overpopulation, famines, pollution, and what not—while disagreeing among themselves as to whose evil is the mightiest. Like other pessimists I, too, have my own diagnosis of the disease process inherent in the present civilization and I, too, have my own advice on how to combat it. And the name of the miracle medicine with which I propose to save the king is the science of civilization.

First, let me provide a diagnosis. In fact, I don't mean that civilization is sick or diseased in any way. In only mean that it is in danger. And this danger derives from the acceleration of social processes. Is it necessary to demonstrate the fact of acceleration? Perhaps not. In any society where important social indicators like gross national product (GNP), population and many others are discussed in terms of their *growth rates*, one can deduce that social processes are accelerating. For example, let me compare the lives of my Japanese contemporaries with that of my great-grandfather. He was born a *samurai* and died a *samurai*, and he would never have dreamed that the society he lived in and its social institutions could be any different. My grandfather experienced the *Meiji* revolution when all his beliefs must have been over-turned; but any experience as shattering as this would have happened only

192   *M. Toda*

once in his whole lifetime. On the other hand, both my father's generation and
mine had to revise our beliefs and value systems every ten years, on average;
and the environment we live in, for instance the houses and cities, apparently
has little in common with the environment in which we were born. I don't
mean that life in the past was uneventful. Wars, accidents, fires, famines—
most of these are old, familiar, recurrent crises. Today, however, changes are
quick and irreversible, and crises often have unfamiliar and unprecedented
characteristics.

So let me take the acceleration as a fact. But is it temporary or permanent?
Such a question is absurd, however. Someone demonstrated by curvilinear
extrapolation that some of these social indicators will reach infinity before the
year 2000. Obviously this is impossible and the acceleration will inevitably
slow down. But how? There are two ways. The acceleration of a high-speed
sports car may be arrested by depressing the brake pedal, or by an accident.
It is true that, at least in the so-called developed countries, we have so far
enjoyed the acceleration of this sports car named civilization. However, some
of the passengers, cowards like myself, have begun to feel a little uneasy
about the speed it has acquired. The vision through the front window becomes
blurred, and as a result, one observes another unprecedented event: that many
serious adults are beginning to argue seriously about the future of mankind!
This scene may look comical, but it may foreshadow the panic of the majority.
Sooner or later most passengers will begin to realize that no one knows the
location of the brake pedal, or even that of the steering wheel, of this super-
automated machine. Since they cannot jump off this accelerating vehicle, the
first thing they will do in the ensuing panic, human nature being what it is,
will be to attack directly the vital parts of the car, either the engine or the
carburettor. And it requires little imagination to recognize that the engine of
the present civilization is 'technology', and the carburettor feeding the engine
is 'science'. Destruction of the engine of the carburettor of a sports car accelerating at high speed is fatal. The car is likely to blow up. And should there
be any injured survivors left after the explosion, they could perhaps console
themselves by observing the ruined car named civilization and acknowledging,
'Now at last we are free from acceleration and pollution. Let's walk slowly'.

So this is my contribution to the school of pessimism. Whether or not you
believe that such a black prediction will come true, I think you will agree
with me that it is the duty of the passengers, or at least some of them, to know
more about the structure and functioning of the vehicle in which they are
riding. While there is still some time left, we should try hard to establish the
science of civilization. This science will not only give us radar equipment to
improve our forward vision, but it will also enable us to control the course

and the acceleration of the car. I am by no means contending that acceleration is evil in itself. Denying acceleration would be equivalent to denying the basic virtues of man. However, there is no doubt that acceleration must be put under the control of mankind for the benefit of mankind.

Now that I have uttered this nice slogan, I feel obliged to reply to the cynic who will say: 'It would be wonderful to have such a science. But you are a psychologist who has hardly succeeded in explaining the behaviour of even a single man. How brave you are to propose a science of such a complicated entity as civilization, which is a product of billions of people, alive and dead'. I would reply that the complexity in the behaviour of an object is not necessarily a reflection of the number of its constituent elements. If it were, then physics would have been the most hopeless science of all—and I was a physicist before becoming a psychologist. So, if the number of constituent elements is the only obstacle to obtaining a science of civilization, we may happily dismiss it as a fallacy. Unfortunately, however, the real difficulties seem to lie somewhere else. Otherwise, it is inconceivable that the avaricious breed called scientists would have so long missed the chance of preying upon such a fascinating subject as civilization, and of digesting it into a neat set of formulae. So the first step towards this science must be to discover the real cause of the difficulties, for, if one can believe what some optimistic philosophers say, a problem is half solved once one knows what it really consists of.

One of the difficulties, which I think crucial, is that it is hard for us to look at civilization in the right way. Let me find an analogy. We psychologists often use so-called 'ambiguous figures' for classroom demonstration purposes. Such a figure is one that doesn't make sense at all, at first glance, but appears as a jumble of meaningless blocks and lines. Then after one has looked at it for a while, one suddenly says 'I've got it!' The proper structure of the figure is there, without any ambiguities. The figure is entirely meaningful, and one can no longer recall the old ambiguities.

For the moment civilization is a gigantic ambiguous figure. We can all look at it because we are in the middle of it. But however long and hard we may look at it, no one has ever said 'I've got it!' with utter conviction. But remember that we are looking at our civilization from inside that civilization. It is as if we were rubbing our eyes against a picture, picking up only minute details, so no wonder the moment of revelation has never come.

Let me put it in another way. The science of physics was first developed at the macroscopic level and then gradually advanced down into the realm of microscopic entities. The reason why it has taken that course is no mystery. We can see an apple with the naked eye, but not the atoms inside it. Both man and apples are macroscopic objects, but with the science of civilization, the situation is reversed. We can see the atoms of civilization, but it is hard to conceive what civilization looks like as a whole. Does it look like an apple? Unfortunately no one has invented a macroscope. So the difficulty is that, for us, the macroscopic concepts needed to construct the science of civilization are hard to come by.

There is another source of difficulty, equally grave. We, the observers of civilization, are also a part of that civilization. But man as a being is basically utilitarian: he does not observe what he does not need to, or what he does not want to. This has seldom been a serious problem in the natural sciences, but as a psychologist I know very well that even a scientist cannot be entirely free from his *personal* beliefs and value systems in evaluating scientific hypotheses, and that he may turn a blind eye towards facts which may go against his personal interests.

Compared to these two major sources of difficulties, the others appear relatively minor and easier to overcome. For instance, this science cannot be based upon data obtained from large-scale controlled experiments. However, we already have large amounts of data in the form of historical documents. Indeed human history can be considered as an experiment on the grand scale unintentionally conducted for the benefit of the science of civilization. Even though the Experimenter (with a capital E) who conducted this experiment obviously had no idea of controlled experiments, and even though the Experimenter's human assistants who wrote the observation reports were appallingly poorly trained in the disciplines of the science of civilization, still there is information awaiting reprocessing by 'civilization scientists' to confirm or disprove their hypotheses. Of course, the sheer bulk of the information with which this science should deal will pose another difficulty. Obviously no existing computer can handle it. However, this is a difficulty that money and technology can solve, and so it will be solved as soon as the realization dawns on people that the destiny of mankind is at stake.

Two important points should be made about the nature of the predictions with which the science of civilization will provide us. First, the predictions should all be conditional in nature. For instance, they should be conditional on what people want to do about civilization today, allowing them to choose their own futures. They should also be conditional upon very important scientific breakthroughs, technological innovations and similar social events which will critically influence the future course of our civilization. Technically, the occurrence of these events may be dealt with by models based on the laws of chance, but the fact remains that our future may take an entirely different course depending on exactly when a particularly important event takes place.

If these uncertainties are taken seriously, it will soon become obvious that predictions for more than a few years ahead are hopeless if they are made by the ordinary method of extrapolation. This will be true even when the method is improved drastically by the science of civilization. No extrapolation method, however elaborate, can exhaust all the factors that might influence our civilization. It must at least assume that all the factors left out will remain constant or stable. Civilization is an organized whole, and world civilization today is spreading and unifying all the local civilizations with ever-increasing speed. No assumption could be more wrong than that of stability. An alternative method to this sort of extrapolation is to take civilization as a whole and try to find out where it will eventually stabilize. If one can somehow define a generalized potential energy for a society, a stable society will be characterized by its local minimum. Once a set of such solutions is found, our long-range predictions may be made by indicating which of these solutions we are now heading towards, and how much shift of course is currently within our control.

So much for the need for and difficulties involved in the science of civilization. To complete the story, it is of course desirable to go one step forward and prove that this science is obtainable. Regrettably, the impossibility of proving this is obvious, and as a substitute I should like to present some of my working hypotheses, or rather images, concerning it. I do this only because I think even the worst images will be better than none, although I have to suppress a fleeting suspicion that this supposition may be vastly mistaken.

Since the primary purpose of my attempt is to obtain some useful macroscopic notions of the principal dynamics of society or civilization, I must drastically simplify my argument, sometimes even to the point of absurdity. So let me happily announce that to begin with I have simplified man into an agent who transforms energy into work according to some master programme characteristic to himself. The notion of energy I use here is not that of the conserved energy of physics. Rather, it is more or less our everyday notion of energy that is consumed. I think it will eventually be possible to put this notion of consumable energy on a sounder base by generalizing the notion of negative entropy or free energy in thermodynamics. For the time being, however, allow me to define it indirectly as the energy that man can turn into work.

For a very long time the major supply of this energy to man was through his food. The use of energy was also limited mostly to the obtaining of food. The cycle was thus closed in the simplest possible way. There must, however, have been fluctuations in the amount of the input and output energies; when the balance was negative people would die and the population decrease; when it was positive, the population would increase and use up the excess energy. In any case, the increases and decreases in population should have worked as a negative feedback mechanism to restore the energy balance per head. Unlike other animals, however, man would occasionally have shown a slight but odd deviation from this pattern when the master programme cut in; then he built systems, material and non-material, using that excess energy. As a material system, man made tools for hunting, for instance. This increased his efficiency in obtaining food, and must have produced more excess energy. Even if the proportion of excess energy used in this way was very slight, it was a positive feedback process, leading up to today's visible acceleration.

With this last statement my oversimplification may appear to have gone too far. Let me elaborate this point a little. Between the activity of hunting and the activity of making tools for hunting there is no clear gap. Both require first the acquisition of information and then the use of it for control. But the latter includes one more inductive step in the links connecting the starting line with the goal. The new connection, borne by whatever neural network, is a new system and needs some energy for its formation. I shall not ask how man does it. I only want to note that man's brain has not only the capacity but also a programme for using excess energy this way, at least occasionally. In other words, he first acquires information and then uses it, if possible, to control his environment for his own benefit. In simple terms, the benefit is his own preservation or, a little more generally, the preservation of the organization with which he identifies himself. Because of the inexorable second law of thermodynamics, any system tends to disintegrate unless one works on it constantly to restore it. So my assumption is that man is so programmed as to use excess energy to build systems—neural, material, interpersonal or otherwise—which counteract, in one way or another, the negative entropy decay of the system involving himself. So men build houses, wear clothes, form groups and learn how to fight.

These systems not only help man to preserve the internal energy of his systems but also produce more excess energy by improving the control of his environment. Better control, in turn, helps us to acquire better information.

This is a typical positive feedback mechanism, and it will act as a force that constantly accelerates the fly-wheel of civilization. Of course, the wheel has not always turned as smoothly as my simplified argument might suggest. Nature was resourceful in providing negative feedback means to counteract the acceleration—overpopulation, conflicts, epidemics and so on. In most cases, however, man sooner or later found the causes of the troubles and used the information to control them on later occasions. So the causes of friction in the mechanism of civilization were lubricated out one by one, leaving the information-control positive feedback as the sole agent operating. As there seems to be no built-in stopping mechanism in the programme that makes man work this way, we now arrive at the not-yet-famous second law of civilization dynamics: *in an isolated human system, the negative entropy it contains has a tendency to increase.* God knows what the first law is.

These two second laws, that of thermodynamics and that of civilization dynamics, will naturally compete in determining the actual historical processes in each civilization. Consider the local civilizations of the past. In the first phase of a civilization the second law of civilization dynamics must be working at full force. Gradually social systems will develop, expand and become firmly established. Material systems become abundant and non-material systems like art begin to flourish. However, sooner or later this civilization reaches its prime and passes into its second phase, when the omnipotent power of the second law of thermodynamics will begin to be felt. No system, whether material or non-material, or however well preserved it may be, can permanently evade the fate of negative entropy decay. Perhaps the most important consequence of such decay in a civilization is the decline in the efficiency of social systems. The solidity of the social systems acquired through toil in the first phase then suddenly becomes a defect rather than a merit, for this makes it harder for the systems to adapt to the new conditions. Any effort as great as that needed to abolish and renew the well-established central social system of a civilization requires a tremendous amount of energy, and the malfunctioning of the system will also make it difficult to recruit and organize so much excess energy. At this stage revolutions will often be planned as unsanctioned attempts to reach a similar end. Even though some may succeed, resulting in a partial renewal of the whole system, these attempts will hardly be sufficient to undo the already reversed direction of positive feedback operation, and the whole civilization will gradually decline and fall as the output of excess energy dwindles.

This scheme, however, will not apply to our present civilization or to its foreseeable crises—not because the scheme itself is a vast oversimplification, but because of the entirely new factors present. These new factors are science and science-based technology. In the civilizations of the past the central social system, in which I am of course including political and military systems, exploited excess energy mainly from external sources, distributed it to the members of the civilization, and then reabsorbed it to enforce and expand the system itself. However, the external resources which were exploited were mostly limited to human resources: the excess energy of people who did not properly belong to that civilization, such as enemies, barbarians and slaves. As long as the energy resources are limited to manpower, the total excess energy accumulated in a civilization cannot amount to much. In our present civilization, on the other hand, science has enabled us to tap entirely different kinds of non-human energy resources, such as fossil, fission and—in the near future—fusion fuels. The amount of excess energy liberated from these resources has already been enormous, and some time ago this apparently made us cross the point of no return at which the precarious balance between positive and negative feedback was lost and the monopoly of acceleration began.

One obvious consequence of this is that the social systems of our civilization, formed primarily according to the old principle of rigid preservation, will hardly be able to catch up with the ever-gathering speed of change. Every day, science and technology produce innovations with which the social systems must somehow cope. Military systems must be revised as new weapons are developed, industrial systems should be altered to handle new products and production facilities, laws must be changed following changes in value systems, and political systems must adapt themselves to all these changes. The systems are certainly undergoing all these modifications, but the time lag is now apparent and the gap is increasing. The social systems become inefficient in a new way. They distribute an unprecedented amount of excess energy to the people in developed countries, but they begin to fail to reabsorb it.

Now recall my assumption that people are so programmed as to use their excess energy to build systems to the benefit of a greater system to which they belong. One of the primary functions of social systems should be to provide people with means to comply with this programme. So when social systems fail to perform this function properly, people begin to get frustrated in spite of their affluence—the affluence typically represented by spare time and freedom from worries about their livelihood. Or rather they are frustrated because of the affluence in the excess energy which they do not know how to use.

This type of frustration will not directly lead to revolutions, however, for although people in affluent societies can easily get frustrated they can hardly become desperate. So, for the time being, the abundant excess energy will remain unabsorbed and unorganized. Even without organized large-scale attacks upon the established social systems, however, the abundance of unorganized energy will probably have a peculiar but far-reaching effect upon their structures. In the first place, people will begin to lose respect for inefficient social systems. This will result in the decline of the authority these systems once had over people. What political systems in rich nations now have the authority they had at the time of the Second World War? Military systems begin to lose their once-characteristic power-enforced relations between officers and soldiers. In many countries the authority of educational systems has vanished into thin air. In Japan it is the authority of the law courts that is now being seriously questioned. Industrial systems have been left relatively intact, but their authority, too, is apparently beginning to suffer over the issue of industrial pollution.

It now strikes me that the effect of abundant and unorganized excess energy appears to resemble somewhat that of heat energy on physical systems. They both melt systems rather than break them down. If there is anything substantial in this analogy we may entertain a notion which might be called the *social temperature*. When the central social system complex functions properly, it will absorb excess energies and grow, while keeping the social temperature low. When it fails to do so under a high energy input, however, the temperature will increase and gradually melt its structures.

What will happen after systems begin to melt? New and efficient systems may emerge eventually, if we can wait long enough. Again the critical factor is time. In a civilization saturated with energy, anything may happen at any time, as the whole civilization is in a state of something like a high explosive. When frustration becomes much deeper, the suspicion might prevail that the source of all evils is material abundance, and claims would be made that the activities of the scientists, the evil masters, should be restricted. Though it is a false idea, there is some element of wisdom in this suspicion because if one wants to maintain a stable society it certainly ought to be easier with al low energy level than with a high one. I can even visualize that such an anti-science movement, in the form of some fanatic religion, would spread like wildfire, collecting the excess energy of many unsatisfied people, and then, after considerable violence and destruction, our civilization would backslide into another civilization of a mediaeval type, though this time with a highly sophisticated structure for maintaining itself.

As I am tired of describing the black picture alone, I feel happy to replace it now with a new one with colours a little brighter. Let us suppose that we have succeeded in obtaining the science of civilization and that civilization has been smoothly steered to the stable solution preferred by mankind. The problems facing such a society then need to be considered as follows.

As I am assuming that this society is on a high energy level, science should remain advanced and be at the core of civilization. This in turn implies that every individual will be allotted a large sum of excess energy. In order to keep the social temperature down, the energy should then be reabsorbed by the social system, but in an entirely new way. This is necessary because the social system cannot turn the absorbed energy into its own internal energy, since the structure of a stable society cannot change very quickly and acceleration must be put under control. On the other hand, no rigid social structure will be able to maintain itself at a high energy level. These requirements seem to be satisfied only by a society with a fluid sort of structure, whose stability will be based on a form of dynamic balance. In other words, such a society should be able to change its apparent form very easily as it absorbs excess energy. However, the excess energy will soon be reabsorbed by another system which I may call the *energy sink*, and society will regain its balance. The energy sink will consist of projects in which everyone participates, but which will not immediately reproduce energy. For instance, there should be projects concerned with activities in all branches of the arts. Such projects would make our civilization more balanced, while keeping the energy output moderate. For scientifically minded people, scientific projects on a really grand scale should be provided. These projects would have to be important enough to let people devote their entire energy to them, and at the same time be on a scale grand enough to give the civilization scientists time to prepare for the shock their eventual completion will give to civilization.

Anyway, the excess energy problem may be solved even though the solution is only temporarily effective. The most difficult part of the problem is how to provide every individual, even those who are not gifted, with ways of participating or ways of using their excess energy in a meaningful way. My tentative solution is to construct society not on the basis of individual men but on the basis of *teams* of men. From *n*-person games theory it is known that players who are relatively weak in a game tend to form coalitions to acquire greater power as a team. In this society of the future a team is a qualified one only when it is capable of participating as a team in any one of the many projects provided by society. As teams will be organized freely and disintegrate freely, and as there will be many kinds of teams, everybody will have a chance to join the ones that suit him best and to make an important contribution to society through them.

Although it is doubtful that such a wild idea alone will solve all the problems of advanced civilization, it is also true that the combination of elements greatly increases the variety of things that can be done, compared to what can be done by single elements, and the possibilities of achieving a more stable and prosperous society through the free cooperation of many different types of people have yet to be seriously investigated.

The science of civilization should be the key to solving all the vital problems we face today, the key that will open up a new vista of a sound and prosperous civilization of tomorrow; and I am, to tell the truth, an optimist at heart.

Discussion

Weinberg: Dr Jay W. Forrester's schematic approach[1] to the creation of a science of civilization is similar to yours, Dr Toda. It is surprising that you as a professor of psychology basically shove under the carpet all the detailed psychological questions that a physicist like me thinks are the essence of a science of civilization.

Toda: It is perhaps because I was also trained as a physicist! I really believe that the major obstacle to the rapid advancement of the social sciences is the fact that we see too many details. In order to provide psychology as well as other social sciences with structural, theoretical frameworks, we should deliberately try to observe things more macroscopically than we do now.

Weinberg: So you don't concede that a science of civilization is impossible?

Toda: There is no alternative but to believe that it is possible.

Weinberg: I believe it is impossible, but people should try to prove that I am wrong. For a long time I thought that thermonuclear energy was impossible; but I hope to live long enough to see my doubts disproved.

Thiemann: Institutions today are created mainly by lawyers, and the lawyers defend the past; they are not instructed in or dedicated to thinking of the future. Thinking of humanity or civilization as a thermodynamic group with a large number of individuals brings in the analogy of the phase changes or phase transitions of physics and physical chemistry. New phase changes may also happen to civilization.

Toda: I certainly think that civilizations have phases, not only in the simple-minded sense I used in my paper, but also in the stricter sense of the term. Since man himself, the basic constituent element of each civilization, remains the same, we may analyse historical processes to try to discover the conditions most likely to cause a certain phase-shift in any civilization. We would then know the conditions needed to create a desirable phase-shift in our present civilization. There may be other concepts like this one of phases in the natural sciences which would also be useful in the social sciences. Analogy alone may not be sufficient, but the resources of the natural sciences have not yet been fully explored for the benefit of the social sciences.

Rathenau: If one type of energy sink could consist just of doing science, aren't such sinks already at work in our present society, where so many people are doing science?

Toda: Yes. But in our present society most scientific projects are related, directly or indirectly, to the production of energy.

Mathur: You referred to civilization as subject to scientific laws, Professor

Toda, and human communities do indeed exhibit some of the attributes of living organisms, their behaviour being to some extent modelled on that of biological organisms. Physical laws also apply to them but have to change their content and interpretation. One basic physical law to which they are subject is the Maupertuisian Principle of Least Action[2] that I referred to earlier (p. 174). The objective of effort is survival of the organism, that is the prevention of permanent equilibrium with the environment—only inanimate objects such as stones are in equilibrium with the environment.

When living organisms combine with others to form the bigger living organisms called 'central subjects' (see p. 175), the survival of the main body becomes the objective of each of the parts. In terms of the biological system, those who are the fittest in terms of having claws, so to speak, to deal with nature, are the fittest to survive. One way in which a society keeps itself flexible in operation and changes its structure is by investing in science and technical progress so that it is not overwhelmed by a changing environment.

Bloch: In Japan in a short hundred years a transition has occurred which was spread over many more centuries in Europe and the Western world. Yet the conflicts Japan is experiencing today between her traditional society structure and the changes due to scientific or technological innovation seem to be the same. Does this mean that these changes are so overwhelming in their impact that the background against which they occur can almost be neglected?

Toda: It is very difficult to describe what has happened in Japan in the past hundred years, because we ourselves are not quite sure what the underlying processes have been. It is true that the Japanese are adaptive and industrious. In our long history we have mostly been busy in assimilating foreign cultures, typically Chinese, and we have done it with the least possible conflict with our traditional culture. Whether this history and experience alone can explain the mystery, frankly I don't know.

The adaptability, or low amount of cultural inertia, of our nation will, however, make Japan very sensitive to the phase-shifts of contemporary civilization. My impression is that now even the superb adaptability of the Japanese has been stretched rather thin, and the unease of the general public seems to be spreading. We may get over the coming crisis as we have before, or we may not. But it is true that now an entirely new element has been introduced into our culture.

Freeman: This last point seems to be in conflict with your basic aim, Dr Toda. You were arguing that the problem with the social sciences is that they see too much detail, and they need broader generalizations, disregarding the infinite complexity of detail. I am very much in sympathy with you on this point: one would love to be able to disregard the complexity and have the simplicity the hard sciences appear to have. But is it possible?

It seems to me that the social scientists haven't yet achieved this grand simplification, not because they are obtuse or because they have no 'macroscope', but because the situation really is different, for the reasons you have just given. Human societies are changing very rapidly and therefore one cannot generalize as much as one can about phenomena showing greater uniformity and stability of behaviour. Human societies also show a great variety of behavioural responses. The interaction of cultural change and science and technology is very different in different circumstances. Therefore I rather doubt whether either the kind of scheme that you are suggesting or Dr Forrester's model [1] will actually achieve their objectives.

Malthus tried to make a grand simplification of this kind and, given his assumptions, his argument was logically correct. But he ignored something that was extremely important: technical progress. Of course technical progress is now being incorporated into more sophisticated models of social development, but I would be willing to bet that a great many other things are being ignored, and that the unexpected will prove very important in social development.

So the 'science of civilization' must take into account the rapid rate of change in human society and in human behaviour systems, individual and social, and it must reckon with the fact that there are alternative ways in which humanity can develop. There is no single direction of development but a range of possibilities, and some degree of freedom of choice is one of the factors in the situation.

Toda: Those points do not seem to conflict with my argument. We must certainly pay attention to cultural and other differences. The main thing is that we should find numerical indicators to describe cultural and other macroscopic differences. The acceleration of change will most naturally be dealt with in numerical terms, and even the qualitative changes which come after acceleration may be amenable to numerical treatment. The number of such indicators may be very large, but we can let the computer handle them.

I cannot prove that this kind of science can be obtained, but I also believe that no one can produce arguments strong enough to show that it is impossible. Many problems that have been thought of as impossible have been solved when the situation really presses scientists to solve them. Our situation now is very pressing indeed, and I believe, and hope, that in a rather short time this problem will attract many good scientific minds.

Thiemann: Certainly the models you and Dr Forrester suggest are still extremely primitive, but their aim is to find some invariants. In thermodynamics we can describe the maximum efficiency by only two temperatures; this is also extremely primitive but it is the result of very sophisticated research by physicists. In these extremely primitive models the invariants are not as simple as two temperatures because the human being is involved, and it all depends on what the human being finally wants to have.

Discussion

1. FORRESTER, J. W. (1971) Counterintuitive behavior of social systems. *Technology Review, 73*, 52–68.
2. MATHUR, G. (1959) Economics of the living organisms. *Science and Culture, 24*, 249–253.

Summing up

HUBERT BLOCH

This conference began with discussions of the responsibility of the scientist to the public as regards the consequences of his work and its general impact on society. Our concern about these matters is justified but we must take care not to drown ourselves in feelings of guilt. A feeling of responsibility is quite distinct from one of guilt. For the scientist, responsibility must be a continuing process whereby his goals and the means of reaching them are continually adjusted in response to the changing needs of society and increasing stores of knowledge.

We then attempted to come together on a common terminology, but in this we were not very successful. Civilization was defined fairly adequately, but paradoxically we could not agree on what is science or what are scientists. Is the so-called scientific method the common link that holds together science and scientists, is there a common scientific ethic and are there some goals shared by the entire scientific community? These questions remained unanswered. We also asked whether a single species of scientists exists, or whether scientists are merely professionals lumped together in various groups according to the scientific disciplines they represent.

In our discussions, the term science was mostly used in the sense of 'big' science, or was equated with the natural sciences. We seemed to have almost forgotten that the humanities, too, belong to the sciences. Of the social sciences only economics, education and psychology were touched on. Was this because they are relatively cheap and do not cost the public much money, or because their consequences are considered potentially less dangerous for humanity? Since we failed to agree on terminology, our usage of the term 'science' was rather loose and was allowed to overlap with 'technology' and even 'engineering'!

There was general agreement that science can create significant social and human problems, but there was much less agreement about whether these problems can also be solved by science. Not everybody thought that the application of scientific methods is suitable for getting us out of impasses created by science. Rather, it was said that in many instances compromises would have to be made, as some of the problems were regarded as 'trans-scientific' in nature.

Are civilization and science then in conflict or collaboration? Dr Roche cited an example where a remarkable civilization grew and existed entirely without science, and we were presented with many instances where science is being used, and abused, for clearly uncivilized goals. Nevertheless, there was general agreement that science is an essential and noble part of civilization and that the two are in collaboration more often than in conflict.

Surprisingly, throughout most of these discussions science was talked of as a clearly goal-oriented enterprise: science for health, science for economic needs, science for national power. This is particularly true of the demand for more science now emanating from the developing world. Science, there, should bring better crops, more energy supplies, less disease, higher standards of living. To me, many of our discussions were reminiscent of debates in an industrial rather than an academic science-policy-making context. In the developing countries, it seems natural that the betterment of socio-economic conditions and raising the standard of living should rank highest on the lists of national priorities. But the problems here are not really scientific in nature, or only marginally so. They are problems of engineering, of finance, of vocational training and education and of political implementation. With so many pressing technological problems to be solved, is not the pursuit of pure science a luxury that poor countries can ill-afford? And is it uncivilized if these countries turn their attention first to the solution of down-to-earth practical, rather than scientific, problems? Should India, for instance, divert a substantial percentage of her meagre resources to high energy physics and molecular biology when the primary needs of that country are in quite different areas and so obvious for everybody to see? If being civilized means that a country has to put the pursuit of purely scientific goals before the solution of the most urgent material problems of the people, then the definition of civilization needs to be reconsidered. This dilemma was not exhaustively dealt with, which is the more surprising in view of the rather practical and often utilitarian undertone characterizing much of what was said.

We had a lengthy discussion on today's anti-science movement—its significance, its character, whether or not there is a crisis and, if there is, whether it represents merely a particular aspect of the general counter-culture of our time. Seen in this context, science would indeed be a part of civilization, be-

cause it is rejected by some on the same grounds as other previously un-
contested pillars of civilization are now being rejected!

Serious as it is, the anti-science movement should probably not be over-
rated and if it impels scientists to do some soul-searching about the justification for and significance of their own work, it may not be as bad as might
appear at first sight.

A recurrent theme concerned the well-known side-effects of science and
technology—pollution and all the rest. We agreed that all or most of these
problems can and must be solved, that what we most need are political acts to
implement effective control measures, and that these are more likely to happen
now because the public has been aroused and is ready to take action, including
footing the bills where necessary. It was recognized, however, that not all
problems can be solved yet as the necessary technology is not always available.
More research is needed in many areas and it must be done. Public awareness
of the imminent dangers is a powerful force indeed and it is only to be hoped
that emotional pressures will not force decisions that could not pass the test of
cool scientific scrutiny.

To most of us it seemed that, since science has invaded the field of government, scientists have no choice but to take a more active part in the shaping
of policy; they cannot shun this responsibility. To limit their role to that of
advisers without a share of the responsibilities no longer seems permissible.

The formidable amounts spent every year on military research were
mentioned. These sums of money are as difficult to visualize as Dr Weinberg's
millions of mice. In view of the sheer size of the world-wide military research
budgets, it might seem that we have spent three days discussing the role and
usage of a ridiculously low percentage of total world expenditure on science.
Yet all the money spent on military research is spent with our consent by
governments we have elected. Not only do our parliamentary representatives
vote the necessary appropriations, but hundreds of thousands of our scientific
colleagues collaborate and contribute actively. If we consider war as the
enemy of civilization, there ought to be no choice for scientists but to oppose
military research actively, not merely by attending Pugwash Conferences, but
by refusing to work in military research establishments. Perhaps this is too
simplistic a view. I know the issue is more complex, but the fact remains that
all the problems we have concerned ourselves with are dwarfed by this one
reality: that an overwhelming proportion of all scientific expenditure and
efforts in manpower, money and facilities is used to attain goals of which
scientists ought not to approve or which they should at least question seriously.

To reach such a conclusion at the end of this meeting is rather sad and
unsatisfactory. But I cannot help being stunned by the disproportion between

the destructive ends for which so much of the money allocated to scientific research is used, and the relatively small sums of money controlled by the scientific community and used to finance the type of research we have discussed here. As long as this disproportion is permitted to stay, it is indeed legitimate to ask whetherscience and civilization are in conflict or collaboration.

At the beginning of this meeting, I made some suggestions which I felt might help to lead science and technology out of the impasse in which they find themselves. Although these proposals did not all meet with approval, I should nevertheless like to repeat the one that in the light of our discussions seems to be the most essential. It is the plea to widen the training of scientists to include the study and analysis of the contradictions among various technological systems, and to establish closer working relationships between different scientific disciplines which are traditionally separated and segregated. Their training must instil in scientists a sense of wider responsibility, not only for their work but also for its impact on society; at the same time it must give them the necessary professional tools to deal with their extended range of tasks in an efficient and truly scientific manner.

Contributors to the Symposium

Sir ERIC ASHBY, FRS, has been Master of Clare College, Cambridge since 1959 and Chairman of the Royal Commission on Environmental Pollution since 1970. He graduated in botany at Imperial College, London and taught there and at the Universities of Chicago, Bristol, Sydney and Manchester from 1926 to 1950. He was President and Vice-Chancellor of Queen's University, Belfast from 1950 to 1959 and Vice-Chancellor of Cambridge University from 1967 to 1969. He has been chairman or a member of many government councils and committees on science policy, education and grants. He is a Trustee of the Ciba Foundation.

Publications include: papers on aspects of experimental botany and on education; *Technology and the Academics*, 1958; *Community of Universities*, 1963; *African Universities and Western Tradition*, 1964; *Universities: British, Indian and African*, 1966 (with Mary Anderson); *Masters and Scholars*, 1970; *The Rise of the Student Estate*, 1970 (with Mary Anderson); *Any Person, Any Study*, 1971; Science and antiscience (Bernal Lecture to the Royal Society), in *Proceedings of the Royal Society*, Series B, 1971, *178*, 29–42.

HUBERT BLOCH, chairman of this symposium, is Director of the Friedrich Miescher-Institut in Basle and a member of the Research Council of the Swiss National Science Foundation (Schweizerischer Nationalfonds zur Förderung der wissenschaftlichen Forschung). He studied medicine in Basle and lectured in microbiology there from 1940 to 1946. He was visiting investigator at the Rockefeller Institute, New York, from 1947 to 1948 and a member of the Public Health Research Institute, New York, from 1948 to 1956. From 1956 to 1961 he was Professor of Microbiology at the Pittsburgh University Medical School. In 1961 he became Director of Biological Research and then Director of Research for CIBA Limited, Basle. The Friedrich Miescher-Institut, of which he became the first Director in 1969, is an Institute for fundamental biomedical research, sponsored by CIBA-GEIGY Limited.

Publications include numerous papers on pathology and immunology in infections, especially in tuberculosis, and the following publications more closely related to the theme of this symposium: The drawbacks of medical progress, in *CIBA Journal* 1966, No. 37; Hochschulaufgaben in der heutigen Welt der Technik, in *Bildungs-anforderungen in der industriellen Welt. Schriften zur Zeit*, 1969, *32/33*, 25–43; Gedanken zur schweizerischen Wissenschaftspolitik, in *Chimia* 1970, *24*, 321–327; Umwelt und Gesundheit, in *Gesundheitspolitik Heute*, Jahrbuch 1971 der Neuen Helvetischen Gesellschaft, *42*, 35–43.

HERMANN BONDI, FRS, is Chief Scientific Adviser, Ministry of Defence, London, and was Director-General of the European Space Research Organization from 1967 to 1971. He studied at Trinity College, Cambridge and lectured in mathematics at Cambridge from 1945 to 1954 before becoming Professor of Mathematics at King's College, London, in 1954.

He was Chairman of the National Committee for Astronomy from 1963 to 1967 and secretary of the Royal Astronomical Society from 1956 to 1964. He is Vice-President of ACE (Advisory Centre for Education), and a member of the Rationalist Press Association Ltd, the Advisory Council of the Science Policy Foundation Ltd, the Executive Council of PEP (Political and Economic Planning) and the Delegacy of King's College, London.

Publications include: papers on astrophysics etc.; *Cosmology*, 1952, 1960; *The Universe at Large*, 1961; *Relativity and Commonsense*, 1964; *Assumption and Myth in Physical Theory*, 1968.

FRANÇOIS BOURLIÈRE is Professor of Medical Biology in the Faculty of Medicine, University of Paris and also Lecturer in Mammalian Ecology in the Faculty of Sciences. He is Chairman of the ICSU International Biological Programme and was President of the International Union for the Conservation of Nature from 1963 to 1966. He studied medicine and biology at the University of Paris and his research work is on the biology of ageing and the ecology of mammals. He has edited and lent his support to *La Terre et la Vie*, the French quarterly journal on applied ecology, for the last 20 years.

Publications include: *The Natural History of Mammals*, 1954, 1956 and 1964; *Sénescence et Sénilité*, 1958; *African Ecology and Human Evolution*, 1963 (co-editor with F. Clark Howell); *Problèmes de Productivité Biologique*, 1967 (co-editor with M. Lamotte); *Problèmes d'Ecologie*, vols. 1–3, 1971 (co-editor with M. Lamotte).

JOHN F. BROCK is now Honorary Professor of History and Philosophy of Medicine at the University of Cape Town, where he was for 33 years Professor of Medicine.

He was a Rhodes Scholar at Oxford, studied medicine in London and was Assistant Director of Research in Medicine at Cambridge from 1936 to 1938. His research work for over 30 years has been on the effects of human malnutrition.

Publications include: *Kwashiorkor in Africa*, 1951; *Recent Advances in Human Nutrition*, 1961; and many articles in medical and scientific journals.

Sir ALAN BULLOCK has been Vice-Chancellor of Oxford University since 1969 and Master of St. Catherine's College since 1960. He studied classics and history at Oxford and is a Fellow of the British Academy.

Publications include: *Hitler, a Study in Tyranny*, 1952, revised edn 1964; *The Liberal Tradition*, 1956; *The Life and Times of Ernest Bevin*, vol. 1, 1960, vol. 2, 1967; *The Oxford History of Modern Europe* (general editor with F. W. Deakin); *The Twentieth Century* (editor), 1971.

CHRISTOPHER FREEMAN has been Director of the Science Policy Research Unit at the University of Sussex since it was set up in 1966. He is also the Reginald M. Phillips Professor in Science Policy. He graduated in economics from the London School of Economics and has followed a career mainly in teaching and research. Before joining the University of Sussex, he worked at the National Institute of Economic and Social Research in London where he was responsible for a series of studies on research and innovation in British industry and for the Institute's annual industrial inquiries. He has undertaken consultancy for a number of international organizations on the standardization of research and development statistics.

Publications include: surveys on research and innovation in the plastics industry, economic capital goods industry and the chemical process plant industry (*National Institute Economic Reviews*, Nos. 26, 34 and 45); *The Research & Development Effort in Western Europe, North America and the Soviet Union: An Experimental International Comparison of Research Expenditure and Manpower in 1962* (with A. Young), OECD, 1965; The goals of R & D in the 1970s, in *Science Studies*, November 1971 (co-author); *Measurement of Output of Research & Experimental Development*, UNESCO, 1970; *The Measurement of Scientific & Technological Activities*, UNESCO, 1969; *Science & Technology for Development*, U.N. New York, 1970 (co-author).

JUNE GOODFIELD-TOULMIN was Professor of Philosophy and Human Medicine at Michigan State University from 1969 to 1971. She graduated at the University of London and after a period of research at Oxford University she taught and lectured at Cheltenham Ladies' College, Benenden School and the University of Leeds from 1949 to 1960. She was Assistant Director of the Nuffield Foundation Unit for the History of Ideas from 1960 to 1965, lecturer at Wellesley College from 1965 to 1969, and Visiting Lecturer at Harvard University in 1968. In addition to the history of medicine and science, she is much concerned with the visual presentation of science and scientific ideas and has written and directed, or produced, a number of films (*The Ladies' College of Cheltenham*, 1953; *Earth and Sky*, 1958; *The God Within*, 1962; *The Perfection of Matter*, 1964; *The Perception of Life*, 1964).

Publications include: *The Growth of Scientific Physiology*, 1960; *The Ancestry of Science*: vol. 1, *The Fabric of the Heavens*, 1961, vol. 2, *The Architecture of Matter*, 1962 and vol. 3, *The Discovery of Time*, 1965 (all three with Stephen Toulmin). Her most recent work is a novel, *The Natural Reaction*, 1972. Within this new format, she explores her long-standing interest in the delicate relationship between science and government.

HARRY G. JOHNSON has been Professor of Economics at the University of Chicago since 1959 and also Professor of Economics at the London School of Economics since 1966. He studied at the University of Toronto, Cambridge University and Harvard University and held various university teaching posts from 1943 to 1949. He was a Lecturer in Economics at Cambridge from 1950 to 1956 and Professor of Economic Theory at Manchester from 1956 to 1959.

Publications include: articles on monetary theory, international trade and banking in various journals of economics; *The Canadian Quandary*, 1963; *The World Economy at the Crossroads*, 1965; *Economic Policies towards the Less Developed Countries*, 1967; *Essays in Monetary Economics, 1967*; *Money in Britain*, 1959–1969, 1970.

FRANKLIN A. LONG is Henry R. Luce Professor of Science and Society and Director of the Program on Science, Technology and Society at Cornell University, Ithaca, New York, where he has been Professor of Chemistry since 1946. He graduated in chemistry at the University of Montana, with a Ph. D. from the University of California, and lectured in chemistry at the Universities of California and Chicago before going to Cornell in 1937. He was a member of the President's Science Advisory Committee in 1961 and 1964-67, and was Assistant Director of the U.S. Arms Control and Disarmament Agency in 1962 and 1963.

Publications include: Support of scientific research and education in our universities, in *Science*, 1969, *163*, 1037–1040; Strategic balance and the ABM, in *Bulletin of the Atomic Scientists*, 1969, *24* (12), 2–5; The industrial aspects of Apollo, in *Bulletin of the Atomic Scientists*, 1969, *25* (7), 70–73; Preparing chemists to meet society's future needs, in *Journal of Chemical Education*, 1971, *48*, 17–21; Growth characteristics of military R & D, in *Impact of New Technologies on the Arms Race*, 1971.

GAUTAM MATHUR has been Professor and Head of the Department of Economics, Osmania University, Hyderabad, since 1964. He studied at Punjab University, Lahore and at Cambridge University. He worked for the Burmah Shell Company before becoming a Senior Lecturer and later Reader at Punjab University. He was Dean of the Faculty of Social Sciences at Osmania University from 1966 to 1970. He specializes in growth economics and perspective planning and is establishing the Centre for Special Assistance in Economic Planning at Osmania University. He is a member of several Government of India advisory committees and editor of the New Cambridge Economics Series published by the Cambridge University Press.

Publications include: *Planning for Steady Growth*, 1965; Investment criteria in a platinum age, in *Oxford Economic Papers*, 1967, *19*, 199–214; Economic development and the ivory tower, in *Education and Society*, 1968, pp. 349–363; *Human Capital Formation*, in preparation; *Economic Logic*, in preparation (New Cambridge Economics Series).

Lady MEDAWAR was formerly Chairman of the Family Planning Association of England, and is now Executive Chairman of the Margaret Pyke Centre in London.

She studied zoology at Oxford University and took a research degree on the behaviour of lymphocytes.

Publications include: *Family Planning*, 1971 (co-editor with D. Pike).

Sir PETER MEDAWAR, FRS, Director of the National Institute for Medical Research, Mill Hill, London from 1962 to 1971, is now doing research in transplantation biology at the Medical Research Council's Clinical Research Centre at Northwick Park, Harrow. He studied at Oxford and became Lecturer in Zoology there in 1944. From 1947 to 1951 he was Mason Professor of Zoology at the University of Birmingham and from 1951 to 1962 Jodrell Professor of Zoology and Comparative Anatomy at University College London. He has been a member of the Agricultural Research Council and the University Grants Committee. In 1960 he received the Nobel Prize for medicine, jointly with Sir Macfarlane Burnet.

Publications include: papers on growth, ageing, immunity and tissue transplantation; *The Future of Man* (1960, Reith Lectures); *The Art of the Soluble*, 1969; *Induction and Intuition in Scientific Thought*, 1969; *The Hope of Progress*, 1972.

The Honourable GERARD PELLETIER has been Secretary of State of Canada since July 1968. He studied at the University of Montreal Faculty of Literature and from 1939 to 1943 was Secretary General of the youth movement, Jeunesse étudiante catholique. From 1945 to 1947 he worked for the World Student Relief Fund in Geneva and then returned to Canada to work as a reporter for the Montreal daily, *Le Devoir*. In 1950 he became public relations officer of the Confederation of National Trade Unions and director of its official paper, *Le Travail*. At this time he also worked on several radio and television series. From 1961 to 1965 he was editor of the daily *La Presse*, Montreal, and in 1965 he was elected Member of Parliament for the Montreal-Hochelaga riding. He was chairman of the Standing Committee on Broadcasting, Films and Assistance to the Arts in 1966 and in 1967 was appointed Parliamentary Secretary to the Secretary of State for External Affairs, in which capacity he visited a number of Latin American countries and attended the 22nd session of the United Nations General Assembly. In April 1968 he was appointed Minister without Portfolio, with special responsibility to the Secretary of State.

G. W. RATHENAU has been Director of Philips Research Laboratories, Eindhoven and a special professor at the University of Amsterdam since 1967. He studied physics at the Institute of Technology, Berlin, at the University of Berlin and at Göttingen. Later he did research on the spectroscopy of molecules and solids at the University of Groningen and at the Physics Laboratory of Teyler's Foundation, Haarlem, The Netherlands. From 1938 to 1952 his research was mainly on magnetism and metals, at Philips Research Laboratories. He was a professor at the University of Amsterdam from 1952 to 1963 and then returned to Philips Research Laboratories. He has been a member of the Royal Netherlands Academy of Science and Letters since 1960.

MARCEL ROCHE has been President of the Consejo Nacional de Investigaciones Científicas y Technológicas, Caracas, Venezuela, since 1969. He studied at Johns Hopkins University and the Harvard School of Medicine, and after working at the Johns Hopkins Hospital, Baltimore and at the Peter Bent Brigham Hospital in Boston he became a research worker at the New York Public Health Research Institute. From 1952 to 1958 he was Director of the Luis Roche Institute for Medical Research in Caracas. In 1958 he was made Chief of the Department of Physiopathology and Director of the Venezuelan Institute for Scientific Research. He was Simón Bolívar Professor of Latin American Studies at Cambridge University from 1970 to 1971.

Publications include: *Bitácora*-63, 1963; *La Ciencia entre Nosotros*, 1967, and 88 scientific papers.

EDWARD SHILS has been Professor of Sociology and Social Thought at the University of Chicago since 1951; he is a Fellow of Peterhouse, Cambridge, and has

been Visiting Professor of Social Anthropology at University College London since 1970. He was formerly a Fellow of King's College, Cambridge (1960-69), and before that Reader in Sociology in the University of London (London School of Economics, 1946–50). He is the founder and editor of *Minerva: A Review of Science, Learning and Policy*. His research has been on intellectuals in Europe, Asia, Africa and America.
Publications include: *The Intellectual between Tradition and Modernity; The Indian Situation*, 1960; *Political Development in the New States*, 1961; *The Torment of Secrecy*, 1956; *Towards a General Theory of Action* (with Talcott Parsons), 1951; *The Intellectuals and the Powers (Selected Papers, vol. 1)*, 1972; *Criteria of Scientific Development* (ed.), 1968 and numerous papers on sociological theory, mass society, science policy, higher educational institutions in Europe and Asia.

HUGO THIEMANN has been Director-General of the Battelle Research Centre in Geneva since 1954. He is a graduate in electrical engineering and Dr ès Sciences Techniques of the Federal Institute of Technology of Zurich (E.T.H.), where he was assistant to the director of the Department of Industrial Research of the Institute of Applied Physics. He has worked on various fields of applied physics, optics and television and headed research on the development of the large-screen TV projection system later called Eidophor. Subsequently, he was responsible for Eidophor's first demonstration in New York in sequential colour on behalf of CIBA Ltd.
In 1953 he established the Division of Applied Physics and Electrical Engineering at Battelle-Geneva. In 1965, the degree of Dr *honoris causa* was conferred upon him by the University of Geneva.

Publications include: Changing dynamics in research and development, in *Science*, 1970, *168*, 1427–1431; Innovation et entreprise, in *Les Problèmes de Gestion dans l'Entreprise*, 1970; New frontiers for research and development, in *Proceedings of the Royal Institution of Great Britain*, 1971, *44*, No. 204; and many other articles in various journals.

MASANAO TODA is Professor of Psychology in the Faculty of Letters, Hokkaido University, Japan. He graduated in physics, did graduate work in physics and then in psychology at the University of Tokyo, and has been teaching psychology at Hokkaido University since 1952. He was a Research Fellow at Harvard University, Visiting Research Associate Professor at the University of North Carolina, and Visiting Professor at the University of California, Los Angeles. He has been working mostly in the fields of decision making and mathematical psychology.

Publications include: The design of a fungus-eater: a model of human behavior in an unsophisticated environment, in *Behavior Science*, 1962, 164–183; About the notion of communication and structure: a perspective, in *Communication:*

Concepts and Perspectives, 1967; *The Theory of Games and Theories of Behavior*, (co-author with J. Nakahara), 1968; Possible roles of psychology in the very distant future, in *General Systems*, 1970, *15*, 105–108.

Lord TODD, FRS, Master of Christ's College, Cambridge, since 1963, was Professor of Organic Chemistry, Cambridge University, from 1944 to 1971. He studied at the Universities of Glasgow, Frankfurt and Oxford, and was on the staff of Edinburgh and London Universities before becoming Sir Samuel Hall Professor of Chemistry and Director of Chemical Laboratories, University of Manchester, in 1938. He was Chairman of the Advisory Council on Scientific Policy from 1952 to 1964 and of the Royal Commission on Medical Education from 1965 to 1968. He has been President of the Chemical Society (1960–62) and of the International Union of Pure and Applied Chemistry (1963–65). He was made a Life Peer in 1962. In 1963 he became a Trustee of the Ciba Foundation, and is Chancellor of the University of Strathclyde, Glasgow. He was awarded the Nobel Prize for Chemistry in 1957.

Publications include: numerous papers in chemical and biochemical journals.

STEPHEN TOULMIN was Professor of Philosophy at Michigan State University from 1969 to 1971, and is a Visiting Professor in the Science Policy Research Unit at the University of Sussex. He read mathematics and physics at Cambridge from 1940 to 1942 and worked on radar research for the Ministry of Aircraft Production from 1942 to 1945. From 1947 to 1951 he was a Research Fellow in Philosophy at King's College, Cambridge, and from 1949 to 1955 he was Lecturer in the Philosophy of Science at Oxford University. In 1955 he became Professor of Philosophy at the University of Leeds and in 1960 Director of the Nuffield Foundation Unit for the History of Ideas, London. He was Professor of Philosophy and History of Ideas at Brandeis University, Massachusetts, from 1965 to 1969, and has been a Counsellor of the Smithsonian Institution since 1966. He has also acted as a consultant on science policy questions for the Office of Science Resources Planning, National Science Foundation, Washington, D.C.

Publications include: *Reason in Ethics*, 1950; *The Philosophy of Science*, 1953; *The Uses of Argument*, 1958; *Foresight and Understanding*, 1961; *The Ancestry of Science*, vols. 1–3, 1961, 1962, 1965 (with June Goodfield-Toulmin); *Human Understanding*, vol. 1, 1972.

ALVIN WEINBERG has been Director of Oak Ridge National Laboratory, Tennessee, since 1955. He studied at the University of Chicago and was a member of the war-time team of theoretical physicists who designed the first nuclear reactors. He joined the Oak Ridge National Laboratory in 1945 and was designated Research

Director in 1948. He has written extensively on some of the difficult problems of public policy posed by the growth of modern science. He coined the phrase 'big science' to describe the new kind of large-scale scientific enterprise exemplified by Oak Ridge.

For his contributions to the theory and development of fission reactors, in 1960 he received both the Atoms for Peace Award and the United States Atomic Energy Commission's E. O. Lawrence Memorial Award.

Publications include: *Physical Theory of Neutron Chain Reactors*, 1958 (with E. P. Wigner); *Reflections on Big Science*, 1967; In defense of science, in *Science*, 1970, *167*, 141–145.

Sir JOHN WOLFENDEN became Director and Principal Librarian of the British Museum in 1969. He studied at Oxford and was Fellow and Tutor in Philosophy, Magdalen College, from 1929 to 1934. He was Headmaster of Uppingham School from 1934 to 1944 and of Shrewsbury School from 1944 to 1950. From 1950 to 1963 he was Vice-Chancellor of Reading University. He acted as chairman of the Secondary Schools Examination Council from 1951 to 1957, of the Departmental Committee on Homosexual Offences and Prostitution from 1954 to 1957, of the University Grants Committee from 1963 to 1968, and of many other committees. He is President of Aslib.

Publications include: articles, lectures, reviews, and *The Approach to Philosophy*, 1932; *How to Choose Your School*, 1952; chapters in *The Prospect Before Us*, 1948; *Education in a Changing World*, 1951.

Index of Contributors

Entries in **bold type** *refer to papers; other entries are contributions to discussions.*

Indexes compiled by William Hill.

Subject Index